# THE MEANING OF JESUS

MARCUS J. BORG

N. T. WRIGHT

# THE MEANING OF JESUS

TWO VISIONS

HarperSanFrancisco

*A Division of HarperCollinsPublishers*

HarperCollins books may be purchased for educational, business, or sales promotional use. For information please write: Special Markets Department, HarperCollins Publishers, 10 East 53rd Street, New York, NY 10022.

HarperCollins Web Site: http://www.harpercollins.com

HarperCollins®, ▆ ®, and HarperSanFrancisco™ are trademarks of HarperCollins Publishers Inc.

FIRST EDITION

*Library of Congress Cataloging-in-Publication Data*
Borg, Marcus J.
    The meaning of Jesus : two visions / Marcus J. Borg and N. T. Wright—
    1st ed.
        p.    m.
    Includes bibliographical references and index.
    ISBN 0–06–060875–7 (cloth)
    ISBN 0–06–060876–5 (pbk.)
    1. Jesus Christ—Person and offices. I. Wright, N. T. (Nicholas Thomas) II. Title.
BT202.B646    1998                                        98–30672
232—dc21                                                            CIP

99 00 01 02 03  RRD(H)  10 9 8 7 6 5 4 3 2 1

# ∘ CONTENTS

# ○ INTRODUCTION

THIS BOOK HAS grown out of a friendship. We first met in 1984, after Tom Wright had read Marcus Borg's book *Conflict, Holiness, and Politics in the Teachings of Jesus.* As Tom has described elsewhere, he found this book exciting and illuminating, and he sought out Marcus to congratulate him as well as to explore some "matters arising" and to ask why the book had ended as it did rather than in certain other possible ways.

Since our friendship thus grew out of the fascinated study of Jesus within his historical context, it is appropriate that it should give birth, some fourteen years later, to a book in which we put down some markers indicating where the conversation has led. During this period, we both have published several books and articles, many of them about Jesus. It is impossible in a work of the present size to rehearse all the arguments and to set out all the documentation, which are the normal requirements of scholarship. The main lines of most of what we here summarize have been set out and argued for in these other works, though at various points we both go beyond what we have said elsewhere, not least as a result of our own continuing dialogue.

Our personal stories are both interestingly similar and interestingly different. Marcus Borg grew up in a traditional and conventional Midwest Lutheran church, Tom Wright in a traditional and conventional Anglican one in the north of England. Marcus found increasing difficulties with his tradition in his teens and twenties, though he never lost his fascination with its central figure, and through that he has come back into a lively and active Christian faith. Tom, at the equivalent period of his life, found the tradition coming alive in fresh ways through some fairly un-Anglican styles of spirituality, though he never lost his instinctive rootings in the liturgical life of the church, and he has faced the predictable challenges that arise through the study of history and philosophy. Both of us went to Oxford University, and both, though at different times, ended up studying under the late Professor George B. Caird; our indebtedness to him has been recorded elsewhere. Marcus, however, continued to pursue the study of Jesus, whereas Tom at that stage focused almost entirely on Paul, coming to the historical study of Jesus in the late 1970s.

We are both committed to the vigorous practice of the Christian faith and the rigorous study of its historical origins and to the belief, which we find constantly reinforced, that these two activities are not, as is often supposed, ultimately hostile to each other. Rather, we find them mutually informative and supportive. To put this another way: we both acknowledge Jesus of Nazareth as Lord, and we regard the no-holds-barred study of his actual history as a vital part of what we mean by that. For precisely this reason, we deliberately began the work for this specific project in shared eucharistic worship, when Marcus visited Tom in Lichfield (England) in September 1997. The plan for the book took shape within the framework of participating together in morning and evening prayer in Lichfield Cathedral during the following five days. We believe that this setting, so far from prejudicing the "objectivity" of our work, was and is the most appropriate context for it. There is, after all, no such thing as objectivity in scholarship. Anyone who supposes that by setting scholarship within a modern secular university, or some other carefully sanitized, nonreligious setting, they thereby guard such work against the influence of presuppositions that can seriously skew the results should, we suggest, think again.

This is not to say, of course, that we find ourselves in substantial agreement on the majority of issues. If that were so, there would hardly be a book to write. Indeed, within the bounds of friendship and shared Christian faith and practice, we have both frequently been puzzled, and even disturbed, by some of what the other has said. Working on this book has at least enabled us to understand each other a lot better, to explain to each other (and perhaps to our readers) things that we each had thought were clear but that apparently weren't, and to remove impressions that had been unwittingly given. Inevitably, this has left the remaining disagreements posed more sharply. We have not flagged them all the way through the book, since to do so would become complex and tedious. The reader will quickly see where they are to be found. What results is, as it were, a single-frame photograph taken from a long sequence, freezing one moment in our conversation in the hope that others will find it interesting and helpful.

We envisage at least three categories of interested readers.

First, we hope that those who would not call themselves Christians will find the conversation interesting and refreshing. We both believe strongly that what we say about Jesus and the Christian life belongs, not in a private world, inaccessible and incomprehensible except "from faith to faith," but in the public world of historical and cross-cultural study, in the contemporary world as well as the church.

Second, we hope to shift logjammed debates into more fruitful possibilities. Much current writing about Jesus falls into rather sterile either-or distinctions (such as the classic fundamentalist versus modernist debates); we venture to suggest other ways in which the issues might be lined up. We hope thereby to advance an ecumenical dialogue that is often ignored. Liberal Lutherans, for instance (to use a broadbrush term for the moment), have more in common with liberal Anglicans or Presbyterians than with the more conservative members of their own denominations. Our dialogue might provide stimulus for such groups to begin to talk to each other afresh. While hard-line fundamentalists and radicals will both perhaps gnash their teeth, we hope that this book will serve as a bridge between many other groups of Christians.

On this point, it might appear at one level that Tom is a traditionalist in his views and Marcus a revisionist. There is a grain of truth in this, but we regard these labels, and similar ones, as quite misleading. Tom has come, through wrestling with the history and culture of first-century Judaism, to a picture of Jesus that is seriously at odds with traditional Christian views on some matters (for example, Jesus' supposed predictions of his second coming), while supporting the tradition in other matters, though from quite new angles. Marcus has come, through wrestling with cross-cultural issues of how to describe appropriately a figure like Jesus, to a picture that is firmly supportive of the tradition on some matters (for example, Jesus' healings, his spirituality, and his founding of a movement), while questioning it on many others, though by no means always in what has become the standard, dare one say traditional, revisionist fashion. Tom feels able, as a historian, to attribute more of the gospel material to Jesus than Marcus does, though the meaning Tom suggests for the material is by no means always what the traditionalist would expect. Marcus, in suggesting that less of it goes back to Jesus himself, nevertheless insists upon its importance, its truthfulness in senses other than historical, and its validity within a contemporary Christian vocation to follow Jesus.

Third, we hope to open up more specifically the perennially important question of how different visions of Jesus relate to different visions of the Christian life. Many who are deeply concerned with issues of justice, spirituality, pastoral care, and other matters within the churches do not always relate these issues to the question of Jesus. We propose some ways in which this might be done.

Neither of us is content to let things rest with a cheap and easy suggestion that, since we are both practicing Christians, our two positions are equally valid—whatever that might mean. It might be that both our positions are equivalent and fairly adequate expressions, from different points of view, of the same underlying reality. Neither of us quite thinks that. It might be that we are both wrong, and that some quite different position is truer. Neither of us thinks that, either. It might be that one of us is closer to the truth in some areas, and the other in others; and that by our dialogue we may see more clearly things that the other has grasped more accurately. We are both prepared for that eventuality.

Where we do agree, however, is on the following point. Debate about Jesus has recently been acrimonious, with a good deal of name-calling and angry polemic in both public and private discourse. We hope in this book to demonstrate that this is not the only way of doing things. Of course, it is comparatively easy for us: our positions, though very different in many ways, are not at opposite poles in the current debate, and we share, as we have said, both friendship and overlapping personal histories. But we hope, and indeed pray, that in this book we will be able to model a way of conducting public Christian disagreement over serious and central issues that will inspire others to try the same sort of thing. If, in the process, we help both Christians and non-Christians, and those uncertain which of these two brackets they belong in, to grapple with points of view they might otherwise have dismissed without serious thought, we shall be delighted. If, in addition, both of us grow, through this process, in our understanding of the subject matter, and enable others to do so as well, we shall have succeeded in our deepest underlying aim.

Our process, for those who may be interested, has been as follows. We had already read each other's work, as it had appeared, over many years, and had had many conversations, public and private, about broad outlines and numerous details. When we met in September 1997 we discussed some of the most central topics and managed to eliminate some initial puzzles and misunderstandings as well as to pose new questions to each other. We then agreed on the outline of the chapters for the book—the topics for each chapter and the order in which we would take turns in addressing them. We then each drafted what we wanted to say on the topic in question, without further reference to the other, though of course with many memories of the issues the other had raised. We then read each other's chapters, commented on them, and redrafted our own in dialogue. We could, of course, have doubled the size of the book by taking matters further at each point, but we have felt that the reader would not easily follow to-and-fro discussion of detailed points. Though we have not, of course, reached agreement, we are satisfied that we have eliminated misunderstandings, that is, that neither of us has misrepresented the other. We offer the result to the reader as the celebration of shared friendship, faith, and scholarship.

M. J. B.
N. T. W.

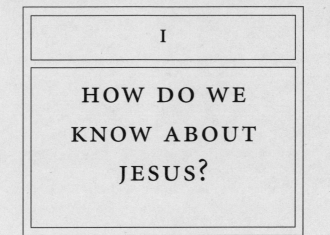

I

# HOW DO WE KNOW ABOUT JESUS?

# SEEING JESUS: SOURCES, LENSES, AND METHOD

*Marcus Borg*

---

H OW DO WE KNOW about Jesus? What are our sources, what are they like, and how do we use them?[1] For most of the Christian centuries, the answers to these questions seemed obvious. Our sources? The New Testament as a whole, and the four gospels in particular. What are they like? The gospels were seen as historical narratives, reporting what Jesus said and did, based on eyewitness testimony. How do we use them? By collecting together what they say about Jesus and combining them into a whole. Importantly, it did not require faith to see the gospels in this way; there was as yet no reason to think otherwise.

This way of seeing the gospels led to a common Christian image of who Jesus was and why he mattered. Who was he? The only Son of God, born of the virgin Mary. His purpose? To die for the sins of the world. His message? About many things, but most centrally about the importance of believing in him, for what was at stake was eternal life.

But over the last two hundred years among historical scholars, both within and outside of the church, this common image of Jesus has dissolved. Its central elements are seen no longer as going back to the historical Jesus, but as the product of the early Christian movement in the decades after his death. Jesus as a historical figure was not very much like the most common image of him.

As I write these words, I am sitting on the shore of the Sea of Galilee. I am here with a group of thirty Christians assisting my wife, Marianne, an Episcopal priest who leads educational-spiritual pilgrimages to Israel. My role is to provide historical background and commentary. As I do so, I often feel like the designated debunker. Again and again I find myself saying about holy sites associated with Jesus, "Well, it probably didn't happen here," or, "Well, it probably didn't happen at all." Of course, I have more to say than that, but it is a frequent refrain.

For example, today as we drove past Cana, I told the group that the story of Jesus changing water into wine at the wedding at Cana is most probably not a historical report but a symbolic narrative. At the site marking the Sermon on the Mount, I said that it was unlikely that Jesus ever delivered the Sermon on the Mount as a connected whole, even though many of the individual sayings probably go back to him. In Nazareth, I said Jesus probably was born *here,* and *not* in Bethlehem.

I sometimes feel like a debunker in my writing as well. A significant portion of what I have to say is, "This story is probably not historically factual," or, "Jesus probably didn't say that." And yet, for reasons I will explain later, I also find the nonhistorical material to be very important and meaningful. I am not among the relatively few scholars who think that *only* that which is historically factual matters.

## THE NATURE OF THE GOSPELS

But for now I want to explain why the issue comes up so often, whether on pilgrimage to the Holy Land or in my work as a Jesus scholar. The issue arises because of the nature of the Christian gospels, our primary sources for knowing about Jesus. Two statements about the nature of the gospels are crucial for grasping the historical task: (1) They are a developing tradition. (2) They are a mixture of history remembered and history metaphorized. Both statements are foundational to the historical study of Jesus and Christian origins, and both need explaining.

### The Gospels as a Developing Tradition

The four gospels of the New Testament are the product of a developing tradition. During the decades between the death of Jesus around the year 30 and the writing of the gospels in the last third of the first century (roughly between 70 and 100), the traditions about Jesus developed. More than one factor was responsible. There was a need to adapt the traditions about Jesus to new settings and issues as early Christian communities moved through time and into the broader Mediterranean world. Moreover, the traditions about Jesus grew because the experience of the risen living Christ within the community shaped perceptions of Jesus' ultimate identity and significance.

As developing traditions, the gospels contain two kinds of material: some goes back to Jesus, and some is the product of early Christian communities. To use an archaeological analogy, the gospels contain earlier and later layers. To use a vocal analogy, the gospels contain more than one voice: the voice of Jesus, and the voices of the community. The quest for the historical Jesus involves the attempt to separate out these layers or voices.

## History Remembered and History Metaphorized

The gospels combine history remembered with history metaphorized. By the former, I mean simply that some of the things reported in the gospels really happened. Jesus really did do and really did say some of the deeds and teachings reported about him.

By history metaphorized, I mean the use of metaphorical language and metaphorical narratives to express the meaning of the story of Jesus.[2] I define *metaphor* broadly to include both symbol and story. Thus the category includes individual metaphors, such as Jesus is the light of the world, and metaphorical narratives, where the story as a whole functions metaphorically. Metaphorical language is intrinsically nonliteral; its central meaning is "to see as"—to see something as something else. To say Jesus is the light of the world is not to say that he is literally a light, but means *to see him as* the light of the world. Thus, even though metaphorical language is not literally true, it can be powerfully true in a nonliteral sense.[3]

As I use the phrase, history metaphorized includes a wide variety of gospel material. Sometimes a story combines both history remembered and history metaphorized. For example, Jesus really was crucified. But the stories of his death, as I shall argue in chapter 5, are to a large extent history metaphorized: the meanings of his death are expressed in metaphorical language and narrative. A second example of history metaphorized based on history remembered: Jesus probably did restore sight to some literally blind people. But the way the stories are told in the gospels gives them a metaphorical meaning as well.[4]

The category of history metaphorized also includes stories of events that most likely did not happen. I see the story of Jesus changing water into wine at the wedding in Cana in its entirety as history metaphorized; I do not think a historical event lies behind it. As the opening scene of the public ministry of Jesus in John's gospel, the author uses it (and perhaps created it) to invite us to see the story of Jesus as a whole as the story of a wedding banquet at which the wine never runs out and at which the best is saved for last.

So also with the stories of Jesus feeding the multitude in the wilderness with a few loaves and fishes. They are, almost certainly, not historical reports but metaphorical narratives using imagery from Israel's story of the Exodus. The association invites us to see Jesus as one like unto Moses, to see what happened in him as like a new exodus, and (as the gospel of John puts it) to see Jesus himself as the bread of life, the true manna sent from God to feed us in the midst of our journey from bondage to life in the presence of God.

In short, the gospels do not simply report the history of Jesus, they metaphorize it.[5] For me as a Christian, both matter. For me as a historian, the realization that the gospels are a developing tradition containing both history remembered and history metaphorized points to the historical task. It also leads to the distinction that has been foundational to the modern discipline of Jesus scholarship.

## A CRUCIAL DISTINCTION

The name *Jesus* has two referents. On the one hand, *Jesus* refers to a human figure of the past: Jesus of Nazareth, a Galilean Jew of the first century. On the other hand, in Christian theology, devotion, and worship, the name *Jesus* also refers to a divine figure of the present: the risen living Christ who is one with God.

These two referents have been variously named in the history of Jesus scholarship. The first is commonly spoken of as "Jesus of

Nazareth" or "the Jesus of history" or "the historical Jesus." The second is "the Christ of faith" or "the biblical Christ" or "the canonical Jesus." My own preferred terminology is "the pre-Easter Jesus" and "post-Easter Jesus."

By the pre-Easter Jesus, I mean of course Jesus during his historical lifetime: a Galilean Jewish peasant of the first century, a flesh-and-blood figure of the past. This Jesus is dead and gone—a claim that does not deny Easter but simply recognizes that the "protoplasmic" Jesus isn't around anymore.

By the post-Easter Jesus, I mean *what Jesus became after his death.* More fully, I mean the Jesus of Christian tradition and experience. Both nouns, *tradition* and *experience,* are equally important. The former includes the Jesus of the developing Christian tradition in its pre-canonical, canonical, and ultimately creedal stages. The latter is the Jesus whom his followers (in the first century and in the centuries since) continued to experience after his death as a living, spiritual, and ultimately divine reality. As the Jesus of Christian experience, the post-Easter Jesus is an experiential reality, not simply an article of belief. ⅄

Both the pre-Easter and post-Easter Jesus are the subject of this book. How they are related to each other will be treated in later chapters. For now, I want to emphasize the importance of making the distinction between the two. When we don't, we risk losing both.

Such was my experience. I didn't know the distinction when I was growing up in the church, and so I combined everything I heard about Jesus into a single image: stories from the gospels, texts from the rest of the New Testament, doctrinal statements from the creeds, affirmations from Christian hymns and preaching. My uncritical synthesis generated what might be called "the composite Jesus."

I thus thought of Jesus as a figure of history as more divine than human. That's because I took it for granted that he was all of the things that the New Testament and the creeds say about him: Son of God, Word of God, Wisdom of God, messiah; very God of very God, begotten before all worlds, of one substance with God, the second person of the Trinity. And I took it for granted that he knew all of these things about himself.

Moreover, I thought of him as having the mind and power of God. It was because he had a divine mind that he knew things and could speak with authority. Because he had divine power, he could do spectacular deeds such as multiplying loaves and walking on water.

But note what had happened: I lost the historical Jesus as a credible human being. A person who knows himself to be the divinely begotten Son of God (and even the second person of the Trinity) and who has divine knowledge and power is not a real human being. Because he is more than human, he is not fully human. As the South African scholar Albert Nolan has remarked, we consistently underrate Jesus as a figure of history.[6] When we emphasize his divinity at the expense of his humanity, we lose track of the utterly remarkable human being he was.

Less obvious but equally important, I also lost the living risen Christ as a figure of the present. Because I had uncritically identified the divine Jesus with the human Jesus, Jesus as a divine figure became a figure of the past. He was here for a while, but not anymore. For thirty years, more or less, Jesus a divine being walked the earth. Then, after he had been raised from the dead, he ascended into heaven, where he is now at the right hand of God. He will come again someday—but in the meantime, he is not here. Jesus had become for me a divine figure of the past, not a figure of the present.

Thus failing to distinguish between the pre-Easter and post-Easter Jesus risks losing both. When we do make the distinction, we get both.

## MY LENSES FOR SEEING JESUS

How we see Jesus is to a large extent the product of the lenses through which we see him. So I turn to describing the lenses—the intellectual factors—that most affect how I see Jesus and Christian origins. Four are most important.

The first lens is the foundational claim of the modern study of Jesus, and this has already been described. Namely, the gospels are the product of a developing tradition, and they contain both history remembered and history metaphorized.

The second lens is the study of ancient Judaism. Like most scholars, I emphasize Jesus' rootedness in his own tradition. Jesus must be understood as a Jewish figure teaching and acting within Judaism, or we will misunderstand what he was about.

The third lens is the interdisciplinary study of Jesus and Christian origins, especially the social world of Jesus. A recent development with great illuminating power, it is one of the central features of the current renaissance in Jesus research. John Dominic Crossan most fully embodies this approach, and I have learned much from him.[7]

My fourth lens is the cross-cultural study of religion. To the interdisciplinary approach of Crossan and others, I add studies of religious experience (its varieties and effects) and types of religious figures known cross-culturally. I emphasize especially ecstatic religious experience and the nonordinary states of consciousness associated with it. Indeed, to the extent that my own sketch of Jesus is distinctive within the discipline, it is because of the weight that I give to ecstatic religious experience and its effects.

## THE IMPORTANCE OF WORLDVIEW

One more crucial factor affects how we see Jesus: our worldview. It could be understood as a fifth lens, but is better understood as a "macro-lens" affecting all of our seeing. A worldview is one's most basic image of "what is"—of what is real and what is possible.[8]

Individuals have worldviews. We all live our lives on the basis of what we think is real and possible. Cultures also have worldviews; indeed, one of the primary elements of a culture is its worldview.[9] Thus there are a multitude of worldviews.

Nevertheless, and broadly speaking, worldviews fall into two main categories: religious and secular. For a secular worldview, there is only "this"—and by "this" I mean the visible world of our ordinary experience. For a religious worldview, there is "this" and "more than this." The "more than this" has been variously named, imaged, and conceptualized; I will simply call it "the sacred." A religious worldview sees reality as grounded in the sacred. For a secular worldview, there is no sacred ground.

Modernity is dominated by a secular worldview. This image of reality began to emerge in the Enlightenment of the seventeenth and eighteenth centuries with the birth of modern science. Sometimes called the Newtonian worldview or simply the modern worldview, it sees what is real as the world of matter and energy, space and time; and it sees the universe as a closed system of cause and effect, operating in accord with natural laws. This vision of reality took the Western world by storm, to a large extent because of the impressive accomplishments of the science and technology that it generated. By this century, it had become the worldview of mass culture in the West, and most of us were socialized into it.

Like all worldviews, it functions in our minds almost unconsciously, affecting what we think possible and what we pay attention to.[10] It is especially corrosive of religion. It reduces reality to the space-time world of matter and energy, thereby making the notion of God problematic and doubtful. It reduces truth to factuality, either scientifically verifiable or historically reliable facts.[11] It raises serious doubts about anything that cannot be accommodated within its framework, including common religious phenomena such as prayer, visions, mystical experiences, extraordinary events, and unusual healings.

This worldview has very much affected the modern study of Jesus and the Bible. Not all scholars operate within it, but it has been the majority mind-set of the modern academy. When we try to see Jesus within this framework, it radically reduces what we will take seriously. There is much that we will miss, including the centrality of God for Jesus. We focus instead on what makes sense within our way of seeing.

So it was for me. There was a prolonged period in my life when the modern worldview functioned in my mind as the final arbiter of what can be taken seriously. The process was gradual. Raised as a Christian in the middle of this century, I grew up with both a religious and a secular worldview. By early adolescence, the secular worldview had begun to cause problems for my religious worldview. By my late teens and twenties, the problems had become acute. Indeed, the modern worldview had essentially crowded out the religious worldview.

But I now see things differently. In my thirties, I became aware of how uncritically, unconsciously, and completely I had accepted the modern worldview. I saw that most cultures throughout human history have seen things differently.[12] I realized that there are well-authenticated experiences that radically transcend what the modern worldview can accommodate. I became aware that the modern worldview is itself a relative cultural construction, the product of a particular era in human intellectual history. Though it is still dominant in Western culture, I am confident that the time is soon coming when it will seem as archaic and quaint as the Ptolemaic worldview.[13]

The change in my worldview has made it possible for me once again to take God seriously. I am convinced that the sacred is real. I see reality as far more mysterious than the modern worldview (or any worldview) affirms. I do not know the limits of what is possible with any precision. To be sure, I am reasonably confident that some things never happen, but I am convinced that the modern worldview draws those limits far too narrowly. All of this has strongly affected my work as a historian of Jesus and Christian origins. I can take much more of the tradition seriously.

## METHOD: EARLY LAYERS PLUS CONTEXT

Constructing an image of Jesus—which is what the quest for the historical Jesus is about—involves two crucial steps. The first step is discerning what is likely to go back to Jesus. The second step is setting this material in the historical context of the Jewish homeland in the first century.

### Step One: Discerning What Is Early

The quest involves discerning the early layers of the developing traditions about Jesus. What is early? What is later? I accept these common scholarly conclusions about our sources of material about Jesus:

- Paul is our earliest New Testament author. All of his genuine letters were written before any of the gospels; his earliest ones are from around the year 50, and they predate Mark by about twenty years. Yet Paul says relatively little about the historical Jesus, so he is not a major source.

- Q is the earliest written layer in the gospels, put into writing most likely in the fifties. A hypothetical document reconstructed by scholars from material found in Matthew and Luke but not in Mark, it is about two hundred verses long. An early collection of teaching attributed to Jesus, it contains very little narrative material. It was used by both Matthew and Luke when they wrote their gospels.[14]

○ Mark is the earliest of our existing gospels, written near 70 C.E. It provides the narrative framework for the other two synoptic gospels, Matthew and Luke.

○ Matthew and Luke each had a copy of Mark when they wrote their gospels later in the century. They also had a copy of Q, and they knew or created other traditions now found in them.

○ John's gospel is very different from the synoptic gospels and is not a primary source for the historical Jesus. It is, however, a powerful witness to what Jesus had become in the early Christian community in which John was written, about which I will say more later in this book.

○ The gospel of Thomas, discovered about fifty years ago in Egypt, is (like Q) a collection of sayings (114 in all). In present form, Thomas probably dates to the first half of the second century. I am inclined to see Thomas as independent of the synoptics and containing some early traditions not found elsewhere. But it is not a major source in my work.

Thus I see Mark and Q as the two primary documents behind the synoptic gospels. This widely accepted position is commonly known as "the two-source theory" or "the two-document hypothesis."[15]

Given the above view of our sources, how does one discern what is early? First, the most objective test is multiple attestation in two or more independent sources, at least one of which is early. In practice, it most commonly means "double attestation," for we have relatively few traditions with three or more attestations. The logic is straightforward: if a tradition appears in an early source *and* in another independent source, then not only is it early, but also it is unlikely to have been made up.

Second, when a core of material has been established through multiple attestation, texts that have only single attestation can be accepted if they are coherent with this core. Coherence might be argued on the basis of common subject matter. It might also be argued on the basis of common form. For example, many of the parables that have only single attestation are accepted as going back to Jesus because they reflect a perception and voice already established by multiple attestation.

A third factor involves a complication. Namely, one can discern demonstrable tendencies of the developing tradition. This functions both negatively and positively. When a saying or story reflects such a tendency, one must be suspicious of it. Alternatively, one that counters a demonstrable tendency of the developing tradition may well be historical, a survivor from an earlier stage.

## Step Two: Historical Context

Historical context is crucial, for words spoken and deeds done take on meaning only in context. They mean little, or remain ambiguous, apart from context. The same gesture can have very different meanings in different cultures, and the same saying can mean very different things in different contexts.

For reconstructing the meaning of things said and done by the historical Jesus, the crucial context is not the literary context of the gospels, but a cultural context, a social world. The context in which early Jesus material is to be set is the social world of the Jewish homeland in the first third of the first century.

There are several resources for knowing about the world of Jesus. Some of what we know comes from literary sources: early Christian literature, mostly canonical but also noncanonical; Jewish literature, both ancient and contemporary with Jesus; and (to a lesser extent) non-Jewish sources. Some comes from archaeological investigation. And some comes from the interdisciplinary study of his world. There are things we can know about his world that our ancient sources do not explicitly say. For example, none of our sources says that the world of Jesus was the world of a preindustrial agrarian society, yet we can be quite sure that it was. Knowing the economic and political dynamics typical of such societies can help us understand what the world of Jesus was like. Indeed, knowing those characteristics enables us to recognize data in our sources that point to such a world.

This is not the place to try to describe the world of Jesus in a comprehensive way. I content myself with noting that the Jewish social world in the time of Jesus was undergoing significant social change and sharp tensions. The Jewish homeland fell under Roman imperial control in 63 B.C.E., about sixty years before Jesus was born. The combination of Roman rule and Hellenistic cultural influences meant that traditional ways and identities were in question. Ethnic identities were in tension with more cosmopolitan visions of human life. The commercialization of agriculture led to the dislocation of peasants from land that they had owned. It was a restive time. Jewish revolts against Rome broke out around the time of Jesus' birth. Forty years after his death, the calamitous war of Jewish rebellion climaxed in the Roman destruction of Jerusalem and the temple, changing Jesus' native religious tradition forever. Jesus thus lived in a watershed century. In this setting, he did what he did. And everything we can know about his world is relevant to the study of the historical Jesus.

Because much of this chapter has focused on how to go beneath the surface level of the gospels in order to discern the historical Jesus, I want to emphasize as I conclude that both the historical Jesus and the canonical gospels matter to me as a Christian.[16] The pre-Easter Jesus, as we can discern him through historical research, is a remarkable and compelling figure, and our glimpses of him can help provide content for what it means to take him seriously. The canonical Jesus discloses what Jesus had become in the experience of early Christian communities near the end of the first century. Independently of their historical factuality, the stories of the canonical Jesus can function in our lives as powerfully true metaphorical narratives, shaping Christian vision and identity. It is not an either-or choice; both the pre-Easter and post-Easter Jesus matter.

What we see is to a large extent the product of how we see. Thus our understanding of the sources, as well as the lenses through which we see both them and the world of Jesus, will decisively affect what we see in the figure behind the gospels. What all of this means will, I trust, become clear in the rest of this book.

# KNOWING JESUS:
# FAITH AND HISTORY

*N. T. Wright*

W E KNOW ABOUT Jesus in two ways: history and faith.

People regularly try to eliminate one on the basis of the other, dismissing combinations as compromise. This separation belongs to the Western world of the last three centuries. It goes with the split of religion and politics, with the dismissal of "God" into a remote deist heaven (leaving humans to organize the world as they pleased), and with the definition of *religion* as "that which humans do with their solitude." These and similar phenomena of the so-called Enlightenment have created a climate in which history has been used as a weapon against faith, and faith as an escape from history.

Like Marcus, I grew up with this split implicit in my worldview. One used a different tone of voice for God, and even for Jesus ("Our Lord"). Fascinated as I was by ancient history, when I first studied the New Testament, the closest I got to integrating the two worlds was when Paul appealed to Nero. The early Christians lived, one assumed, primarily in a world of faith, hammering out issues such as justification and Christology. Their theology hardly impinged even on their thinking about their own corporate life, let alone on world politics, except as a distant implication.[1]

But around the time that I began to study Jesus in his historical context (the late 1970s), I also began to study Judaism. Not the idealized Judaism I had thought of before, in which people carried in their heads a set of abstract ideas and expectations, but the rough-and-tumble Judaism of the Maccabees and Herod, of the wars of 66–70 and 132–135, of Qumran and Masada. It was a world in which Philo of Alexandria could write learned works of philosophy and exegesis and then act as an ambassador at the imperial court on behalf of his beleaguered community. It was the world of the learned and devious Josephus, the general, aristocrat, and historian who spoke of Israel's God going over to the Romans—and then did so himself. It was the world of the Dead Sea Scrolls. I began to read them, and the pseudepigrapha, too, (a motley and disparate collection of Jewish writings from the last few centuries B.C.E. and the first few C.E.) not simply as collections of dreams and visions, encoding abstract theological ideas that could then be lined up either as precursors of Christian beliefs or as evidence of that which Christian theology opposed, but as Jewish tracts that used the language of symbol and myth to stake out positions in a very this-worldly political history. At every point in this reading I found material that illuminated Jesus and the texts that spoke of him. At no point did I detect the familiar split of history and faith.

It took some years, and various crises exegetical and personal, to show me that this integrated world of history and faith was more true to the rest of human life, including my own, than I had dared to suppose. Study of ancient integrations led me to conjecture, then to celebrate, analogous contemporary integrations. Led me, in other words, first to name and then to rebel against the tyrannical thought-forms in whose split-level world I had grown up. Led me, at length, out into fresh epistemological air, and the new, risky choices of a single world with multiple interlocking dimensions.

I regard this move as the most liberating moment in my intellectual development. I react against attempts to pull me back into the old split-level world—attempts made, of course, from both levels—with the vigor of one who does not want to be imprisoned again in the attic (faith divorced from history) or the dungeon (history divorced from faith). This reaction will be understood, perhaps, by those who have experienced other liberations, for instance from heavy-handed traditional Protestantism or Catholicism; though from where I sit it often looks as though those who trumpet loudest about such liberations have sometimes merely exchanged the attic for the dungeon.

All historians have theological presuppositions. Atheism and agnosticism count as well as faith; refusing to declare one's own interests, or assuming an unargued modernist or secularist stance a priori, is either naive, or mischievous, or a naked power play. We all see the world through the colored spectacles of our own personal histories, backgrounds, assumptions, and so on. History is precisely a matter of looking, *through one's own spectacles,* at evidence about the past, trying to reconstruct the probable course of events and the motivations of the characters involved, and defending such reconstructions against rival ones, not on the grounds of their coherence with one's own presuppositions, but on the scientific grounds of getting in the data, doing so with appropriate simplicity, and shedding light on other areas of research.[2] Part of the process is becoming aware that one's spectacles are almost certainly distorting the picture, and becoming ready to let puzzles within the evidence or the reconstruction, or the alternative theories of one's colleagues, alert one to such distortion and enable one to clean or replace the offending lens. Those who are unaware that they are wearing spectacles are merely less likely than their colleagues to know when they need cleaning. My own major book on Jesus[3] grew to the length it did precisely because I was determined to allow this process of dialogue to occur at every stage of the research and to be visible at every stage of the argument.

My view, that we come to know Jesus by both history and faith, is itself a product of a lifelong attempt to do just this, which I believe to have been sufficiently successful (though constantly in need of improvement) to encourage me to press on. When, during this attempt, I have found from time to time that the Jesus I knew by faith seemed less and less like the Jesus I was discovering by history, I have found that by living with the problem, turning it this way and that in the complex and often hidden world of personal and communal consciousness and reflection, faith has been able to discover not just that the new, and initially surprising, historical evidence was capable of being accommodated, but also that it could actually be turned to advantage. Alternatively, there were times when faith stood its ground and, by looking at the challenge from all angles, was able to show that the historical evidence was as well if not better interpreted within a different framework.

Part of the challenge of history comes from allowing suspicion a proper role. Suspicion, that is, of the texts themselves, of one's colleagues' readings, and particularly of one's own. However, a caution is necessary. The guild of New Testament studies has become so used to operating with a hermeneutic of suspicion that we find ourselves trapped in our own subtleties. If two ancient writers agree about something, that proves one got it from the other. If they seem to disagree, that proves that one or both are wrong. If they say an event fulfilled biblical prophecy, they made it up to look like that. If an event or saying fits a writer's theological scheme, that writer invented it. If there are two accounts of similar events, they are a "doublet" (there was only one event); but if a single account has anything odd about it, there must have been two events, which are now conflated. And so on. Anything to show how clever we are, how subtle, to have smoked out the reality behind the text. But, as any author who has watched her or his books being reviewed will know, such reconstructions again and again miss the point, often wildly. If we cannot get it right when we share a culture, a period, and a language, it is highly likely that many of our subtle reconstructions of ancient texts and histories are our own unhistorical fantasies, unrecognized only because the writers are long since dead and cannot answer back. Suspicion is all very well; there is also such a thing as a hermeneutic of paranoia. Somebody says something; they must have a motive; therefore they must have made it up. Just because we are rightly determined to avoid a hermeneutic of credulity, that does not mean there is no such thing as appropriate trust, or even readiness to suspend disbelief for a while, and see where it gets us.

I propose, then, a no-holds-barred history on the one hand and a no-holds-barred faith on the other. This, I believe, is to live in the uncomfortable real world, where such things do not shout challenges at each other from behind locked doors but meet, merge, fuse, question each other, uncouple again, swirl round each other, undergird and undermine each other, examine each other's foundations and set about demolishing or reconstructing them, appearing at one moment inseparable and at the next in an embarrassingly public family squabble. This is, after all, inevitable if we reflect on what doing history actually involves, and on what faith—the Christian faith, at least—is all about.

One important feature of bringing together the worlds of history and faith, and recognizing that other people (notably first-century Jews) did so, too, is that we should make ourselves conscious of the way in which we, and they, use language to do both at the same time. George Caird, with whom Marcus and I both did our graduate work, argued in a famous book that when people come face-to-face with ultimate and personal reality, this event "can be adequately viewed only through the lenses of myth and eschatology."[4] These are both, Caird argues, varieties of metaphors. But, as he also argues, to say that a particular set of language is "mythological" or "eschatological" is by no means to say that it does not intend to refer to actual people, actual events, actual history. What it does, rather, is to invest that history, those people, with a significance that a bald and unadorned narrative would lack. To allow bare history, or a "truth" that was entirely divorced from history, the last word would be to cave in and admit that the Enlightenment's split world had won after all. The attic or the dungeon.

How then do we proceed with the tasks? What do history and faith look like when pursuing these goals?

First, history. I take it as basic that the historian of any period covets, dreams about, lusts after *evidence*. Every coin, every half-erased inscription, every fragment of papyrus is precious. Who cares whether the evidence comes from a "heretical" sect? If it is evidence, we want it. If this is true for any historian, it is even more so for the ancient historian, who often has to piece together random fragments and make bold hypotheses about whole decades for which little or no evidence has survived. When it comes to knowing about Jesus, we have a good deal of evidence at one level and precious little at another. We have a fair amount of material produced by Jesus' avowed followers, and very little produced by anyone else. Any fresh clues, from whatever source, are to be welcomed, studied, sifted, and used to their full potential.

The historian of Jesus, using all available material and coveting more, will try to answer questions such as: What can be known about Jesus? Where does he belong within the world of his day (the world of Greco-Roman antiquity and of first-century Judaism in particular)? What were his aims, and to what extent did he accomplish them? What caused him to meet an early death? And, not least, why did a movement claiming allegiance to him spring up shortly after his death, taking a shape that was both like and significantly unlike other movements of the time? These are questions that *any* historian, not just Christians, must ask. All will want to use the same data to answer them.

The question then is: do the available data offer us, as they stand, a coherent picture which makes sense historically? If not, how do we evaluate them? Which pieces of data take us closer to Jesus, and which ones lead us away from him?

The available sources do not offer a coherent picture. The Jesus of the canonical material is in certain respects quite different from the Jesus of at least some of the noncanonical documents (for example, the Nag Hammadi codices). The Jesus of both of these is scarcely recognizable in the veiled picture of Jesus in the later rabbinic material. Add to this the picture of Jesus in Tacitus, Josephus, and elsewhere. How do we decide? What do we make of the evidence?

Almost all scholars still believe that the earlier the material, the more likely it is to bring us into contact with historical bedrock. This assumption is by no means always justified, but let us remain with it for the moment. It at once opens up the long-standing problem about the sources that, whatever one's prejudices, are bound to play a large role at some point: the synoptic gospels (Matthew, Mark, and Luke).

It has long been assumed among New Testament scholars that in order to work back from our sources to find Jesus himself we must first solve the problem of the literary relationship between these gospels. This is notoriously complex. (The question of the relationship between them and John, and between all four canonical gospels and Thomas, is more complex still.) If they used sources (including one another), can we reconstruct them?

Further stages of investigation are frequently undertaken. Prior to the writing of the gospels and their sources, the material probably circulated in oral forms, which can be studied in terms of their likely settings. When the gospel writers used their sources, they can be presumed to have selected, adapted, and arranged the material. A three-stage development can then be postulated: (1) the shaping of preliterary oral traditions; (2) the collecting of oral traditions into literary sources; (3) the collecting and editing of these literary sources into polished gospels. In case this were not already sufficiently complex, it is frequently supposed that we can and should also investigate further hypothetical stages of the history of Jesus traditions in between these three.

If all this worked, and if most scholars agreed about it, it would be fine. But it doesn't, and they don't, and it isn't. Despite frequent claims, a century of research has failed to reach anything like consensus on a single one of the stages in question, let alone on the hypothetical developments in between. Thus:

1. There are dozens of different proposals about how to analyze the forms of the early tradition and about what elements of the life of the early church they may reflect. None commands widespread agreement.

2. There are at least two widely held, variously developed, and mutually incompatible theories about the literary sources of the synoptic gospels: (a) The majority still hold that Mark was written first and that behind the passages in which Matthew and Luke overlap with each other but not with Mark was a source that scholars call Q. A vocal minority within this majority claims to distinguish different stages in the development of Q; many others, though believing firmly in Q, offer radically different explanations of its origin or, alternatively (like Marcus), regard all such further theories as at best unprovable. (b) A minority, however, hold that Matthew was written first and was used by both Mark and Luke (so that Q never existed). Further, several who agree with the majority on Marcan priority agree with the minority that the overlap between non-Marcan passages in Matthew and Luke is better explained by Luke's use of Matthew than by a common source.

3. Mutually incompatible theories abound as to where, when, and why the synoptic gospels came to final form. Since there is no agreement about sources, there is no agreement as to how and why the different evangelists used them. If, for instance, we believe that Matthew used Mark, we can discuss Matthew's theology on the basis of his editing of Mark. If we don't believe Matthew used Mark, we can't.

4. In the nature of the case, if there is no agreement about how the tradition developed in these major stages, there is no chance of agreement on possible levels or layers in between.

One reason for the continuing impasse on these questions is that they are often addressed, and solutions to them proposed, with more than half an eye on the probable outcome for the supposedly second-order questions concerning Jesus. The Q theory came to birth as part of a conservative response to radical nineteenth-century skepticism; it provided, so it was said, a reliable and early source for Jesus' sayings. Now, however, some who promote it do so in the hope that, by isolating a hypothetical "early Q," they may offer a radically alternative vision of Jesus and early Christianity to that which appears in the synoptic tradition as a whole. Similarly, Marcan priority has sometimes been used as a way of affirming that the early church preserved a memory of Jesus' career, at least in outline; Matthean priority is now sometimes presented as a way of ensuring the authenticity of sayings (parables, for instance) which might otherwise be suspect as occurring only in one source, and that a late one. And so on, and so on.

All such questions, however, are to be seen in their wider context, which is a part of the large question: why did Christianity begin, and why did it take the shape it did? This includes questions about Jesus and John the Baptist; it includes questions about Paul, John, and the gospel of Thomas; it includes, particularly, questions about the nature of the synoptic material and the way in which it reached its present form. And the way to solve all such questions, whether to do with Jesus or to do with the sources, is once more the scientific method of hypothesis and verification.

There still seems to be considerable confusion as to how this method, which I have consciously tried to use through all my historical work, actually functions. The researcher, after a period of total and sometimes confusing immersion in the data, emerges with a hypothesis, a big picture of how everything fits together. The hypothesis is proposed, spelled out as fully as possible. In the process, it is tested against three criteria: Does it make sense of the data as they stand? Does it have an appropriate level of simplicity, or even elegance? Does it shed light on areas of research other than the one it was designed to cover? History diverges from the so-called hard sciences, not in the use of this method and in the asking of these questions, but in that there are no agreed-on criteria for what counts as "making sense" of the data or, for that matter, what counts as the appropriate level of simplicity. Real life, which history purports to describe, is often bitty and messy, with loose ends and inconsistencies.

This method is quite different from that frequently proposed within some circles of Jesus study. It is proposed that the way to study Jesus is to break the material down into its component parts and to evaluate these on the basis of certain rules. Only when we have done this will we be allowed to put together the jigsaw puzzle of what we have discovered and see what sort of a coherent picture it might produce. This apparently scientific proposal hides two unproved assumptions: (a) the belief that isolated fragments of Jesus material circulated, and developed, in the early church divorced from narrative frameworks; (b) a quite well worked out theory about Jesus and the early church which actually dictates the rules proposed for assessing material.

If we are to be thorough and disciplined about the total historical task, however, it is important that we recognize that *all* the pieces of the puzzle, including every question about Jesus and every question about the sources, belong together within the overall hypothesis. We are not in a position to solve one part of the puzzle first and then use it as a fixed point from which to tackle the rest. In particular, we are not (despite repeated assertions) in a position to solve the question of synoptic sources first and then use this to reconstruct Jesus. As I have argued elsewhere, we actually know more securely that Jesus of Nazareth was a Jewish prophet announcing the kingdom of God than we know almost anything about the history of traditions that led up to the production of the gospels as we have them.[5] And we can fill in this picture of Jesus step-by-step, as I have tried to show in my writings, in such a way as to draw in more and more of the evidence within a growing hypothesis about both Jesus himself and Christian origins, *including the writing of the gospels*. The coherence and simplicity of the resulting picture, the sense that is made of the data, and the light that is shed on many other areas enable us to state with confidence that this, or something like it, is indeed how it was. Whether or not my own reconstruction is accepted in detail, this is the method that we must use, as historians, in coming to know about Jesus.

What is more, we cannot settle in advance the question of how much, if any, of the gospel material belongs to a period later than that of Jesus himself. We cannot, that is, *assume,* ahead of the reconstruction, that quite a lot of the gospel material was invented by the early church and then argue implicitly from that assumption that anyone who comes up with a historical proposal about Jesus which gets in most of the data cannot be considered a serious historian. This is precisely the sort of move, a kind of hedge around the critical Torah, made by paradigms under threat to protect themselves from the possibility of an imminent shift. Of course the early church used and shaped the gospel stories for their own ends. But of course we do not know, ahead of time, whether they invented any stories wholesale and, if so, which bits are which. Only if we presuppose a view of Jesus—if, in other words, we secretly decide the question before we start—could we know that. This, of course, is often done, particularly by those still wedded to an older liberal picture of "Jesus the teacher" who (unlike several leaders of first-century Jewish movements) would be shocked to think of himself as, for instance, messiah. I do not know in advance, more specifically, that a considerable gulf exists between Jesus as he was (the "pre-Easter Jesus," in Marcus's language) and Jesus as the church came to know him and speak of him (the "post-Easter Jesus"). We might eventually wish to reach some such conclusion; we cannot build it into our historical method.

So much for history. What then can we say about faith in itself, a no-holds-barred Christian faith of which I have already spoken? What is it, and what sort of knowledge of Jesus can it provide? It has been inherent in Christianity from the beginning that the believer "knows Christ";[6] Jesus, as the good shepherd, knows his own sheep, and his own know him.[7] This is regularly described in terms borrowed from ordinary interpersonal relationships: believers are aware of Jesus' presence, his love, his guidance, his consolation, his rebuke, and even perhaps his laughter. They are aware of being in touch with a personality that is recognizable, distinct, frequently puzzling and unpredictable, always loving and lovable, powerful and empowering, loyal and calling forth loyalty. This awareness is regularly generated and sustained through certain activities, notably worship, prayer, the sacraments, suffering, the reading of scripture, Christian fellowship, reflection on the world as created and redeemed in and through Jesus Christ, and perhaps particularly the service of those in desperate need, those in whom Christians believe they meet Jesus in a special way.

At the same time, as with any relationship, there can be problems, misunderstandings, and difficulties. Almost all Christians report experiencing from time to time a sense of distance or even the apparent withdrawal of Jesus' presence. Christian teachers and spiritual directors have long recognized that this may happen through one of, or a combination of, various factors, including depression, tiredness, rebellion, sin, misinformation, wrong expectations, and many others. Equally, they may happen for none of those reasons, and there may be times when all one can do is to wait in the darkness. But after the waiting, again and again, comes fresh "knowledge"; granted the way the English language works, one cannot call it anything else. It is not just "belief." It is natural to say "I believe it's raining" when indoors with the curtains shut, but it would be odd to say it, except in irony, standing on a hillside in a downpour. For many Christians much of the time, knowing Jesus is more like the latter: being drenched in his love and the challenge of his call, not merely imagining we hear him like raindrops on a distant windowpane. (For many, of course, the latter is the norm; hinting, promising, inviting.)

But what does it mean to "know" someone? Humans being what they are, this is a great mystery. It is, clearly, different from knowing *about* them. When we "know" a person (as opposed to, say, knowing the height of the Eiffel Tower), we imply some kind of relationship, some mutual understanding. We are used to each other; we can anticipate how the other will react; we accurately assess their wishes, hopes, and fears. We could perhaps have arrived at the basic facts by careful detached study, but when we say we "know" someone, we assume that this knowledge is the result of face-to-face encounter.

When someone claims to "know" Jesus of Nazareth in this sense, they are making a claim about other things as well: the existence of a nonspatiotemporal world; the existence of Jesus within that world; the possibility of presently alive human beings having access to that world, and of this being actually true in their case. They are claiming, more particularly, to know one person in particular, a distinctive and recognizable person, within that world, and that this person is identified as Jesus. This knowledge is what many people, myself included, are referring to when we say that we know Jesus "by faith."

And, in that knowledge, we come also to know *about* Jesus: in the context of the personal relationship, we discover more about who Jesus is, what he is like, what gladdens him and grieves him, what he longs for and laughs at, what he offers, and what he challenges people to do. And, at the heart of it all, less easy to express but deeply important, one is confronted with a love rooted in historical action and passion, a love that has accomplished for us something that we desperately needed and could not have done for ourselves.

In saying all this, I open myself, of course, to the full hermeneutical fury of the modernist, who says I have renounced objectivity, and the postmodernist, who says it's all wish fulfillment. Equally important, I open myself to the comment that plenty of people have used the word *Jesus* to denote figures so different from one another that the possibility of self-delusion is strong. All this I acknowledge. Yet at precisely this point history comes to the help of faith. The Jesus I know in prayer, in the sacraments, in the faces of those in need, is the Jesus I meet in the historical evidence—including the New Testament, of course, but the New Testament read not so much as the church has told me to read it but as I read it with my historical consciousness fully operative. The Jesus whose love seems to go deeper and reach more of me than the deepest human loves I know (and I have been blessed with much human love) converges remarkably with the Jesus whom I have tried to describe historically in chapter 12 of *Jesus and the Victory of God* and, more briefly, in chapter 6 of the present book—the Jesus, that is, who found himself possessed of a very first-century Jewish vocation, to go to the place where the world was in pain and to take that pain upon himself. The more I find out *about* Jesus historically, the more I find that my faith-knowledge of him is supported and filled out. These knowings are indivisible. I see why some people find themselves driven to distinguish the Jesus of history and the Christ of faith, but I do not think the early Christians made such a distinction, and I do not find the need to do so myself. This Jesus of whom I speak still comes to meet us, sometimes bidden, sometimes not, sometimes despite the locked doors of an enclosed epistemology, always recognizable by the mark of the nails. And he thereby raises most of the questions that the rest of this book will examine.

History, then, prevents faith becoming fantasy. Faith prevents history becoming mere antiquarianism. Historical research, being always provisional, cannot ultimately veto faith, though it can pose hard questions that faith, in order to retain its integrity precisely as *Christian* faith, must struggle to answer, and may well grow strong through answering. Faith, being subject to the vagaries of personality and culture, cannot veto the historical enterprise (it can't simply say "I don't like the Jesus you write about, so you must be wrong"), but it can put hard questions to history, not least on the large topic of the origins of Christianity, and history may be all the better for trying to answer them.

All of this means, I realize, that the question this chapter sought to address—that of *how* we know about Jesus—interacts in all sorts of ways with the rest of the book, which deals with *what* we know about Jesus. We cannot find a neutral place on which to stand, a theory of knowledge, or a theory of knowledge-about-Jesus, which can be established independently of its object. History and faith (taking *faith* in its broadest sense, as whatever worldview-commitment or metaphysical assumption one may make) need each other at every step, and never more so than here. This inclines me to suppose that the category of knowledge itself is actually a branch of another category—that, as in some parts of the Hebrew scriptures, "knowing" is part of "loving" rather than the other way around. But since this is a book about Jesus, not about epistemology, this topic must be left for another day.

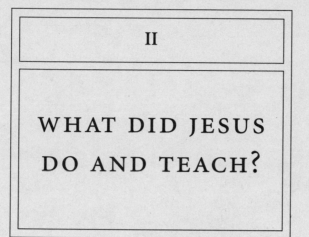

II

# WHAT DID JESUS DO AND TEACH?

## CHAPTER 3

# THE MISSION AND
# MESSAGE OF JESUS          *N. T. Wright*

I F WE ARE to talk meaningfully about Jesus, there is no question
where we must start. We must study him within the Jewish world of
Palestine in the first century.

## JESUS THE PALESTINIAN JEW

Jesus was a first-century Palestinian Jew. Whatever he said and did
must have made sense, even if disturbing sense, within that context.
However many other grids of reference we bring to him, we cannot
skip this one. Certain specific things follow at once from this.[1]

Jesus belonged within a world where (what we call) theology and
politics went hand in hand. Granted the particular theology and the
particular politics, that is hardly surprising.

The theology was Jewish monotheism, whose first-century shape
had been forged in the fires of persecution in the centuries since the
Babylonian exile. First-century Jewish monotheism was not an abstract
theory about there only being one god. The Jews believed *their* god,
YHWH, was the only god, and that all others (including the "one god" of
Stoics and other pantheists) were idols, either concrete creations of
human hands or abstract creations of human minds. Jesus shared the
belief that Israel's god was the only true god.

Monotheism went hand in hand with "election." The Jews believed
themselves to be the chosen people of this one god. What happened to

Israel was therefore of universal significance. Many Jews of Jesus' day therefore supposed (for instance) that when YHWH finally acted to vindicate them, this would be the means of judgment and/or mercy coming upon the rest of the world. Jesus shared the belief that Israel had been chosen to be YHWH's special people, through whom the world would be addressed by its creator.

If there is one god, and you are his one people, but you are currently suffering oppression, you must believe that the present state of affairs is temporary. Monotheism and election thus give birth to (what I call) eschatology: the belief that history is going somewhere, that something will happen through which everything will be put right. First-century Jewish eschatology characteristically claimed that the one god would soon act within history to vindicate his people and to establish justice and peace once and for all. Jesus shared this belief.

More specifically, for many Jews in what we call the second-temple period (covering the last four centuries before Jesus and the first century after him), this hope was held within an implicit larger story, a metanarrative about YHWH, his people, and the world. This story, echoing the great foundation narrative of the Exodus from Egypt, had been decisively reshaped by the experience of the Babylonian exile and by the persistent belief, visible in texts and movements of various sorts, that this exile, in its deepest reality, was not yet over. Just as the language of exodus continued to dominate eschatology, so the language of return came to function as a second, and decisive, layer of metaphor, a lens through which Jesus' contemporaries viewed God's plans for their future.

They had, of course, returned home long since from Babylon. But exile was about more than geography. Exile was the state of political servitude, cultural domination, and above all theological unredeemedness that Israel continued to experience. It was a punishment for Israel's sin, the symbolic outworking of their god having given them up to their own devices, first copying, then suffering under, pagan idolatry. Thus, if foreigners were still their overlords, Israel's punishment was continuing. The great promises of forgiveness articulated by the prophets of the exile, notably Isaiah, Jeremiah, and Ezekiel, had not yet been fulfilled. The so-called postexilic writings speak of a liberation still to be accomplished. They employ, to describe this liberation, the language of return from exile, of new exodus.[2] Jesus shared this prevailing understanding of Israel's story and hope.

It was within this context, within a world on tiptoe with expectation, that Jesus began to announce, after the manner of a would-be prophet, that YHWH, Israel's God, was now at last becoming king. The first of these points is easily established: Jesus spoke of himself as a prophet, he behaved as a prophet, and when others referred to him in this way he did not correct them. The early church, which believed a good many other things about Jesus, would have had no interest in inventing this characterization.[3] The first stroke in my historical sketch of Jesus as a first-century Palestinian Jew is therefore: Jesus was *a first-century Jewish prophet.*

The second follows closely on the first: Jesus was a first-century Jewish prophet *announcing God's kingdom.* This was the very center of his mission and message. If he was indeed a first-century Jew, living, believing, and hoping within the worldview I have just outlined, we should be able to see something of what he meant.

The meaning of the phrase "kingdom of God" within first-century Judaism is of course a huge topic in itself. I propose to cut through the jungle of texts and discussions by highlighting two interesting phenomena from key moments in the story of the Jews in this period.[4]

The first is Josephus's description of the rebellion of Judas the Galilean, which took place in 6 C.E. The revolutionaries were inspired, says Josephus, by the belief that they should have "no master but God."[5] This attitude seems to have been quite widespread. Many, perhaps most, Jews longed for the day when they would not be ruled by the Roman emperor or even by the pseudoroyal house of Herod but would have God alone for their sovereign. The phrase "kingdom of God" (and such similar reverential phrases as "kingdom of heaven") denoted, not a *place* where God ruled, but rather the *fact* that God ruled—or, rather, that he soon would rule, because he certainly was not doing so at present in the way he intended to do. Other lords had usurped his unique role as the sovereign of Israel.

This hope was not merely political. It grew directly out of Jewish monotheism: YHWH, Israel's God, was the one God of all the world. Theology and politics, piety and revolution, went hand in hand.

The second moment which illustrates the same point comes from a hundred years after Jesus' day. The last great would-be messiah of the period, Simeon ben-Kosiba, led a rebellion in 132 C.E. It lasted for three years, until he and his followers were rounded up and killed by the

Romans. Ben-Kosiba had been hailed by the greatest rabbi of the period, Rabbi Akiba, as "Bar-Kochba," "son of the star," messiah.[6] But after
his defeat the rabbis, in a move that would determine the shape of Judaism from that day to this, turned their faces away from revolution
and focused instead on the private study and practice of Torah, the
Jewish law. This move was summed up neatly by one of Akiba's disciples, Rabbi Nehunya ben ha-Kanah, who said, "He who takes upon
himself the yoke of the Law, from him shall be taken away the yoke of
the kingdom and the yoke of worldly care."[7] In other words, devotion to
Torah, studied and practiced within the Jewish community, offers a
safe alternative to revolution. And the code ben ha-Kanah used for revolution is the phrase "the kingdom," or "the kingdom of God."

These two examples (which are of course only the tip of the iceberg)
explain the popularity of the view that Jesus was a Jewish revolutionary. He announced the kingdom of God; he gathered followers around
him; he marched on Jerusalem; he died the death of the failed revolutionary leader. What could be more simple?

But even a modest acquaintance with the complex gospel tradition
suggests that things were never that simple. Jesus seems to have drawn
not merely upon the current revolutionary ideology, but on the idea of
the "gospel," the good news, which traces the kingdom theme back to
the prophets, and particularly to Isaiah.[8] It will help to introduce a passage which draws together a good deal of the theology of Isaiah 40–55
and, in doing so, provides a central biblical statement of the coming
kingdom of God, namely, Isaiah 52.7–12:

> How lovely upon the mountains are the feet of the one
> who brings good news, who publishes salvation, who says to Zion
> "Your God reigns!"
> Listen! Your watchmen lift up their voices and shout for joy,
> because in plain sight they see YHWH returning to Zion.
> YHWH has bared his holy arm in the sight of all the nations, and all
>     the ends of the world shall see the salvation of our god.
> Depart, depart, go out thence, touch no unclean thing . . . for YHWH
>     will go before you, and the god of Israel will be your rearguard.

Here are the three main strands of second-temple hope. When
YHWH becomes king, Israel will return from exile, evil will be defeated,

and YHWH himself will return to Zion. None of this had happened in Jesus' day. Israel had not been restored. As long as pagans ruled, evil had not been defeated. Similarly, at no point in the second-temple period do we find any statement that YHWH has returned to dwell on Zion, in the renewed temple.[9] To invoke the Isaianic gospel, then, was to go beyond mere military revolution. It was to speak of the return from exile, the defeat of evil, and the return of YHWH to Zion.

The coming kingdom of God was not, then, a matter of abstract ideas or timeless truths. It was not about a new sort of religion, a new spiritual experience, a new moral code (or new strength to observe existing ones). It was not a doctrine or a soteriology (a systematic scheme for individual salvation or a general statement about how one might go to heaven after death). It was not a new sociological analysis, critique, or agenda. It was about Israel's story reaching its climax, about Israel's history moving toward its decisive moment.

The historian must assume that Jesus of Nazareth was gripped by a strong sense of vocation. All that we know about him suggests that he was powerfully aware, not just of a general numinous quality to the universe, but of the deeply personal presence and purpose, strength and guidance of the one he called "Abba," Father. If that makes him a "Spirit person," in Marcus's phrase, so be it, though I myself prefer to use as far as possible language that reflects the culture under discussion rather than importing categories from elsewhere, useful though that sometimes is. It also means that Jesus was aware, as many other Jews down the years—most recently his own cousin John—had been, that he had a particular vocation, a role to perform. That, we must insist, is not Christian retrojection. It is first-century Jewish history.

## ANNOUNCING THE KINGDOM

What, then, did Jesus mean by his kingdom announcement? Let me anticipate my conclusion. Jesus was telling his contemporaries that the kingdom was indeed breaking into history, *but that it did not look like what they had expected.* The time of restoration was at hand, and people of all sorts were summoned to share and enjoy it, but Israel was warned that its present ways of advancing the kingdom were counterproductive and would result in national disaster. Jesus was therefore summoning his hearers to *be* Israel in a new way, to take up their proper roles in God's unfolding drama, and he assured them that if they followed him in this way, they would be vindicated when the great day came. A good many of the parables not only articulate this message but also, in their very form, embody it.[10] This explains, among other things, why the announcement was so often made in a cryptic fashion: "If you have ears, then hear!"

In the course of all this, Jesus was launching the real battle for the kingdom. But it was a battle, not against Rome, but against the enemy that stood behind Rome. This battle, which would reach its own climax in events to take place in Jerusalem, was even now beginning in his public career, as his symbolic actions, and the teaching that surrounded them, generated opposition at various levels. His kingdom announcement itself would lead to the victory through which Israel's god would become king; but this victory, and the resulting kingdom, would not look like what Jesus' contemporaries had in mind.

Jesus' announcement was thus revolutionary indeed—doubly revolutionary, in fact. Not only did the kingdom challenge the power and policies of Herod, of Caiaphas, and of Rome itself, as the revolutionaries would have insisted, it also challenged the militant aspirations of the revolutionaries themselves. And it challenged, within all of that, the injustice and oppression that Jesus saw as endemic within his own society. These things hung together: a society that insisted angrily on its own purity toward outsiders would also maintain sharp social distinctions, and perpetuate economic and other injustices, within itself. At the purely political level, one could have predicted that someone who put his finger on all this would end up being attacked from all sides and even misunderstood by his own followers. But more of that anon.

We should not be surprised that Jesus, in making his kingdom announcement, kept on the move, going from village to village and, so far as we can tell, staying away from Sepphoris and Tiberias, the two largest cities in Galilee. He was not so much like a wandering preacher giving sermons or a wandering philosopher offering maxims as like a radical politician gathering support for a new and highly risky movement. But, again, we should not imagine that politics here could be split off from theology. Jesus was doing what he was doing in the belief that by following this way, rather than the others, Israel's God was indeed becoming king. He was saying what people wanted to hear but challenging the ways they had heard and meant it.

Jesus was therefore announcing that the long-awaited kingdom was being inaugurated through his own work. The example of Bar-Kochba a century later serves to clarify a point that has long puzzled historians: someone doing what Jesus was doing was bound to be speaking of the kingdom as *both* present *and* future.[11] The "presence," though, was not simply an inner personal event, a new way of ordering one's private religious experience, nor was it yet a new way of understanding and reorganizing social or cultural conditions. Likewise, the "futurity" was not the expectation of the end of the world. Bar-Kochba believed that the kingdom was already present. He had, after all, already raised the flag of liberation. That is why he not only minted coins (itself a revolutionary act, a declaration of independence), but dated them with the year 1—much like the French revolutionaries, who in 1793 decided to restart the calendar.[12] Bar-Kochba also believed, however, that the kingdom was still future: he had not yet defeated the Romans or rebuilt the temple. Once he had accomplished those tasks, the world would see that the kingdom had in fact begun with his initial announcement. So it was with Jesus. He saw his initial announcement as the real beginning of the kingdom (a very different interpretation of the kingdom from Bar-Kochba's, but on the same historical map), even though major tasks were still to be accomplished—tasks that, he believed, would retrospectively validate his earlier paradoxical claim.

Jesus, then, was not just a prophet announcing the kingdom. He believed *that the kingdom was breaking in to Israel's history in and through his own presence and work.* This is the third layer of my historical portrait of his mission and message.

## GATHERING SUPPORT

When Jesus told the story of the kingdom, it functioned as an invitation to his hearers to become kingdom people themselves, to seize the chance and to become the real returned-from-exile people of God. We can study this in a sequence of four moves: invitation, welcome, challenge, and summons. At this point Marcus and I more or less agree: Jesus was, in his phrase, a "movement initiator."[13]

First, invitation. Jesus invited his hearers to "repent and believe the gospel." In our world, telling people to repent and believe is likely to be heard as a summons to give up personal sins and accept a body of dogma or a scheme of religious salvation. This is a classic occasion where we have to unlearn our normal readings (including our faith readings) of first-century texts and allow the first century itself to tell us what to hear instead. As we see in Josephus, the phrase means, basically, "Give up your agendas and trust me for mine."[14] This is not to say that Jesus did not give this challenge what we would call a religious or spiritual dimension. It is to insist that we cannot use that to screen out the practical and political challenge that the words would convey.

He was telling his hearers, in other words, to give up their agendas and to trust him for his way of being Israel, his way of bringing the kingdom, his kingdom agenda. In particular, he was urging them, as Josephus had, to abandon their crazy dreams of nationalist revolution. But, whereas Josephus was opposed to revolution because he was an aristocrat with a nest to feather, Jesus was opposed to it because he saw it as, paradoxically, a way of being deeply disloyal to Israel's God: specifically, to Israel's vocation to be the light of the world. Within that, Jesus challenged his contemporaries to abandon the attitudes and practices toward one another which went with that xenophobic nationalism, especially the oppression of the poor by the rich (a constant strand in much of his teaching). And, whereas Josephus was offering as a counteragenda a way that many must have seen as compromise, a shaky political solution cobbled together with sticky tape, Jesus was offering as a counteragenda an utterly risky way of being Israel, the way of turning the other cheek and going the second mile, the way of losing your life to gain it, the way of a new community in which debts and sins were to be forgiven. But before we get to this challenge, we must notice the welcome.

Jesus offered to all and sundry a welcome that, as we have already seen, shocked many of his contemporaries to the core. It was not that he, as a private individual, was associating with the wrong sort of people; that would not have angered the Pharisees. He was welcoming sinners into fellowship with himself *precisely as part of his kingdom announcement;* he was declaring that this welcome constituted them as members of the kingdom. In Judaism, repentance and forgiveness were focused, ultimately, on the temple itself, where the sacrificial system existed to provide the way of restitution for those who, through their sin, had stained, fractured, or jeopardized their membership within Israel. Jesus was offering forgiveness to all and sundry, out there on the street, without requiring that they go through the normal channels. That was his real offense.

With the invitation and welcome went a challenge. Subsequent generations of Christians have long allowed themselves to treat Jesus' challenge as simply a timeless ethic, a new moral code. But this misses the point. The challenge was grounded in eschatology. Jesus was challenging his contemporaries to live as the new covenant people, the returned-from-exile people, the people whose hearts were renewed by the word and work of the living God. Call Jesus a "social prophet" if you will; but his social prophecy grew directly out of his sense of what time it was. His critique of, and warning to, his contemporaries, and his challenge to a different way of being Israel, were based on his firm belief that he was charged by Israel's God with inaugurating the kingdom.

Not all of Jesus' hearers could literally follow him on his travels. But all could practice his way of life, a way of forgiveness and prayer, a way of jubilee, a way which renounced xenophobia toward those outside Israel and oppression of those inside. This is the context, I suggest, within which we should understand the material in what we call the Sermon on the Mount. It is not simply a grand new moral code. It is, primarily, the challenge of the kingdom: the summons to Israel to be Israel indeed at the critical junction of her history, the moment when, in the kingdom announcement of Jesus, the living God is at work to reconstitute his people and so fulfill his long-cherished intentions for them and for the whole world.

Ultimately, the challenge Jesus offered was the challenge to a crazy, subversive wisdom in which ordinary human wisdom, and conventional Jewish wisdom, would be stood on its head. To take up the cross and follow Jesus meant embracing Jesus' utterly risky vocation: to be the light of the world in a way the revolutionaries had never dreamed of. It was a call to follow Jesus into political danger and likely death, in the faith that by this means Israel's God would bring Israel through its present tribulations and out into the new day that would dawn. Again, call Jesus a "wisdom teacher" if you wish; but his utterly subversive wisdom was not a generalized teaching about how to live counterculturally, but the challenge to recognize God's moment and act accordingly.[15] This challenge belongs exactly on the map of first-century Jewish kingdom expectations.

In and through this kingdom agenda, we glimpse Jesus' further goal, out beyond the reconstitution of Israel. Here we need to remind ourselves of the fundamental Jewish perception that, when YHWH does for Israel what he has promised to do, this action will spill over to the Gentile world. Sometimes in second-temple Jewish thought this results in a purely negative picture: when Israel is restored, the nations will be condemned. At other times, notably in Isaiah, the vision is positive: God's rescue of Israel will mean that salvation itself spreads to the whole world. Jesus seems to have envisaged the latter alternative. Many will come from east and west and sit down at table with Abraham, Isaac, and Jacob in the kingdom of God.[16]

All this means that we can add a fourth stroke to our historical portrait of Jesus. He was a first-century Jewish prophet, announcing God's kingdom, believing that the kingdom was breaking in through his own presence and work, and *summoning other Jews to abandon alternative kingdom visions and join him in his.* But what would happen if they refused?

## WARNING OF IMPENDING JUDGMENT

Many of Jesus' contemporaries looked eagerly for the judgment of their God to fall on the nations, on the Babylons and Romes that had oppressed Israel. In such coming judgment they would find their own vindication, as when a defendant in a lawsuit sees her or his attacker condemned. In classic prophetic style, however, Jesus announced that God's judgment would fall first and foremost on Israel itself, because it had failed to respond to the summons to be the light of the world, living instead by oppression and injustice within its own society and by violence, actual or intended, toward those outside. The vindication of God's true people would consist, therefore, in God's endorsement, not of the nation, but of those who followed the true way; these consisted, basically, of himself and his followers, seen as the true representatives of Israel.[17]

Many have traditionally read Jesus' sayings about judgment either in terms of the postmortem condemnation of unbelievers or of the eventual destruction of the space-time world. The first-century context of the language in question, however, indicates otherwise. Jesus was warning his contemporaries that if they did not follow his way, the way of peace and forgiveness, the way of the cross, the way of being the light of the world, and if they persisted in their determination to fight a desperate holy war against Rome, then Rome would destroy them, city, temple, and all, and that this would be, not an unhappy accident showing that YHWH had simply forgotten to defend them, but the sign and the means of YHWH's judgment against his rebellious people. This was not simply the present and local aspect of Jesus' opposition to a more general phenomenon called "the domination system"; it was the unique and decisive challenge to the people of God at the crucial point in their history.

Jesus' warnings are focused in the so-called Little Apocalypse of Mark 13 and its parallels. I have argued elsewhere, against the trend of much twentieth-century scholarly and popular readings, that the chapter is to be read as a prediction not of the end of the world, but of the fall of Jerusalem.[18] When the Old Testament prophets speak of the sun and the moon being darkened, the stars falling from heaven, and so forth, they do not intend that this language be taken literally. They are using well-known metaphors to *denote* concrete events—major political or social upheavals—and to *connote* thereby the cosmic or theological significance which they believe those events to possess.

In the same way, the language in Mark 13.24–27 about the sun and the moon being darkened, and particularly about the Son of Man coming on the clouds, should not be taken in a crassly literalistic sense.[19] This language is borrowed from Isaiah 13, Daniel 7, and elsewhere, passages that refer to the collapse of great pagan empires and the vindication of God's people. "The Son of Man coming on the clouds" in Daniel would not be read by a first-century Jew as a reference to a human figure floating downward toward the earth on a concrete cloud. It would be read as the vindication—the coming to God—of his true people, after their suffering at the hands of the great

Beast, the evil empire that had opposed God, his purposes, and his people. Without going into more detail about the usage of the much-debated phrase "Son of Man," I submit that this reading makes sense within both first-century Judaism and the work of Jesus. Unargued attempts to continue to read the phrase in the old way, whether (as with many conservatives) to insist that Jesus must therefore have predicted his second coming or (with many others) that, because that is what the words mean, Jesus could not have spoken them, need to address this detailed historical argument.

Thus, a fifth stroke in the sketch. Jesus was a first-century Jewish prophet announcing the kingdom of God, believing that this kingdom was inaugurated with his own work, summoning others to join him in his kingdom movement, *and warning of dire consequences for the nation, for Jerusalem, and for the temple, if his summons was ignored.*

## THE CLASH OF SYMBOLS

It is scarcely surprising, in view of all that has been said so far, that Jesus clashed with his contemporaries on many points. There were, after all, plenty of other first-century Jews with agendas, aspirations, and ambitions, most of which Jesus was cutting across. It is vital to realize, though, that such clashes have to do with eschatology, not ethics or religion. Jesus was not "attacking Judaism" but telling his fellow Jews that their moment had come and that they were in danger of missing it. He was not criticizing Jewish religion and offering a different variety, but appealing to Israel's own story and foundation texts to criticize what he saw as deep corruption both within the Jewish society of his day and in widespread Jewish attitudes toward the rest of the world. He stood, in other words, within the noble Jewish tradition of *critique from within.*

He was not, then, in any shape or form, anti-Jewish. Jesus clearly knew that there was a wide spectrum of belief and practice among his contemporaries; nevertheless, like the biblical prophets before him, he denounced "the nation" for its widespread rejection of what he saw as God's will, and its embracing of ways of being Jewish which he regarded as unwarranted, disloyal to YHWH, and disastrous. The prophets had spoken out against the nation, and, though they sometimes were denounced as disloyal,[20] they always claimed the high ground of speaking YHWH's word to his people. The Pharisees were deeply critical of most of their contemporary Jews. The Essenes regarded all Jews except themselves as heading for judgment; they had transferred to themselves all the promises of vindication and salvation, while they heaped anathemas on everyone else, not least the Pharisees. Jesus belongs within the first-century world of rival eschatologies, not within the twentieth-century world of "patterns of religion." Like other would-be reformers, he claimed that he was the one who was truly loyal to Israel's God and his purposes, warning the others about the perils of disloyalty, challenging them to join him in the true way of being Israel at the vital turning point of history, and declaring that he, and his way, would be vindicated by God.

The clashes took place, as clashes often do, over symbols rather than ideas.[21] The beliefs of Judaism I outlined at the start of this chapter were encoded in a variety of symbolic practices that flew the flag of national identity. Supremely, of course, Jews kept the Torah and revered the temple.

Torah meant, not least, sabbath and food laws. Worshiping in the temple in Jerusalem, when one was able to get there (which many did, particularly for the great annual feasts), made the same point: this was the city where the one God had promised to dwell forever.

Adherence to, and defense of, the land of Israel functioned in the same way. So did loyalty to the family: the one God had made promises to "Abraham and his seed." Family members could ultimately opt out, and outsiders could opt in by abandoning idolatry and, in the case of males, becoming circumcised. But Israel, the people of the one God, thought of itself as a blood family. The symbols encoded the theology, and turned it into flesh and blood. This was the symbolic universe that Jesus lived within, and which his form of loyalty to Israel's God and ancestral heritage would turn upside down.

In particular, Jesus' clash with the Pharisees came about not because he was an antinomian, or because he believed in justification by faith while they believed in justification by works, but because *his kingdom agenda for Israel demanded that Israel leave off its frantic and paranoid self-defense, reinforced as it now was by the ancestral codes, and embrace instead the vocation to be the light of the world, the salt of the earth.* To do this would mean, also, abandoning the practice of oppression and violence within the society itself: inward corruption was the other side of the coin of militant nationalism. Jesus was announcing the kingdom in a way that did not reinforce but rather called into question the agenda of revolutionary zeal that dominated the horizon of many of his contemporaries, not least the leading group within Pharisaism.

The various clashes reported during Jesus' itinerant public career reached their head when he arrived in Jerusalem and confronted the temple. The temple was the symbolic heart of Judaism: by design and in hope the dwelling place of YHWH himself; the place of sacrifice, to forgive sins and celebrate the fellowship between God and Israel. In consequence, it was the center of Israel's political life, the power base of the priestly elite who, along with the Herodian house, ran second-temple Judaism at this time.

The temple possessed enormous royal significance, and here we begin to see where these clashes were ultimately leading. David had planned the first temple, Solomon had built it; their two greatest preexilic successors, Hezekiah and Josiah, had restored it. The Maccabees cleansed the temple, and thus, despite having no Davidic connection, became kings for a hundred years. Herod, having received the throne from the Romans, was eager to make it good by rebuilding the temple. The messiahs of the war years, Menahem and Bar-Giora, appeared in the temple, the former to be killed by a rival group, the latter to be taken captive by the Romans and killed during Titus' triumph in Rome. The last great messiah, Bar-Kochba, minted coins depicting the facade of the temple, which, no doubt, he was planning to rebuild. Temple and kingship went hand in hand.

There was, simultaneously, a popular critique of the temple. The Essenes believed in the temple but were passionately opposed to the present regime and hence to the present temple. The Pharisees in this period were beginning to develop the view that study of Torah would count as the equivalent of worshiping in the temple—a helpfully democratic ideal, especially for Jews in Diaspora. Many poorer people in Judaism regarded the temple as a symbol of corrupt and economically oppressive power structures; when the rebels took over the temple early on in the war, one of their first acts was to burn the records of debt kept there. Jesus' action in the temple has some relation to this larger picture of Jewish disquiet, though it transcends it. Once again, we are dealing not with religious or ethical critique so much as eschatological agendas.

What then did Jesus do in the temple, and why did he do it?

Jesus' temple action was an acted parable of judgment. In casting out the traders, he effected a brief symbolic break in the sacrificial system that formed the temple's main raison d'être. As Josephus realized in a similar context, the cessation of sacrifice meant that Israel's God would use Roman troops to execute upon the temple the fate that its own impurity, its legitimation of oppression, and its sanctioning of nationalist resistance, had brought upon it. Israel's God was in the process of judging and redeeming his people, not just as one such incident among many but as the climax of Israel's history. Jesus saw the present grievous distortion of Israel's vocation, outward toward foreigners, inward toward the poor, symbolized catastrophically in the present attitudes toward the temple: a symbol that had gone so horribly wrong could only be destroyed.[22] This judgment would take the form of destruction by Rome. (No wonder people said Jesus was like Jeremiah.)[23] This would be followed by the establishment of the messianic community, focused on Jesus himself, that would replace the temple once and for all.

Jesus' action symbolized his belief that when YHWH returned to Zion he would not after all take up residence in the temple, legitimating its present functionaries and the nationalist aspirations that clustered around it and them. Jesus' symbolic actions, and the sayings with which he explained them, undergird the picture of Jesus as a prophet announcing the kingdom of God, but in a deeply subversive way. The national flags of Judaism may once have stood for Israel's vocation to be the light of the world. Now that they had come to stand for Israel's determination to keep the light for itself, Jesus opposed them on the grounds of loyalty to Israel's deepest traditions and vocations.

Various obvious features of Jesus' public career, such as the call of twelve disciples, spoke volumes about his aims and agenda. His regular healings were themselves the symbolic expression of Jesus' reconstitution of Israel. In the so-called messianic rule from Qumran, the blind, the lame, the deaf, and the dumb are excluded from membership in the eschatological community of the people of God.[24] Qumran tried to create a restored community by keeping people out. Jesus created his by healing them and so bringing them in. His healings were the sign that the kingdom of God, the real return from exile, was happening in and through his own work.[25]

Along with this agenda went Jesus' creation of what the anthropologists might call a fictive kinship group. "Here are my mother and my brothers; everyone who hears the word of God and does it." The latter group seems, remarkably, to consist of those who hear the word of *Jesus* and do it. This renewed family was open-ended: the poor, the children, the tax collectors, and the general riffraff of society were invited to belong. Jesus' table fellowship with sinners—what John Dominic Crossan refers to as his "open commensality"—became one of the central symbols of his whole agenda. It spoke of the eschatological banquet, the messianic celebration. It challenged, symbolically, other contemporary construals of and agendas for the kingdom of God.

All is focused, once more, on the temple. Jesus acted in such a way as to indicate that he saw his own movement as the god-given replacement for the temple itself. The controversy about fasting points in this direction: Israel's fasts commemorated the temple's destruction,[26] and Zechariah had promised that the great fasts would eventually turn into feasts.[27] This, however, would come true only when YHWH restored the fortunes of his people, when the messianic banquet would take place. That is what Jesus is hinting at when he speaks of the wedding guests not being able to fast while the bridegroom is with them.[28] This is not timeless teaching about religion or morality. It is a claim about eschatology. The time is fulfilled; the exile is over; the bridegroom is at hand. Jesus' acted symbol, feasting rather than fasting, brought into public visibility his controversial claim, that in his work *the temple was being rebuilt*. Metaphorically, of course; but the metaphor denoted something concrete, namely Jesus himself and his community and movement, not something abstract, such as a new ideal or spirituality.

The same must be said of Jesus' offer of forgiveness. The Jerusalem temple claimed control of the means of forgiveness; Jesus challenged this with his actions and sayings. His exchange with a scribe, reported only in Mark 12.32–4, is highly significant: to love God with all one's heart, and one's neighbor as oneself, is worth more than all burned offerings and sacrifices. It is to this man that Jesus says, "You are not far from the kingdom of God." God's kingdom was precisely about replacing the temple system with the renewed heart, which, itself celebrating the forgiveness of God, would love God and neighbor in the way that the Shema, the daily prayer of the Jews to this day, indicated as the heart of Jewish practice. Jesus was claiming to offer all that the temple stood for.

Jesus' critique of his contemporaries' symbol system led, as we saw, to his action in the temple. His own positive symbols led to the Last Supper: the young Jewish prophet reclining in table fellowship with his twelve followers, celebrating (perhaps on the wrong night) the meal that in itself and its biblical allusions spoke of the coming kingdom, of the new exodus, of forgiveness of sins, of covenant renewal, and that did so in a setting and context that formed a strange but deliberate alternative to the temple.

The sixth stroke of my sketch is therefore as follows: Jesus was a first-century Jewish prophet announcing and inaugurating the kingdom of God, summoning others to join him, warning of the consequences if they did not. *His agendas led him into a symbolic clash with those who embraced other ones, and this, together with the positive symbols of his own kingdom agenda, point to the way in which he saw his inaugurated kingdom moving toward accomplishment.*

## JESUS' IDENTITY

When we put together Jesus' temple action and Last Supper, we discover that at the heart of Jesus' prophetic persona lay, not just the simple announcement of God's kingdom, but the claim, implicitly, to be the king that was to come. We know of several other royal or would-be royal movements in the first century; Jesus' movement is not quite like any of them, but it is not that different, either. To suppose that because the early Christians regarded Jesus as messiah, any suggestion that Jesus himself shared this belief *must* be a retrojection from later Christian theology is to let the hermeneutic of suspicion play dog-in-the-manger to actual historical reconstruction.

To address the question historically, we must start with Jesus, as we have seen him, at the head of a movement through which, he believed, the long-awaited kingdom was dawning. All the signs are that he regarded his own work not simply as pointing forward to this kingdom, but actually as inaugurating it: his actions only make sense if he believed that through them the kingdom was in some sense present, not simply future. These two cannot be played off against each other. On the contrary, the strange presence of the kingdom during Jesus' lifetime actually points forward to a crisis event through which it will come in a fuller reality. The example of Bar-Kochba, already noted, not only reminds us of how presence and futurity might go together in a second-temple kingdom announcement; they also reveal the agenda that would carry one from the first to the second. Evil (the Romans) had to be defeated and the temple rebuilt.

Jesus, I suggest, believed himself to be bound by a similar vocation, with the all-important difference that his agenda involved neither violence nor bricks and mortar. He believed himself called to take on the real enemy, of which Rome, as many of his contemporaries would have agreed, was but the symbol and pawn. And what was that real enemy? Evil itself, threatening God's kingdom and people through Rome, but itself a suprapersonal, supranational power, sometimes capable of being referred to under the quasi-personal language of "the accuser" (in Hebrew, "the satan"). There is excellent evidence that Jesus saw himself engaged in a running battle with this enemy throughout his short public career and that he saw these skirmishes pointing toward a greater showdown yet to come.

But what weapons could he use to fight such a battle? As we saw earlier, he denounced the use of military action, and he advocated the deeper revolution of loving one's enemies, taking up one's cross, losing one's life in order to gain it. This, it gradually appears, was not simply a way of life he urged on his followers, an ethic to be implemented at any time and place where people felt bold enough to do so. It was, much more sharply, an agenda and vocation to which he knew himself called, and that he announced as the way of being God's true Israel. It was his own fresh construal of the law and the prophets, the controversial way by which, he proposed, Israel's God would make Israel at last what it had always been called to be, the light of the nations. And, like other Jewish would-be leaders and messiahs before and since, Jesus believed himself called to go ahead of the people and fight the battle on their behalf. Like

David taking on Goliath, he would face the enemy of God's people alone, choosing the strange weapons that matched his own vision.

He would not only fight the true battle; he would also build the true temple. Jesus' action in the temple, complex and controversial though it has proved in historical discussion, seems to me to have been a clear symbolic action designed to declare God's judgment on the present temple.[29] Such an action must have implied, within second-temple Jewish expectations, that some form of replacement temple was envisaged. The symbolism of many of Jesus' actions spoke powerfully about what sort of temple he envisaged. Like the Essenes, he saw his own community as the true temple; or rather, he saw himself as the place and means of doing, decisively and eschatologically, that for which the temple had stood.

Jesus therefore believed himself to be Israel's messiah, the focal point of its long history, the one through whom Israel's God would at last deal with its exile and sin and bring about its longed-for redemption. This, I must stress, is not a particularly odd thing for a first-century Jew with a strong sense of God's presence and purpose, and a clear gift for charismatic leadership, to think. Others thought much the same, with local and personal variations. Of course, saying "Jesus was the messiah" remains controversial and from the historical point of view unprovable: it involves the claim to know that the God of Israel had indeed uniquely anointed Jesus. But to say "Jesus acted and spoke in ways consistent with his launching a veiled claim to be messiah, and inconsistent with his having no intention of making such a claim" is a historical hypothesis that, I believe, can be powerfully sustained.[30]

This, it seems to me, is actually implied in Marcus's account of Jesus. If Jesus was all the things Marcus says he was, then, in a century that saw many would-be messiahs and royal personages come and go, leading movements, announcing the kingdom, going to Jerusalem, saying and doing things about the temple, it is highly likely that Marcus's "Jewish mystic," if he was indeed a Spirit person, a social prophet, and a movement initiator, would have faced the question both from onlookers and from within his own heart and mind: was he, then, the messiah? Several other first-century Jews thought they were and had followers who agreed with them. Why should Jesus not have belonged in their number? I am very happy that we should analyze Jesus with all the tools, cross-cultural and otherwise, at our disposal. But when all is said and done, the categories of Jesus' own world matter, too, as Marcus would be quick to insist.[31] Even Josephus could tell people to believe in him;[32] I can imagine Judas the Galilean and Bar-Kochba telling people to believe in them. If Jesus really was, as Marcus allows, a "movement initiator," why should he not have done the same?

If Jesus did in any sense believe that Israel's God was calling him to take up the vocation of messiah, certain things follow. Any first-century would-be messiah must have believed, as Bar-Kochba a century later than Jesus certainly believed, that if his claim were true it belonged within the larger claim, that this was the moment Israel had waited and longed for. I call this sort of belief eschatological, and I note both that it is sometimes, though not always, expressed in what many call apocalyptic language, and that it always implies some kind of political stance.[33] It has to do with a sense of history reaching its unique climax. A new ethic, social critique, or spirituality can find a home within an eschatological belief and agenda, but by themselves they do not add up to it. Adding "prophet of the kingdom" to the end of a noneschatological list of characteristics of Jesus does not produce convergence with a through-and-through eschatological reading. If Jesus is really to be earthed in first-century Judaism, this seems to me nonnegotiable: the eschatological longing, the readiness to see in a new movement the possibility that this might be God's great, final, decisive hour with Israel and the world. The reason I find myself, as a historian, locating Jesus within this world of eschatology is because nothing else seems to do justice to his context or his position within it.

As I follow this path, I discover a Jesus who was not simply an example, even the supreme example, of a mystic or Spirit person, such as one might meet, in principle, in other cultures. I find, rather, the Jesus I have just been describing: Jesus as a first-century Jewish prophet announcing and inaugurating the kingdom of God, summoning others to join him, warning of the consequences if they did not, doing all this in symbolic actions, *and indicating in symbolic actions, and in cryptic and coded sayings, that he believed he was Israel's messiah, the one through whom the true God would accomplish his decisive purpose.*

That purpose, though, would not be accomplished simply by repeating Jesus' message and symbolic actions until more and more people were persuaded. It would come about through the decisive events to which his two great symbolic actions pointed. If the temple action spoke of messiahship, the Last Supper pointed to the cross. But that is the subject of another chapter.

## KINGDOM THEN—KINGDOM NOW?

This picture, I believe, makes very good sense historically. Jesus' critique of his contemporaries was critique from within; his summons was not to abandon Judaism and try something else, but to become the true, returned-from-exile people of the one true God. He aimed to be the means of God's reconstitution of Israel. He would call into being the true, returned-from-exile Israel. He would challenge, and deal with, the evil that had infected Israel itself. He would be the means of Israel's God returning to Zion. He was, in short, announcing the kingdom of God: not the simple revolutionary message of the hard-liners, but the doubly revolutionary message of a kingdom that would overturn all other agendas, including the revolutionary one. He was a prophet, announcing and inaugurating the kingdom, summoning followers, warning of disaster, promising vindication, clashing symbolically with other agendas, implicitly claiming messiahship, and anticipating a showdown. He was, in other words, a thoroughly credible first-century Jew.

What relevance has such a person for the world, the church, or the Christian today? It all depends. If Jesus' project as I have described it simply led to a messy death and nothing more, not very much. Who wants to follow a two-thousand-year-old failure? Why would anyone take seriously the subversive wisdom of a strange teacher, however fascinating, who believed that Israel's God was going to act through him to save Israel and the world, but who managed not only not to save himself from death but not to deliver Israel and Jerusalem from the crushing disasters of 70 and 135 C.E.?

If, however, Jesus' death did accomplish the real defeat of the evil that had infected Israel along with the rest of the world—if, in other words, his actions in Jerusalem did somehow accomplish the kingdom of God in the revised sense that he had been announcing all along— then this was good news not only for Israel but for the whole world.

The early church, clearly, thought this was the case. They gave as their reason one thing and one thing only: after his shameful death, Jesus had been raised from the dead. The practical, theological, spiritual, ethical, pastoral, political, missionary, and hermeneutical implications of the mission and message of Jesus differ radically depending upon what one believes happened at Easter. That, too, is the subject of another chapter.

## CHAPTER 4

# JESUS BEFORE AND AFTER EASTER: JEWISH MYSTIC AND CHRISTIAN MESSIAH

*Marcus Borg*

THIS CHAPTER'S TITLE compresses how I see Jesus into the most compact crystallization I can muster: Jesus as Jewish mystic and Christian messiah. "Jewish mystic" and "Christian messiah" are both radically shorthand phrases for a fuller understanding, and they are easily misunderstood if their shorthand character is overlooked.

The phrase "Jewish mystic," as I use it, contains the five elements about which I will say more later in this chapter: Jesus as Spirit person, healer, wisdom teacher, social prophet, and movement initiator.

Similarly, the phrase "Christian messiah" is compact shorthand for the exalted status given to Jesus in the New Testament. Expressed in what are sometimes called the "exalted titles" of Jesus (which are really "exalted metaphors"), this status includes "messiah," "Son of God," "Word of God," "Wisdom/Sophia of God," "Lamb of God," "Light of the World," "Bread of Life," "Alpha and Omega," "firstborn of all creation," and so forth. All of this is what I mean by "Christian messiah."

My central claim is that Jesus is *both,* an affirmation that I make as both a historian and a Christian. But the rest of the title points to an important qualification and clarification: Jewish mystic and Christian messiah describe how I see Jesus *before* and *after* Easter. To use language from my previous chapter, I see *the pre-Easter Jesus* as the former and *the post-Easter Jesus* as the latter.

The affirmation in the title thus also includes an implicit negation. Namely, I am not persuaded that the pre-Easter Jesus thought of himself as the messiah, and so I describe him in nonmessianic categories.

Instead of seeing any of the exalted metaphors as reflecting Jesus' own self-awareness or sense of identity, I see them as post-Easter affirmations. They are the early Christian movement's witness to what Jesus had become in their experience, not his own testimony about himself. Such language is "history metaphorized," and in this case it is Jesus himself, his life and his death, who is metaphorized.[1]

As a Christian, I affirm these metaphors to be true. I see Jesus as the messiah, the Son of God, the Word of God, the Wisdom/Sophia of God, and so forth. That affirmation is a defining element of what it means to be Christian: namely, Christians find the decisive revelation or disclosure of God in Jesus.[2] But I doubt that any of these affirmations go back to Jesus himself, and so I do not use them in my exposition of the historical Jesus. I describe Jesus before Easter in nonmessianic terms.

## JESUS' SELF-AWARENESS: MESSIANIC?

The question of Jesus' messianic self-understanding or self-awareness, and the decision whether to describe him before Easter in messianic or nonmessianic terms, is one of the major issues in the history of Jesus scholarship. It is also the single most important difference between Tom and me in our understanding of the historical Jesus. Did Jesus think of himself as the messiah? And did he see his death as part of his messianic vocation? Tom's historical judgment about both questions is yes. It shapes his sketch of Jesus in a comprehensive way: Tom sees Jesus as consciously living out a messianic vocation, including seeing his own death within that framework.

My historical judgment is, "It's possible but very difficult to know with any degree of probability, and if I had to bet, probably not." To be more precise, I am sufficiently doubtful that we can trace a messianic self-awareness back to Jesus so that I do not use the term *messiah* (or any of the other exalted metaphors) in my historical reconstruction of Jesus. I do not see Jesus as seeing himself in messianic terms, and I do not think he saw his death as central to a messianic vocation or as in some sense the purpose of his life.

What's at stake in this question? In what ways does it matter whether or not Jesus thought he was the messiah? For many Christians, especially when they first hear about this possibility, it has seemed that a lot is at stake. The possibility that Jesus didn't think he was the messiah has often seemed to threaten the truth of Christianity itself. Could Jesus be the messiah if he didn't think he was?

But this way of thinking about the question is too limited. Rather, there are four options for thinking about the relationship between Jesus' own self-awareness and his messianic status.

1. Jesus thought he was the messiah, and he was right. Based on what the New Testament itself says, this has been the common Christian position throughout the ages. A considerable body of scholarship also argues for this view.

2. Jesus thought he was the messiah, and he was wrong. Some who hold this position might still grant that he was an impressive historical figure; others would say that he was seriously mistaken, even deluded.

3. Jesus didn't think he was the messiah, and therefore he wasn't the messiah. This sounds like common sense but is actually "fact fundamentalism" or "fact literalism," which exists in both secular and Christian forms: if something isn't factually and literally true, it isn't true. Secular literalism and Christian literalism share this in common.

4. Whether or not Jesus thought he was the messiah, he is the messiah. That is, his messianic status and the truth of the exalted metaphors do not depend upon whether Jesus thought of himself in those terms. Whether any of them go back to Jesus or not, they are the community's testimony to what Jesus had become in their life together.

Of these options, I choose the fourth, and Tom chooses the first. We thus share an important agreement: Jesus is the Christian messiah. We disagree about a particular historical judgment, namely, whether we can be reasonably confident that a messianic self-understanding was part of Jesus' own self-awareness.

My primary reasons for being unable to make that affirmation are twofold. They flow directly out of taking seriously that the gospels are a developing tradition, and that they are a mixture of history remembered and history metaphorized.

First, in our earliest gospel, a messianic self-claim is not part of Jesus' own message. In Mark, Jesus does not teach about being messiah, Son of God, and so forth. To clarify: the issue is not whether Mark thinks Jesus is the messiah and Son of God. For Mark, Jesus is both; indeed, that is his gospel's opening line. Moreover, Mark tells us that the spirit world knew about Jesus' exalted identity during his ministry: his exalted status is declared by a divine voice at his baptism and transfiguration and by evil voices during exorcisms.

But on the human level, only once in Mark does the subject come up during Jesus' public ministry, namely, in the famous interchange between Jesus and his disciples at Caesarea Philippi.[3] As Mark tells the story, it is late in Jesus' ministry, immediately before the final journey to Jerusalem was to begin. Jesus asked his disciples, "Who do you say that I am?" After they reported what others had been saying, Peter responded, "You are the messiah!"[4] The story then concludes on an enigmatic note: Jesus neither accepted nor rejected Peter's affirmation but instead sternly told him to say nothing about it.

To repeat: in Mark's portrait of the teaching of Jesus, this is the first and only time an explicitly messianic interchange occurs. Thus, according to our earliest gospel, an exalted self-claim was not part of Jesus' own teaching.[5] Of course, it is possible that Jesus thought he was the messiah, even though he didn't say anything about it. But how would we know that?

There is a second reason why I cannot with confidence attribute a messianic self-awareness to Jesus. Namely, the gospel traditions as they develop display a demonstrable tendency to add exalted language to earlier texts.

Two texts in which the author of Matthew uses Mark's gospel as a source for his own illustrate this tendency. First, to Mark's story of Peter's messianic affirmation at Caesarea Philippi, Matthew adds two things. To Peter's exclamation, "You are the messiah," Matthew adds a second christological affirmation: "the Son of the living God." Then, rather than ending the story with Jesus' enigmatic command to be silent, Matthew adds a response from Jesus strongly commending Peter and explicitly affirming Jesus' own special status: "Blessed are you Simon son of Jonah! For flesh and blood has not revealed this to you, but my Father in heaven."[6]

Second, Matthew's treatment of Mark's story of Jesus' walking on the water also illustrates this tendency. Mark's story concludes with the disciples confused about what they had just experienced:[7] "And Jesus got into the boat with the disciples and the wind ceased. And they were utterly astounded, for they did not understand about the loaves, but their hearts were hardened."

As Matthew copies this story from Mark, he deletes the disciples' lack of understanding and replaces it with a christological affirmation: "Truly you are the Son of God."

He also adds, "And those in the boat worshiped him."[8] Thus, according to Matthew, recognizing Jesus as Son of God and *worshiping* Jesus as such go back to the ministry itself.[9]

Beyond Matthew, the exalted metaphors of John's gospel provide further evidence that early Christian communities projected post-Easter understandings of Jesus back into the ministry itself.[10] Given this demonstrable tendency of the developing tradition, we have to wonder if the very few references to Jesus' exalted status in early layers of the tradition are also the product of this tendency. In my judgment, historical caution requires that we be skeptical that any of this goes back to Jesus.[11]

I also am not persuaded by an argument from inference. This approach grants that the exalted titles are scarce and perhaps even absent from the early tradition but argues that we may nevertheless infer that Jesus thought he was the messiah from the remarkable things he said and did or from his use of texts from the Hebrew Bible that speak of a time of deliverance and fulfillment. I agree that the early layers of the tradition present Jesus as an utterly remarkable figure, but I think the inference that he was the messiah, Son of God, and so forth, was most likely first made by the early Christian movement after Easter. The argument from inference helps us see why the early movement made the inference, but I am skeptical that it takes us back to the mind of Jesus. Rather, the inference and the exalted metaphors in which it is expressed are most persuasively and powerfully understood as language of the community. In the portrayal of Jesus in the most exalted terms known within the Jewish tradition, we have history metaphorized.

To bring this prologue on Jesus' self-awareness to a close, what is at stake is thus not whether Jesus is the messiah, but whether he thought of himself this way. But there is a second reason why the question matters. Namely, thinking of Jesus as self-consciously the messiah with a messianic vocation easily and naturally leads to the inference that a major part of Jesus' teaching concerned who he was and his purpose. Put most simply: was he part of his own message? Did Jesus want people to believe *in him?*

This is a different question from whether he wanted people to follow him or to take seriously what he took seriously, both of which seem to me to be true. But a positive answer to the question "Did Jesus think he was the messiah?" often shifts the way we see Jesus' message and purpose: namely, that it was (at least in part) *about him.*[12] But I think an emphasis on the person of Jesus is a post-Easter development. My understanding of Jesus before Easter is that he wasn't interested in leading people to believe in him. He was doing something else. To that I now turn.

## JESUS BEFORE EASTER

Like the early layers of the gospel tradition, both Tom and I begin our treatment of Jesus with him as an adult at about age thirty.[13] We do not begin with the birth stories of Matthew or Luke or with Luke's story of Jesus at age twelve in the temple. Though legends throughout the centuries as well as more recent writers have tried to fill in "the missing years of Jesus," most scholars are skeptical that such efforts have any historical value.

All we know about Jesus' life before age thirty is a list of bare facts. He was Jewish; his parents' names were Mary and Joseph; he had siblings. His father was probably a carpenter, and therefore his family was from a marginalized peasant class; and he himself may have been a carpenter.[14] He was from Nazareth, a small peasant village in Galilee, but only four miles from Sepphoris, the largest city in Galilee and the center of Herodian administration during Jesus' youth.[15] There Jesus would have encountered levels of wealth and cultural sophistication unknown in Nazareth. He was not unfamiliar with the ways of the world.

We may also surmise that Jesus as a young man was on a religious quest. It is a reasonable assumption, given who he became. It is also the most probable explanation of his going to John the Baptizer in the wilderness in the late twenties of the first century. There he was baptized by John, who seems to have been Jesus' mentor. John's preaching was marked by themes of crisis, judgment, and renewal. It was also an antitemple movement, replacing the temple's mediation of the forgiveness of sins with the mediation of forgiveness through baptism.

John was soon thereafter arrested by Herod Antipas, the ruler of Galilee. Herod feared John's influence with the people, the Jewish historian Josephus tells us. Moreover, John had criticized Herod's marriage to his brother's wife. According to Mark, John's arrest was the trigger that led Jesus to begin his own public activity. As the gospels tell the story, it was very brief—as little as a year according to the synoptic gospels, and no more than three or four years according to the gospel of John. Either way, it was a remarkably short period of time.[16] Then he was crucified by the empire that ruled his world. But the story did not end there. In one of the most remarkable reversals in history, within three hundred years Jesus had become lord of the empire that had executed him. He became the central figure of the dominant religion of Western culture, and thereby also became the central figure of Western history.

That is a remarkable achievement for a Galilean Jewish peasant. No wonder people, then and now, have been curious about him. What can we say with a reasonable degree of probability about him? As I describe what I think we can know about the historical Jesus, I will focus on two major questions. (1) What was he like? What kind of religious figure was he? What shaped him? (2) And what was he up to? What were his mission and message? What did he proclaim, and what was his aim or purpose or intention?

## JESUS AS JEWISH MYSTIC

What kind of religious figure was he? Though not many of my colleagues begin with this question, I have found it illuminating to do so.

It reflects my conviction that we can know "broad strokes" about Jesus with greater probability than we can know many details.

My broad strokes are drawn from the cross-cultural study of types of religious personality. Five are most illuminating for seeing the kind of person Jesus was: (1) Spirit person; (2) healer; (3) wisdom teacher; (4) social prophet; and (5) movement founder. Each type functions as a template that helps to constellate the traditions about Jesus. Together, these templates generate a *gestalt* of Jesus that not only does justice to early layers of the tradition, but also combines them into a comprehensive image of the kind of religious figure he was.

As cross-cultural categories, these types are not specifically Jewish, and the language is not specifically biblical. But the phenomena are deeply Jewish. Not only are all five types of religious figures known within Judaism, but they are the central and formative figures of the biblical tradition.

My phrase "Jesus as Jewish mystic" is not only radical shorthand for my five-stroke sketch of the pre-Easter Jesus.[17] It is also its foundation, and it points in particular to the first stroke of my sketch: Jesus as Spirit person. In this foundational sense, "Jesus as Spirit person" and "Jesus as Jewish mystic" are interchangeable; by one, I mean the other.

As foundational, my claim that Jesus was a Jewish mystic means Jesus was one for whom God was an experiential reality. He was one of those people for whom the sacred was, to use William James' terms, a firsthand religious experience rather than a secondhand belief.[18] Mystics, as I use the term, are people who have decisive and typically frequent firsthand experiences of the sacred.[19]

The most dramatic of these experiences of the sacred involve a variety of nonordinary states of consciousness. In visions, there is a vivid sense of momentarily seeing into another layer or level of reality. In shamanic experience, one not only sees another level of reality but also enters it and perhaps even journeys within it.

Other nonordinary states involve a strong sense of connectedness with the sacred. This is mysticism in a somewhat narrower sense of the word, namely experiences of communion or union with the divine.[20] Such experiences occur in both "eyes open" and "eyes closed" forms. In the first, often called extravertive mysticism, one sees the same scene one would see in an ordinary state of consciousness, but everything looks different. The world looks exquisite, and it may even appear as if there is light shining through everything or bathing everything in its glow.[21] Moreover, the boundary between self and world, which defines our ordinary subject-object state of consciousness, becomes soft, indeed, less pronounced than a deep sense of connectedness and reunion. "Eyes closed" mystical states (often called introvertive mysticism) also involve a sense of connection and are most often experienced in deep meditation or contemplation. There is a sense of descending (or ascending) beyond the ordinary level of the self to a level where one experiences communion or union with God.[22]

The quality of these experiences is further suggested by the four defining characteristics of mystical states of consciousness as described by James.[23] *Ineffability:* these experiences cannot be described precisely in ordinary language but only with the language of metaphor: "It was like. . . ." *Transiency:* the experiences are typically brief; they come and go. One does not live in a permanent state of mystical consciousness. *Passivity:* they are received rather than achieved. Though spiritual practices may help create the conditions for such experiences, they are not under the control of the person.

Fourth, these experiences are *noetic.* People who have them say they involve a *knowing,* and not just strong feelings such as joy or awe or dread or wonder (though they frequently involve one or more of these as well). Mystics are strongly convinced that they *know* something they didn't know before. What they know is not another bit of knowledge or piece of information, but another reality: they have an experiential awareness of the sacred.

Importantly, such experiences are *transformative.*[24] They transform a person's way of seeing and being. Mystics see the world differently. Rather than seeing the world as "ordinary," they frequently see it as filled with the radiant presence of God. Or, to use Eastern idiom, they see it as "suchness," as the playful and wondrous dance of the void. Moreover, mystical experiences also transform a person's way of being, leading to freedom from conventional anxieties and inhibitions and to compassion as a way of relating to the world.

There is one more important point to make about mystical experiences before we turn specifically to Jesus. Taking mystical experience seriously has direct implications for how we think about God and

God's relationship to the world. Mystical experience implies the immediacy of access to God. If God or the sacred can be experienced, then God is in some sense "right here," accessible and knowable, and not simply elsewhere.

To relate this to how we think about God, mystical experience implies that God is not simply transcendent but also immanent. The transcendence ("beyondness") of God refers to God's otherness or moreness. Mystics know this: they experience "the more." The immanence ("indwelling") of God refers to God's presence in everything. Mystics know this as well: "the more," "the beyond," is accessible. Affirming both immanence and transcendence generates a model of God as both "right here" and "more than right here." It leads to a form of theism called "dialectical theism" or "panentheism."[25]

This form of theism is quite different from a common form of Western theism. "Supernatural theism" conceptualizes God as a personlike being separate from the created world, "out there," beyond the universe.[26] Many Christians (as well as atheists) think this is the orthodox Christian view. After all, imaging God as a personlike being is very common in the Bible. It is also the natural language of worship and prayer, and there is nothing wrong with it in such contexts.

Moreover, the use of personal imagery for God correctly affirms that God is known as a deeply personal presence, as a "you," and not simply as an impersonal force.

But when the imagery of supernatural theism becomes a conceptual model for thinking about God's relationship to the world, it has seriously negative consequences. For many people, it makes the notion of God incredible. Indeed, most modern atheism is a rejection of the God of supernatural theism. It is also theologically deficient: it affirms only the transcendence of God and neglects the immanence of God, despite the fact that the Jewish and Christian traditions have consistently affirmed that God is both.[27] Moreover, this theological deficiency matters deeply: affirming only God's transcendence makes God absent. Mystical experience knows better: God is immanent as well as transcendent, present and not absent. God is the encompassing Spirit in whom we live and move and have our being. God—the sacred—is "right here" as well as "more than right here."

To turn now to Jesus: if one takes seriously that the sacred can be experienced, and that people who have such experiences frequently and vividly may be called mystics or Spirit persons, then it seems apparent that Jesus was one of these. The data supporting the claim that Jesus was a Jewish mystic are early and widespread, particular and general, direct and indirect.

The data are found in the earliest layers of the gospel tradition. Not only do both Mark and Q contain specific texts linking Jesus with the Spirit, but both frame the story of Jesus in such a way as to portray him as a Spirit person. Mark begins his story of Jesus with two experiences common to Spirit persons: Jesus' vision at the Jordan, followed by a "wilderness ordeal" or "vision quest": forty days of fasting and testing in the desert, to which "the Spirit drove him." Mark reports that Jesus spent long hours in prayer, pointing to a form of meditative prayer characteristic of the practice of mystics. Mark's Jesus heals and casts out demons through the power of the Spirit, teaches with the authority of the Spirit, and is accused by opponents of being in league with an evil spirit.

Because Q is largely a collection of sayings and not a narrative gospel, the pattern is not as well defined. But Q also begins with Jesus' association with John the Baptizer and Jesus' visions during his wilderness ordeal. Q contains sayings referring to healings and exorcisms, including the accusation that Jesus was an evil Spirit person. Moreover, most of the teaching attributed to Jesus in Q looks like the wisdom teaching of an enlightened one whose consciousness has been shaped by the experience of the sacred.

Of course, Mark and Q do not take us back directly to Jesus, but to the way the story and message of Jesus were talked about in the 50s and 60s of the first century. But their commonality in portraying Jesus as a Spirit person is striking. How might one account for it? There are two possibilities. First, Jesus was a Spirit person, and that's why Mark and Q in common portray him as such. Second, Jesus was not a Spirit person, and the portrait of him as one is the product of two early Christian communities, independently of each other. For whatever reasons, and whether done at an oral or literary stage of the developing tradition, the communities behind Mark and Q depict Jesus as a Spirit person, even though he wasn't.

This is possible, but I think unlikely. For, quite apart from the impression created by Mark and Q as wholes, both contain multiple individual stories and sayings associating Jesus with the category of Spirit person. In what is almost certainly tradition that they received rather than created, both report visions, healings and exorcisms, the charge of being possessed by an evil spirit, and teachings reflecting a different kind of wisdom. The impression created by Mark and Q and the traditions that they incorporate are thus consistent.[28]

In short, the portrait of Jesus as a Spirit person is history remembered and not simply history metaphorized. This is the basis for my claim that Jesus was a Jewish mystic: for him, God was an experiential reality. He knew the immediacy of the sacred in his own experience. And this claim leads to a second claim: Jesus' experience of God was foundational for the rest of what he was.

## WHAT SHAPED JESUS

I make the transition to Jesus' mission or purpose with some reflections about what shaped Jesus. Three factors seem most important.

The first is what I have just described. Namely, his religious experience as a Jewish mystic was foundational. It decisively shaped who he was. I see his experience of the sacred as the source of his abilities as a healer and exorcist and of his alternative wisdom as a teacher of an enlightenment wisdom. I also see it as the source of his authority, political critique, and social vision as a prophet; and of his charismatic presence, which, combined with the above, accounted for a movement coming into existence around him.

The second factor is the traditions of Judaism. I see him as a deeply Jewish figure, shaped by the traditions of Israel's heritage. I do not have an opinion about whether Jesus could read the Hebrew Bible. This is one of the hot questions of contemporary Jesus scholarship: did Jesus have "scribal literacy," namely, the ability to read and study the Hebrew Bible as a written text? This cannot be assumed, for the ability to find and read a text in an unpointed Hebrew scroll was a skill that required extensive training. The probability of a person from the peasant class having such an ability is low. Yet it is possible that a highly motivated and highly intelligent Jewish peasant like Jesus could have acquired such an ability. But even if Jesus was nonliterate in the sense of not having scribal literacy, he would have known the central traditions of Judaism. He would have known the central stories of the Hebrew Bible (especially the Exodus traditions) through the celebration of the major Jewish festivals. He would have heard Israel's scriptures, Torah and prophets especially, read in synagogue services. These seem to have shaped his sensibility.

A third factor is his experience of injustice. He had a passion for social justice, as we shall see. Such a passion typically arises from the observation or experience of injustice firsthand, as the examples of Gandhi and Martin Luther King in our own century suggest. Jesus was from a marginalized social class in a marginalized village in Galilee, an area undergoing rapid social change and social dislocation in his time. He would have seen injustice happening around him, and whether or not he was personally a victim of it, he had an unusual sensitivity to the poor and marginalized.

## WHAT WAS HE UP TO?

What was Jesus up to? A sense of mission pervades the gospels portraits of him. What was it? What was his purpose or intention, so far as we can discern it? What did he have in mind?

As we think about this question, we must remember that our data for addressing it come from a very brief period in Jesus' life. As already mentioned, his public activity lasted only one to three or four years, depending upon whether we accept the synoptic or Johannine chronology. We are thus trying to discern his purpose from the beginning of a ministry that was cut short. If he had lived and taught for forty more years, as the Buddha did, what more might we be able to discern about his purpose?

Given what we do have, we may surmise the following, which I exposit under the remaining four strokes of how I see Jesus: as healer, wisdom teacher, social prophet, and movement initiator. In my exposition, I will emphasize that he was each of these, and what he was doing as each. We will thereby be given a glimpse of his purpose.

## WHAT HE WAS UP TO: HEALER AND EXORCIST

Not all Spirit persons become healers and exorcists, but some do.[29] Jesus was among them. In his brief reference to Jesus, the Jewish historian Josephus tells us that Jesus was a "doer of mighty deeds."[30]

The gospels agree. They refer to healings and exorcisms in summary form as frequent and typical occurrences:

> That evening, at sundown, they brought to Jesus all who were sick or possessed with demons. And the whole town was gathered around the door. And Jesus cured many who were sick with various diseases, and cast out demons.
>
> And Jesus went through Galilee, casting out demons.
>
> Jesus had cured many, so that all who had diseases pressed upon him to touch him.[31]

The synoptic gospels also contain many individual stories of exorcisms and healings.[32] In addition to possession by evil spirits, the conditions treated included fever, paralysis, withered hand, bent back, hemorrhage, deafness and dumbness, blindness, dropsy, coma, and skin disease.[33]

Behind this picture of Jesus as a healer and exorcist, I affirm a historical core. In common with the majority of contemporary Jesus scholars, I see the claim that Jesus performed paranormal healings and exorcisms as history remembered. Indeed, more healing stories are told about Jesus than about any other figure in the Jewish tradition. He must have been a remarkable healer.[34]

I very deliberately refer to Jesus' healings as paranormal, meaning unusual, alongside the normal, or beyond the ordinary. The word names a phenomenon, but it implies nothing about an explanation. In particular, it enables me to affirm the phenomenon of Jesus as healer without accepting two common explanations. One explanation sees the healings as "miracles" and understands them within the framework of supernatural intervention: God through Jesus intervened in the natural process from "out there" (and often, it is added, as God never intervened before and since). My problem with this view is that I do not accept a supernatural interventionist model of God and God's relation to the world. The model creates more problems than it solves.[35]

I also reject a common modern explanation of Jesus' healings as psychosomatic. Granted, psychosomatic factors may sometimes have been involved, but I think the explanation claims to know too much (just as supernatural interventionism, in its own way, claims to know too much: on this occasion, God intervened in the created order). Thus I use the phrase paranormal healings. Interventions, no. Marvels, yes. Inexplicable and remarkable things do happen, involving processes that we do not understand. I do not need to know the explanatory mechanism in order to affirm that paranormal healings happen. And Jesus seems to have been uncommonly good at them.

What role did Jesus' healings and exorcisms play in his public activity? Do they provide any clues as to his purpose or intention? One might affirm them as central without assigning them any particular significance beyond being deeds of compassion: Jesus discovered he had this ability and used it because he was compassionate and wanted to help people. No doubt that is true. But there are also texts in the gospel that suggest more particular meanings.

First, the healings and exorcisms of Jesus are associated with the coming of the kingdom of God and a time of deliverance. A saying in Q explicitly connects Jesus' practice as an exorcist with the coming of the kingdom of God: "If it is by the Spirit of God that I cast out demons, then the kingdom of God has come upon you."[36] Another Q saying uses language from the prophet Isaiah to signal that the activity of Jesus points to a time of deliverance. To messengers sent to him from the imprisoned John the Baptizer, Jesus is reported to have said: "Go and tell John what you hear and see: the blind receive their sight and the lame walk, lepers are cleansed and the deaf here, and the dead are raised up, and the poor have good news preached to them."[37]

Second, healing may have had a programmatic significance for Jesus. Few scholars have made healing as central to Jesus as John Dominic Crossan, who argues that healing and a shared meal were the two central features of Jesus' public activity. Moreover, healing was also central to the mission on which Jesus sent his followers. In the early and widely attested "mission charge" given to them, they are told to be healers and to share a meal. The two practices involved a sharing of spiritual and material resources, even as they challenged the established religious and social world of Jesus' day. In particular, healing as practiced by Jesus and his itinerant followers pointed to an unbrokered relationship to God, apart from institutional mediation.[38] In short, Jesus' healing activity flowed out of and affirmed the immediacy of access to God.

One further feature of the mission charge to the disciples takes us back to the first point: in addition to healing and sharing a meal, they were to proclaim the kingdom of God. Jesus saw his healings and exorcisms as connected to the kingdom of God.

## WHAT JESUS WAS UP TO:
## WISDOM BEYOND CONVENTION

Teachers of wisdom fall into two categories: teachers of conventional wisdom, and teachers of a subversive and alternative wisdom. The former hand on and sometimes elaborate the received tradition or conventions of a community or group. The latter speak of an alternative path—a way—that leads beyond convention.

Typically, their alternative path is grounded in their own experience of the sacred. Among the world's religions, perhaps the best-known examples are Lao Tzu in China and the Buddha in India. Within the tradition of Israel, the authors of Job and Ecclesiastes are voices of an alternative wisdom that challenged the conventional wisdom of their day.

Jesus also offers an alternative wisdom. As a wisdom teacher, he is more like Lao Tzu or the Buddha than he is like a teacher of conventional wisdom.[39] The basis for my judgment is twofold.

The first is the sheer weight of wisdom teaching attributed to Jesus. Most of his teaching is in the form of memorable short sayings (aphorisms) and provocative short stories (parables), both classic wisdom forms. Most scholars regard these as "bedrock" Jesus material. The second element is an understanding of their function as used by Jesus: namely, he most commonly used aphorisms and parables as perception-altering forms of speech. Aphorisms are compact crystallizations of insight that invite further insight; parables invite the hearer to enter the world of the story and to see something differently because of the story. The primary purpose of both was to invite hearers into a different way of seeing—of seeing God, themselves, and life itself.

The most likely source of such wisdom is mystical experience: enlightened wisdom teachers see and teach as they do because of their own enlightenment experience. Such, I am persuaded, was the source of Jesus' wisdom teaching: he spoke differently because he had seen differently. This, and not the external authority of convention or institution, was the ground of his teaching.

Like enlightened wisdom teachers generally, the way or path that Jesus taught was sharply different from the conventional wisdom of his time. Though its specific content varies from culture to culture, conventional wisdom itself is a cross-cultural phenomenon. Every culture has its conventional wisdom, consisting of its taken-for-granted understandings of what is real and how to live. As "what everybody knows," it is cultural consensus. It is culture or tradition hardened into a description of the way things are, map become reality.[40]

My understanding of conventional wisdom and its role in human life emphasizes that we are all socialized beings. Socialization—the process of growing up within a culture—involves internalizing our culture's way of seeing things. Conventional wisdom thus lives within us. The result is that we do not simply "see" life, but we see it in enculturated ways. It affects not only our seeing but also our identity and self-esteem. We are likely to feel good or not good about ourselves on the basis of how well we live up to the messages and standards of culture internalized within us.

The way Jesus taught led beyond convention. As one who knew God in his own experience, he knew that God was accessible apart from convention and institutions. His wisdom teaching invited a new way of seeing, centering, and living.[41]

*A new way of seeing.* As already mentioned, the forms of Jesus' wisdom teaching—his aphorisms and parables—sought to lead his hearers out of habituated ways of seeing. In addition, many texts explicitly use the language of "seeing" and "blindness." There are those who have eyes but do not see, blind people leading the blind, and people with logs in their eyes. Healing stories about the restoration of sight often also resonate with metaphorical meaning, combining history remembered and history metaphorized. "The eye is the lamp of the body," Jesus said. How we see makes all the difference.

*A new way of centering.* People center their lives in conventional wisdom. This is the natural result of socialization. We pursue the goals and seek the security offered by conventional wisdom. In the time of Jesus, conventional wisdom centered around family, wealth, honor, and religious practice as mediated by "tradition." The wisdom teaching of Jesus, to describe it in abstract terms, invited a radical decentering and recentering, which led from a life centered in convention to a life centered in that which is beyond convention: the sacred.[42]

*A new way of living.* This transformation of seeing and centering led to a new way of living—a new ethic and social vision. The core value of Jesus' ethic was compassion, an unusually rich word with resonances of feeling for people as a mother feels for the children of her womb. "Be compassionate as God is compassionate," Jesus said.[43] In this short verse, theology and ethics are combined in a few words. Moreover, the way of seeing mediated by Jesus' enlightenment wisdom also generated a boundary-shattering social vision. Mystical experience leads not only to a different way of seeing God and the world, but also to a different way of seeing people—not with cultural categories such as beautiful or ugly, important or unimportant, deserving or undeserving, but as beloved of God. Mystics know that culturally conferred social boundaries are ultimately artificial; as human products, they are relative, not absolute. Thus a far more inclusive social vision was possible, one that was to a considerable extent actualized in early Christian communities.

So what was Jesus doing as a wisdom teacher? I see him as inviting his hearers to a way of being in relationship to God that was not dependent upon convention or institutions. Though we need not think he was intrinsically opposed to both, he was critical of the way they functioned in his day, especially among the peasant and marginalized classes. For the most part, his hearers were by the standards of conventional wisdom "not much," or worse. His teaching would have been heard by some of them as "good news." And even as his message was particularly attractive to them, the way of which he spoke was also attractive to at least a few among the elites. In short, he taught a path of transformation centered in the sacred. His wisdom teaching invited people to life in the Spirit.

## WHAT JESUS WAS UP TO: SOCIAL PROPHET

Jesus was a *social prophet*. The type is most clearly found in the social prophets of ancient Israel. They were known for their direct experience of the sacred and for their radical critique of the social-political order. They were God-intoxicated advocates of social justice.

The prophets had visions in which they felt vividly called by God. Their authority and their social passion came from the immediacy of their experience of God and not from institutional authorization. Amos proclaimed:

> The Lord roars from Zion. . . .
> The lion has roared, . . .
> The Lord God has spoken, who can but prophesy?
> The Lord took me from following the flock,
> and said to me, "Go, prophesy to my people Israel."[44]

Those who know the immediacy of God are typically on the side of the marginalized. So Moses and the prophets, the central figures of the Hebrew Bible, suggest. They protested the most common form of economic and political organization in their world, what Walter Wink calls in shorthand the ancient domination system.[45]

In language I owe in part to today's foremost Hebrew Bible scholar, Walter Brueggemann, the social structure of these ancient domination systems had three primary characteristics.[46] They were marked by:

1. A politics of oppression. These societies were hierarchical and patriarchal. They were ruled by a king and a traditional aristocracy, typically called by social historians "urban ruling elites." Ordinary people had no voice in the structuring of society.

2. An economics of exploitation. In these preindustrial societies, the agricultural production of peasants was the primary source of wealth. And these societies were structured so that roughly two-thirds of the wealth generated by agricultural production ended up in the hands of the urban ruling elites, with roughly half going to the wealthiest one to two percent. This was accomplished

through taxation upon agriculture and direct ownership of agricultural land.

3. A religion of legitimation. These societies were commonly legitimated by the claim that the social order reflected the will of God. Kings ruled by divine right, and the powers that be were ordained by God.

This was the world of Egypt as well as the world of the monarchy in Israel itself. The story of ancient Israel begins with liberation from the foreign domination system of Egypt. About three hundred years later, with the rise of kingship in Israel, a domestic domination system emerged. Egypt had been recreated within Israel, and the king had become a new Pharaoh. In royal theology (the theology of the elites), the king of Israel was the Son of God, to whom God had promised an everlasting kingdom. Moreover, God dwelled in the temple in Jerusalem, next to the king's palace. King and temple together stood at the top of the domination system. The social prophets were radical critics of this system. They indicted both king and temple and were advocates of social justice for the marginalized.

The domination system continued into the time of Jesus. There is no reason to think that the Jewish homeland in the first century was an exception to the most common form of ancient social organization. Indeed, the economic situation of peasants may have been worsening in Roman Palestine. The commercialization of agriculture and the vast building projects of the Herods combined to produce a growing class of landless peasants.

In this setting, Jesus was a social prophet like the great social prophets of Israel. Texts in the gospels associate Jesus with these figures. Not only do they speak of the immediacy of Jesus' experience of the sacred and of his authority as flowing from that experience, but also they report that he was thought of as a prophet and may have spoken of himself as one. Moreover, he used prophetic forms of speech and performed prophetic acts, engaging in a radical critique of the domination system of his day. His activity as a social prophet is seen especially in traditions about Jerusalem and the temple, sayings about wealth and poverty, and traditions about purity issues.

According to early tradition, Jesus indicted both Jerusalem and the temple. The point is not that Jerusalem and the temple were the center of Judaism, as if there were something wrong with Judaism. The point, rather, is that Jerusalem and the temple were the center of the ruling elites and thus the center of the domination system. Like Jeremiah before him, he warned of their coming destruction if they did not change.

Jesus spoke harshly about wealth. In our discomfort with these sayings, we have often metaphorized them, as if they refer to spiritual poverty and spiritual wealth, a process that can be traced back at least to Matthew's gospel.[47] But initially they referred to real wealth and real poverty. In that world, to be wealthy meant that one was among the ruling elites. The sayings against wealth are thus part of Jesus' criticism of the domination system.[48]

I also see his critique of the domination system in the many traditions about purity. I am persuaded that purity issues in his time were associated with sharp social boundaries and that the amplification of purity laws was the product of a scribal class attached to the temple. A strong concern for purity was part of the ideology of the elites.[49] Purity was thus, for both Jesus and his opponents, not a matter of piety but of politics.

I am convinced, as I shall argue in my next chapter, that it was Jesus' activity as a social prophet that accounted for his execution. According to the synoptic gospels, his prophetic act of overturning the tables of the moneychangers in the temple court was the trigger for his arrest. His prophetic vocation was that important to him.

## WHAT JESUS WAS UP TO: MOVEMENT INITIATOR

Finally, Jesus was a *movement initiator,* to a large extent because of the combination of all of the above. His healings attracted attention; indeed, without them, it is possible that neither his contemporaries nor we would have heard of him. His wisdom teaching spoke of another "way" that was attractive to the marginalized and even to some of those who were doing well. His social prophecy indicted an oppressive and exploitative domination system. No wonder the common people heard him gladly.

Add to this what seems to have been a charismatic presence, and it is not surprising that he attracted followers. In embryonic form, a movement came into existence around him during his lifetime. Remarkably inclusive and egalitarian, his movement undermined the sharp social boundaries of his day. One of its most striking features was Jesus' inclusive meal practice. The meals of Jesus, ancestors of the Christian eucharist, embodied his alternative social vision. His movement did not move toward institutionalization until quite some time after his death. There was not time for that in his brief life.

*healing & meals*

## JESUS AS PROPHET OF THE KINGDOM OF GOD

I move toward my conclusion with another shorthand crystallization: Jesus as prophet of the kingdom of God. This affirmation is central to Tom's exposition, and I can affirm it as well. Jesus was a spokesperson or messenger for the kingdom of God.[50]

Using the phrase "kingdom of God" brings up the complex question of how we are to understand what Jesus meant by it. For much of this century, a strong majority of scholars understood it within the framework of imminent eschatology: when Jesus spoke of the coming of the kingdom of God, he meant that "the end" was at hand. In the near future, God would dramatically intervene in the world, bring ordinary history to a close, and establish the everlasting kingdom. Scholarly opinion about this has changed in the last twenty years or so. Along with probably a majority of contemporary scholars, both Tom and I (for somewhat different reasons) reject this understanding.[51]

But I do see the phrase "kingdom of God" as central to Jesus. As I have argued elsewhere, I see it as a metaphor or symbol with a range of meanings rather than as a concept with a single meaning. In the message and activity of Jesus, its meanings include the following.

1. In the context of Jesus' activity as a healer and exorcist, it can refer to the power of God. The casting out of demons is the coming of the kingdom of God.

2. In the context of Jesus' wisdom teaching, it can refer to the presence of God as well as to life under the lordship of God. The first

is suggested by sayings like "The Kingdom of God is among you" and "The Kingdom of God is spread out upon the earth, only people do not see it."[52] I see these as reflecting the altered perception of a mystic and teacher of an enlightenment wisdom: for those who have eyes to see, the kingdom (presence) of God is all around us. The second is suggested by the radical recentering that is at the heart of the way of Jesus: there is life in the world of conventional wisdom, and there is life under the lordship of God. The latter is the path of liberation and entry into a new way of being.

3. In the context of Jesus as a social prophet, the emphasis is upon kingdom of God as a social vision. Here it is a political metaphor, and the contrast is to other kingdoms: the kingdom of Herod, the kingdom of Caesar, and so forth. It is what life would be like on earth if God were king, and Herod and Caesar were not.[53] It would be a world of social justice, where the poor are fortunate and the hungry filled.

4. It can perhaps refer to the community of those living under the kingship of God. This is a likely meaning of those sayings that refer to "entering" or being "in" or "out" of the kingdom of God.

5. Though it does not often or primarily have this sense, it can refer to the final or eternal kingdom in which people from east and west banquet with long-dead figures from the past.

As Jesus uses the phrase, kingdom of God is thus a comprehensive metaphor. For this reason, and in this sense, I can affirm that Jesus was "prophet of the kingdom of God." Indeed, I see it as equally as good as my own compact crystallization "Jesus as Jewish mystic." If the latter has an advantage, it is that it calls attention to the centrality of the experience of God for Jesus.


## JEWISH MYSTIC AND CHRISTIAN MESSIAH

As I conclude, I return to the title of the chapter and use it in two ways. Jesus a Jewish mystic became the Christian messiah. The Christian messiah was a Jewish mystic. Both statements, it seems to me, are interesting and illuminating.

As a Jewish mystic, what did Jesus know? He knew how to heal. He knew how to create memorable sayings and stories; he had a metaphoric mind. He knew that God was accessible to the marginalized because he was from the marginalized himself. He knew that tradition and convention were not sacred in themselves but, at best, pointers to and mediators of the sacred and, at worst, a snare. He knew an oppressive and exploitative social order that legitimated itself in the name of God, and he knew this was not God's will. And he knew all of this most foundationally because he knew God.

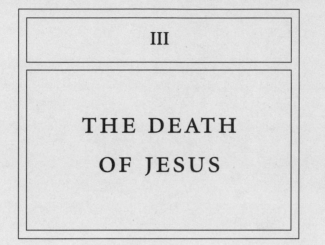

III

THE DEATH
OF JESUS

# WHY WAS JESUS KILLED? *Marcus Borg*

THE STORIES OF Jesus' crucifixion in the gospels are among the most powerful religious narratives in the world. Rich in meaning and metaphorical resonance, the stories of his death have been the subject of theological reflection, liturgy, art, and music throughout the Christian centuries.

In this chapter, I focus on the history behind Good Friday. What happened? And why did it happen? In a later chapter, I will explore the meanings the Christian tradition has seen in Jesus' death. Ultimately I see these meanings as more significant for Christians than the historical reconstruction of what probably happened, but I think the latter is also interesting, illuminating, and important.

## PROLOGUE: JESUS' DEATH AND HIS OWN PURPOSE

Why did it happen? Why did Jesus' life end this way? For centuries, Christians have seen Jesus' death as the very purpose of his life. It was *salvific;* that is, it had saving significance and makes our salvation possible. His death was the fulfillment not only of his purpose but also of God's purpose. In the ancient and familiar language of the gospel of John: "For God so loved the world that he gave his only begotten Son, that whosoever believeth in him should not perish, but have everlasting life."[1] Similarly, the Nicene Creed speaks of the saving significance of

Jesus' death as the very reason he came: "For us and for our salvation he came down from heaven, (and) for our sake he was crucified under Pontius Pilate."

But did Jesus himself see his own purpose this way? According to the gospels in their present form, yes. They portray his death as integral to his vocation, as necessary, and as the fulfillment of prophecy. The central section of our earliest gospel, Mark, is dominated by a threefold prediction of the passion. Jesus is going from Galilee to Jerusalem for the last week of his life: "Then Jesus began to teach his disciples that the Son of Man must undergo great suffering, and be rejected by the elders, the chief priests and the scribes, and be killed, and after three days rise again."[2]

The word *must* points to necessity: Jesus *must* do this. Not only did Jesus speak about his death in advance, but he saw it as something that had to happen.

So also in Luke. In one of Luke's Easter stories, the risen Christ says to the two disciples with whom he has been walking on the road to Emmaus: "Was it not necessary that the Messiah should suffer these things and then enter into his glory?" Moreover, it was foretold by scripture: "'Oh, how foolish you are, and how slow of heart to believe all that the prophets have declared!' Then, beginning with Moses and all the prophets, he interpreted to them the things about himself in all the scriptures."[3]

Older than the gospels themselves, this understanding of Jesus' death is central to the letters of Paul. It is also part of Paul's summary of the tradition he received when he became a follower of Jesus: "For I handed on to you as of first importance what I in turn had received: that Christ died for our sins in accordance with the Scriptures."[4]

Given all of this, it is not surprising that the death of Jesus has been seen as the purpose of his life. But was this how Jesus saw it? Was a salvific understanding of his death in the mind of Jesus himself? Or is it a post-Easter product of the early Christian community?

Of these two options, Tom chooses the first and I choose the second. Tom sees Jesus' death as central to his messianic vocation and purpose: Jesus not only knew that his life would end in crucifixion, but he also saw it as the climactic kingdom action that would defeat the powers of evil and bring about the real return from exile. But I am skeptical that we can trace a salvific understanding of his death back to Jesus himself. Rather, I think it was the early Christian community after Easter that first interpreted it so. Indeed, there is more than one such interpretation of his death in the New Testament, and later I will describe five of them.[5] I see them as powerful and truthful post-Easter metaphors for expressing the significance of Jesus' death and resurrection.

But for several reasons I do not think they go back to Jesus himself. First, with a majority of mainline scholars, I see the passion predictions in Mark as post-Easter creations.[6] The quite detailed correspondence between them and what happens in Mark's passion story suggests so. Moreover, traces in the gospels indicate that Jesus' death was a shock to his followers and a shattering of their hopes. This is hard to understand if Jesus had spoken so clearly about his upcoming execution.[7]

Second, for reasons I will soon explain, I see the use of passages from the Hebrew Bible generally as prophecy historicized rather than as prediction fulfilled.

Third, I have trouble imagining that Jesus saw his own death as salvific. Tom and I differ substantially on this topic. His claim, developed in his next chapter, is that Jesus saw his own death as accomplishing something of utmost importance in the God-Israel relationship, and as "the final battle against the real enemy."[8] Jesus took the suffering and sin of Israel and the consequences of its present historical direction upon himself. He saw his death as atoning for the sin of which Israel was guilty and he himself was innocent.[9]

It seems a strange notion to me: that Jesus thought that his own death would accomplish all of this. Of course, people have thought very strange things about themselves. Moreover, we would be rash to say what a person in a very different culture a long time ago could and could not think. Further, I think Tom's claim in his next chapter is correct: the notion of one's death having an atoning effect for others was present in the Jewish milieu in which Jesus lived and died. I accept that it was possible for a first-century Jew to think this. But I have difficulty affirming that Jesus believed this about himself.

If Tom is saying, "Of course, Jesus was a Spirit person, healer, wisdom teacher, social prophet and movement initiator, and he *also* believed this about his own death," I can imagine that as possible (though I don't think it probable). But if Tom is saying that what really mattered to Jesus—what was most central to his vocation—was what would be accomplished by his death, then I have to demur.

Honesty compels candor: I find this not only a strange notion, but an unattractive notion to attribute to Jesus. I don't want Jesus to have seen his own death as having the significance Tom gives to it. As a Christian, I want Jesus to be an attractive figure.[10] Obviously, wanting Jesus to be attractive cannot be a criterion for making historical judgments, and I must factor this desire into my historical judgment not only about this matter, but about every other historical decision I make about Jesus.

But I also think there is much evidence pointing in the direction I take. There is the body of Jesus' wisdom teaching, his passion for justice as a social prophet, his healings and inclusive meal practice, all of which are difficult to reconcile with the claim that his atoning death was what was most central to his messianic vocation. Was he doing all of these other things "on the side," as it were? Or were they what was central?

In short, I could accept that Jesus saw his own death the way that Tom suggests only if there were very strong historical evidence for it. I find it more historically persuasive, and religiously compelling, to see the purposeful understanding of Jesus' death as post-Easter interpretations, and as history metaphorized, not history remembered. In the language of symbol and story, the five interpretations of Jesus' death and resurrection that I will describe in chapter 8 speak about the defeat of the powers that hold us in bondage, the depth of God's love for us, and the path of transformation that leads to new life.

What is at stake in this difference between Tom and me is thus not the salvific meaning of Good Friday, but a particular historical question: whether Jesus saw his death as having a saving purpose.

My claim that Jesus did not see his death this way does not mean that I think his death took him by surprise. In all likelihood, I think he realized that if he kept doing what he was doing, he risked execution. He knew what had happened to his mentor, John the Baptizer. He may well have known that his journey to Jerusalem could end in his death. But that is very different from saying that he saw his death as central to his purpose.

## THE FINAL WEEK: MARK'S ACCOUNT

As I turn to history behind the stories of his death, I begin with the final week of his life. In the spring of the year 30, Jesus journeyed to Jerusalem in the season of Passover. Jerusalem was the traditional religious and political capital of his people. It was also the center of the domination system in the Jewish homeland. Passover was the most important of the annual festivals, when the city was most crowded with pilgrims from all over the Jewish world. With a group of followers, the Jewish mystic who was a healer, wisdom teacher, and social prophet arrived in the city about a week before the day of Passover itself.

What was Jesus up to in Jerusalem during what turned out to be the final week of his life? Mark's gospel is virtually our only source.[11] Given the nature of the gospels, we cannot assume that he provides us with straightforward historical reporting. But because he is our only source, and in order to say something rather than nothing at all, I begin with a summary of Mark's narrative.

As Mark tells the story, Jesus entered Jerusalem in a provocative manner at the beginning of the week. As he rode into the city from the east on a colt, his followers chanted words that linked his entry with the kingdom of David, the greatest of ancient Israel's kings: "Hosanna! Blessed is the one who comes in the name of the Lord! Blessed is the coming kingdom of our ancestor David!"[12] At approximately the same time, the Roman governor Pilate, with all the pomp and power of empire, would have been entering Jerusalem from the west at the head of a squadron of Roman cavalry.

During the week itself, Mark portrays Jesus primarily as a teacher and social prophet; no healings are reported. As he taught in the temple courts, three Jewish groups engaged him in verbal conflict: Pharisees, Sadducees, and temple authorities.[13]

Pharisees asked him a trap question: is it lawful to pay taxes to Caesar? Sadducees sought to stump him by telling a tale of a woman who was married to seven brothers: in the afterlife, whose wife will she be? A scribe asked him what the greatest commandment is.[14]

Above all, Jesus was in conflict with the temple. Near the beginning of the week, he performed what has been called his most dramatic public act: he overturned the tables of the money changers in the temple court. Understood by scholars in a variety of ways, the action seems to have been a prophetic act like the symbolic acts performed by social prophets in the Hebrew Bible. As such, it was a protest against the temple's role in the domination system and perhaps also a warning of divine judgment against it.[15]

The temple is also the subject of other texts in Mark's account of the final week. Jesus told a parable directed against the temple authorities: they were like the wicked tenants of a vineyard who kept all of the produce of the vineyard for themselves. He indicted scribes, who were employees of the temple elites skilled in the law, for devouring widows' houses. Finally, about the temple itself, Jesus said, according to Mark, "Do you see these great buildings? Not one stone will be left here upon another; all will be thrown down."[16] The centrality of Jesus' conflict with the temple is pointed to by Mark's statement that it was the cause of Jesus' arrest.[17]

In general, I find Mark's account of Jesus' final week historically plausible. Of course, it is not a transcript of what happened, and Mark has shaped the material to fit his narrative development. But the portrait of Jesus acting as a teacher and social prophet embroiled in controversy in Jerusalem the center of the domination system is credible.

## THE FINAL TWENTY-FOUR HOURS: THE PASSION STORIES

The passion stories in the gospels of the New Testament are our primary sources of historical information about the last day in Jesus' life.[18] Beginning with Jesus' last meal with his disciples, the passion stories continue through betrayal, arrest, and trials before Jewish and Roman authorities, and they climax in crucifixion, death, and burial, providing an almost hour-by-hour account of the last evening and day of Jesus' life.[19]

To what extent are they historical reports? Like the gospels generally, the passion stories developed and grew in the decades between Jesus' death and their composition. As developing traditions, they combine four main ingredients: history remembered, prophecy historicized, imaginative elaboration, and purposive interpretation.[20]

*History remembered.* Some of the events in the passion stories really happened and are part of the stories for that reason, a point to which I will soon return. But other factors besides historical remembrance were at work.

*Prophecy historicized.* The Hebrew Bible is frequently quoted or echoed in the stories of Jesus' death.[21] What are we to make of these correspondences between Jewish scripture and the passion stories? Do they appear because of "prophecy fulfilled" or "prophecy historicized"?

That is, do these correspondences appear in the text because the events surrounding the death of Jesus fulfilled prophetic passages in the Hebrew Bible? Or did early Christians create details in the passion stories from passages in the Hebrew Bible, forming "prophecy historicized"? The former was emphasized in my childhood: the detailed correspondences proved that Jesus' death was the fulfillment of prophecy (and therefore also proved that Jesus was the messiah, as well as proving the truth of the Bible as a whole).

Though this approach is still found in some Christian circles today, mainline scholars in general do not see these correspondences as pointing to prophecy fulfilled. Rather, the correspondences appear because of prophecy historicized: namely, early Christians used the Hebrew Bible as they told the story of Jesus' death. It is thus often difficult to know when this use is creating details in the passion narratives rather than mirroring events that actually happened.

The frequent use of Psalm 22 illustrates the issue. According to Mark, Jesus as he died uttered the first verse of the psalm: "My God, my God, why hast thou forsaken me?"[22] But did Jesus actually quote this psalm as his dying prayer, or did Mark attribute these words to Jesus because they seemed appropriate to his anguish? It is difficult to choose; I can easily imagine either. In more language drawn from Psalm 22, Mark reports that people "mocked" Jesus and "wagged their heads" at him.[23] Though there is nothing improbable about this detail, does it appear in the story because of history remembered or because of the use of the psalm in telling the story? Mark echoes the psalm again in the scene of Jesus' executioners gambling for his robe: "They divide my clothes among themselves, and for my clothing they cast lots."[24] But did this happen? Did they really gamble for a peasant's robe, or did the use of the psalm generate the detail? Is this history remembered, or prophecy historicized?[25]

*Imaginative elaboration.* Some parts of the passion stories are imaginative creations. These include details that wouldn't have been known as well as scenes created for apologetic reasons. An example of the former is Jesus' prayer in Gethsemane: "Abba, Father, for you all things are possible; remove this cup from me; yet not what I want, but what you want."[26] But according to Mark, there were no witnesses: Jesus had gone some distance away, and the disciples were all asleep. The point: according to the story itself, nobody would have known what Jesus prayed, and the content of the prayer is thus the product of imaginative elaboration.[27]

An imaginative scene created for apologetic reasons is the story of Pilate washing his hands of the blood of Jesus.[28] Found only in Matthew, it serves the purpose of shifting responsibility for Jesus' death further and further away from Roman authority, a point to which I will return.

*Purposive interpretation.* The interpretation of Jesus' death as serving a divine providential purpose is found in all of the gospels. His death was necessary, foreordained, predicted; it was supposed to happen this way. But this perspective is most likely a post-Easter retrospective interpretation; I don't think Jesus saw his death as the purpose of his life.

These four characteristics combine in various ways. The use of the Hebrew Bible sometimes leads to imaginative elaboration, and both often serve the cause of purposive interpretation. Indeed, the use of the Hebrew Bible can be seen as the spelling out of the early Christian conviction that Jesus' death took place "according to the Scriptures."[29]

## How Much Is Historical?

Thus the passion stories are not straightforward historical narratives but a mixture of history remembered and early Christian interpretation. Given this, what can we say historically about the death of Jesus?

I see Mark's passion story as the earliest. Matthew and Luke each had a copy of Mark, and I see the additions that they made to Mark's passion story as imaginative elaborations.[30] I have no opinion about whether John's passion story shows knowledge of Mark or whether it is completely independent. Thus I see Mark as the foundational narrative, and I turn now to comments about the main elements of his story of the passion.

### From Last Supper to Arrest

*The Last Supper.* Jesus and his followers most likely had a meal together the night he was arrested. It may have been a Passover meal, though this depends on whether we follow the synoptic account or John's account. Jesus may have spoken of his upcoming death; my hunch is that he knew he was in great danger. But I am skeptical that he spoke "the words of institution" over the bread and wine: "This is my body" and "This is my blood." They look to me to be an early Christian ritualization of the death of Jesus, in which the bread and wine of the common meals that marked Jesus' public activity were invested with symbolic meaning.[31]

*Betrayal by Judas.* I think it likely that Jesus was betrayed by a follower named Judas. What Judas betrayed is less clear. Did he simply disclose a location where Jesus could be arrested? But couldn't the authorities have figured that out without a betrayer? Did he betray some confidence about Jesus? That, for example, as Albert Schweitzer suggested, Jesus thought he was the messiah? Or something else? I have no opinion. But the tradition that Jesus was betrayed by one of his own is quite strong.[32]

*Arrest in Gethsemane.* I think it likely that Jesus was with his followers when he was arrested, and I see no reason to doubt that a garden or grove known as Gethsemane on the lower slope of the Mount of Olives was the place. The event that led to his arrest was probably the disturbance Jesus had caused in the temple a few days before.[33]

### From Arrest to Crucifixion

About the events reported between arrest and execution, including the trials before Jewish and Roman authorities, I have little historical confidence. The reason: whatever happened was not witnessed by Jesus' followers; they had fled and were not there.[34] Mark tells us there was an exception: Peter followed from a distance. But even if true, he still could not have witnessed what happened after Jesus was taken away:

the events were essentially hidden from public view until the crucifixion itself.

In particular, I am uncertain about whether there were any formal trials of Jesus before either the high priest or the Roman governor. It is easy to imagine that the order for the arrest and execution of a peasant could have been given and carried out without Jesus ever appearing personally before the highest authorities. And even if there was a trial by either Jewish or Roman authority (or both), I find it difficult to imagine how Jesus' followers could have known what was said: they were not there.[35]

For additional reasons, I am skeptical about the story of the Jewish trial, about which scholars have long noted difficulties. It was against Jewish law to hold a trial at night, and it is virtually impossible to imagine the high priest and Sanhedrin convening on the evening or night of Passover. Moreover, the charge on which Jesus was allegedly condemned by the high priest looks suspect, a point to which I will return in a few pages.

Because of these uncertainties, the details of the passion story from arrest through public execution remain for me in a "suspense account." True, some of what is reported is likely to have happened, even though Jesus' followers lacked firsthand information. For example, it would have been easy for them to imagine the details that routinely happened as part of a crucifixion: scourging, mocking, stripping, and so forth. But I am skeptical that we can say with any degree of probability that Jesus appeared before the highest Jewish and Roman authorities.

## Crucifixion

Despite these uncertainties, quite a bit can still be said historically about Jesus' death. I begin with inferences drawn from the "how" of his execution, and then turn to the questions of "who" and "why."

*How?* That Jesus was executed by crucifixion tells us quite a bit. In the Jewish homeland in the first century, crucifixion was a Roman form of execution. Thus Jesus was executed under Roman authority, whoever else might have been involved, a point to which I will return. Crucifixion was commonly used for two categories of people: political rebels and chronically defiant slaves.[36] The two groups shared something in common: both systematically defied established authority. Because Jesus was not a slave, it follows that he was crucified as a political threat to Roman order.

We also know what typically happened to the corpses of crucified people: they were either left on the cross to be consumed by scavengers or buried in an anonymous grave. We know of at least one exception: the skeletal remains of a crucified man interred in an ossuary have been found near Jerusalem.[37] But the usual practice was to deny a proper burial. It was the final horror of an excruciating form of death designed as a deterrent to rejecting imperial authority.

*Who?* Who was responsible? As already mentioned, the form of execution points to Roman responsibility. But as the gospels tell the story, they portray the Roman governor as reluctant to execute Jesus, and they progressively shift blame to the Jewish authorities and people as a whole. This is most evident in Matthew and John. As Matthew copied Mark, he added the scene of Pilate washing his hands of the blood of Jesus, followed by the exclamation of *all* the people: "His blood be on us and on our own children."[38] The people as a whole become responsible. So also in John: the enemies of Jesus are most commonly spoken of simply as "the Jews."

Was this process of shifting responsibility for the death of Jesus under way by the time Mark's gospel was written? Already in Mark, Pilate doesn't want to crucify Jesus but finally accepts the will of the temple authorities. But is this history remembered, or is the portrait of Pilate's reluctance in Mark an early stage in the process? Choosing seems impossible. It is worth noting that other contemporary sources portray Pilate as a harsh governor not known for sensitivity to either issues of justice or Jewish concerns.

Why did this progressive shifting of responsibility occur? A major reason was the political exoneration of early Christianity. Imagine yourself as a Christian in the Roman Empire in the first century. The central figure of your movement had been crucified as an enemy of Rome; how would you defend yourself against the charge of being part of a politically dangerous movement? Though you couldn't deny the fact of crucifixion, you could say, "The Roman governor didn't want to do it; in fact, he found Jesus innocent. But he was crucified at the insistence of his own people and their leaders."

Unwittingly, early Christians thus created a version of the death of Jesus that has contributed to anti-Jewish attitudes in Christian lands in the centuries ever since. We Christians need to be aware of how the passion stories have become texts of terror for Jewish people, and we need to find ways of correcting the impression generated by an uncritical reading of these stories.

What can we say about what lies behind the gospel picture of responsibility? Though details must remain vague, nearly all mainline scholars see Jesus' arrest and execution as resulting from collaboration between the ruling elites of the day: the Roman governor and a small circle of Jewish temple authorities. This collaboration need not have involved a trial before either; a brief consultation before or after the arrest would have been adequate. The conclusion that Jewish elites were involved is not a way of reintroducing the notion of Jewish responsibility for the death of Jesus. Rather than representing Judaism or the Jewish people, the Jewish temple elites were the oppressors of the vast majority of the Jewish people in the time of Jesus.

*Why?* Why was Jesus killed? Why did it happen? What's the relationship between Jesus' life and his execution? As already argued, I see the understanding of his death as salvific as a post-Easter interpretation generated within the early Christian community, not as the intention of Jesus himself. Moreover, even if we did see his death as Jesus' own purpose, we would still not have an answer to the question, "Why was he killed?"; we would have an answer only to "Why did he die?" The two questions are very different.

According to Mark's account of the Jewish trial, Jesus was condemned to death for a religious offense—indeed, almost a theological one. At the climax of the Jewish trial, as Mark reports it, is the exchange between the high priest Caiaphas and Jesus:

CAIPHAS:  "Are you the Messiah, the Son of the Blessed?"

JESUS:     "I am. And you will see the Son of Man seated at the right hand
               of the Power, and coming with the clouds of heaven."

CAIPHAS:  "Why do we still need witnesses? You have heard his blas-
               phemy." . . . And they all condemned him as deserving death.

According to this scene, Jesus was condemned to death for what looks like a Christian confession of faith: Jesus as messiah, Son of God ("Son of the Blessed"), and soon-to-return Son of Man. Early Christian beliefs about Jesus and expectation of his second coming are combined.[39] As a historical report, it looks suspect to me, and it is more persuasively understood as a post-Easter creation. Thus my historical judgment about the capital offense as "blasphemy" is "Probably not." But even if the judgment could be moved to a strong "Maybe," one could not have much confidence in further hypotheses built upon the supposition.

If the scene of the Jewish trial does not provide the historical reason for Jesus' execution, why then was he killed? For me, the most persuasive answer is his role as a social prophet who challenged the domination system in the name of God. To make the same point differently, if Jesus had been only a mystic, healer, and wisdom teacher, I doubt that he would have been executed. But he was also a God-intoxicated voice of religious social protest who had attracted a following.

In Jesus' world, this was enough to get arrested and executed by authorities who did not care for criticism and who feared popular unrest, as the execution of Jesus' mentor, John the Baptizer, not long before demonstrates. To make the point yet one more way, Jesus died as a martyr, not as a victim. A martyr is killed because he or she stands for something. Jesus was killed because he stood against the kingdoms of this world and for an alternative social vision grounded in the kingdom of God. The domination system killed Jesus as the prophet of the kingdom of God. This is the political meaning of Good Friday.

Of course, the story does not end there. There is Easter, the subject of my next chapter. And there is the rich variety of meanings that the early Christian movement saw in the completed pattern of Jesus' death and resurrection. So Good Friday has more than a political meaning. But it does not have less than a political meaning.

## CHAPTER 6

# THE CRUX OF FAITH                    *N. T. Wright*

---

J ESUS' DEATH IS central to the whole New Testament and to most versions of Christianity from his day to ours. This makes the topic, inevitably, both more complex and more important, more controversial and more exciting.

I come to the issue with four starting points: two about Jesus' context, and two about how oral traditions work.

1. I assume that Jesus, like some other first-century Jewish leaders known to us, believed that in and through his work the biblical prophecies were being fulfilled; Israel's long history was reaching a climactic moment, perhaps *the* climactic moment. Granted my argument in chapter 3, we have good reason to suppose that Jesus knew at least some of the traditions, including biblical passages, that shaped and guided other movements, including messianic movements and movements that resulted in martyrdom. To deny this is, in the last analysis, to split Jesus off from his Jewish context.

2. As historians we must do our best to recreate the way in which first-century Jews, particularly those involved in movements of reform, revolution, or kingdom bringing, would have thought about suffering, death, and martyrdom. First-century Jews were not like comfortable Western scholars, living in a world where the avoidance or mitigation of suffering, especially one's own, is

taken for granted. Traditions existed within first-century Judaism that explained how Israel's God would use even the sufferings and seeming tragedy of his people to bring about the longed-for redemption. The great Exodus story itself, retold in story and symbol each Passover (and evoked in other festivals, too), was all about the long night of slavery getting darker and darker and then God breaking through with freedom and hope. Out of the experience of the Babylonian exile came a whole conglomeration of meditations, finding expression in prophecy, psalm, apocalyptic, and folktale: through the suffering of Israel at the hands of the pagans, Israel's God would somehow bring Israel to redemption.

These traditions were alive and developing throughout the second-temple period. We can see how they were evoked by those who wrote up, in roughly Jesus' own time, the tales of the Maccabean martyrs. Suffering and death were interpreted as effecting Israel's rescue from present and future suffering, from "the wrath of God" in that sense. We can see how these traditions were called upon to explain, and give meaning to, the suffering of the Teacher of Righteousness and perhaps some of his followers. We have no reason to suppose that Jesus would have been either deaf to these voices or incapable of reshaping them around his own particular variety of kingdom agenda and kingdom vocation.[1]

3. We have every reason to suppose that a crowded city at a time of a great religious, cultural, and political festival would have been an ideal time for news to travel fast. Suburban Westerners, used to keeping secrets and having minimal contact or conversation with anyone except the closest friends, colleagues, and relatives, find it hard to imagine, but this is precisely the sort of imagination required by historians all the time. In Jesus' world, as in many parts of the world still, not least in the Middle East, great efforts are required to keep anything at all secret. The "bush telegraph"—what a Jerusalem guide once referred to in conversation as the "Arabic telephone"—is an astonishingly quick means whereby news of people's doings and sayings, movements and

habits, is quickly passed from one person to another. When, therefore, scholars argue, as they do from time to time, that because Jesus' hearings before Caiaphas and Pilate were in secret nobody outside would have known what happened, they are living in a make-believe world. Even today, even in Western societies, even when people are sworn to secrecy in the interests of the church, the state, or the party, secrets have a remarkable habit of leaking out. How much more when the whole city, in eager mood for Passover, was ready to grasp and transmit any snippets of information about the leader whose appearance many thought heralded the arrival of the kingdom of God?

An example from a non-Western context will help. When the Ugandan archbishop Janani Luwum was killed by Idi Amin's soldiers in 1977, his murder was the culmination of several swift nocturnal journeys, kangaroo court hearings, and beatings. No one person was present for more than part of the sequence. Those who were involved had reason to tell nobody what they had done. Yet by the middle of the next day the entire story was told as a connected narrative on the streets of Kampala.[2] The bush telegraph not only transmits snippets of information; it can put them together and make a coherent whole. It simply will not do to say that certain people weren't present so they didn't know. Ask any journalist.

4. Once a story has taken hold of people's minds and imaginations, it is told again and again with minimal alteration. I have spelled this point out more fully elsewhere.[3] Once the story of Luwum's death was put together into a narrative, it did not change. Within the folk cultures that we must assume to have characterized Jesus' context, oral tradition, though informal in process, is very conservative and self-regulating. The stories of Jesus' death, and the events that led up to it, are either extremely clever fictions or probably substantially close to the events.[4] Of course, subsequent literary and theological editing have reshaped and remolded these traditions, so that they now diverge in significant ways. But the inner core of the story has a remarkable convergence.[5]

## THE MESSIANIC TASK OF JESUS

What, then, can be said about these events, so well known at one level in church and Christian tradition and yet so little understood historically? I shall concentrate on Jesus' own understanding, which seems to me both historically recoverable and theologically illuminating. I shall then glance at the political reasons that led the authorities to execute him.[6]

We start with Jesus, as we saw him earlier, at the head of a movement through which, he believed, the long-awaited kingdom was dawning. He regarded his own work not simply as pointing forward to this kingdom, but also as actually inaugurating it: his actions make sense only if he believed that through them the kingdom was in some sense present, not simply future. Yet, as we saw in chapter 3, these two cannot be played off against each other. The strange presence of the kingdom during Jesus' lifetime points forward to a crisis event through which it will come in a fuller reality. Bar-Kochba, like other would-be messiahs, aimed to defeat the Romans and rebuild the temple. Jesus was bound by a similar vocation.

But what weapons could he use to fight such a battle? As we saw, he denounced the use of military action, and he advocated the deeper revolution of loving one's enemies, taking up one's cross, losing one's life in order to gain it. This, it gradually appears, was not simply a way of life he urged on his followers, an "ethic" to be implemented at any time and place where people felt bold enough to do so. It was, more sharply, an agenda and vocation to which he knew himself called, and one that he announced as the way of being God's true Israel. It was his own fresh construal of the law and the prophets, the controversial way by which, he proposed, Israel's God would make Israel at last what it had always been called to be, the light of the nations. Like other Jewish would-be leaders and messiahs before and since, Jesus believed himself called to go ahead of the people and fight the battle on their behalf. Like David taking on Goliath, he would face the enemy of God's people alone, choosing the strange weapons that matched his own vision.

He would not only fight the true battle; he would also rebuild the true temple. Jesus' action in the temple, complex and controversial though it has proved, seems to me a clear symbol of God's judgment. Such an action must, within second-temple Jewish expectations, have implied that some form of replacement temple was envisaged. The symbolism of many of Jesus' actions, climaxing in the meal in the Upper Room, spoke powerfully about what sort of temple he envisaged. The Last Supper traditions, though no doubt shaped in their present form by the early church's varied usage, certainly go back to an actual meal charged with complex and multilayered symbolism. It was not only in the early church that such meal symbolism was understood and valued; as Marcus has argued, in line with John Dominic Crossan, the "open commensality" of Jesus' ministry carried powerful symbolism, and Jesus' last meal simply took this to its logical conclusion.

If, then, Jesus believed himself to be Israel's messiah, the focal point of its long history, the one through whom Israel's God would at last deal with its exile and sin and bring about its longed-for redemption, he also seems to have believed that this messianic task would be accomplished through his own suffering and death. This, I must stress, is not a particularly odd thing to be thought by a first-century Jew with a strong sense of God's presence and purpose and a clear gift for charismatic leadership.

In short, we have every reason to suppose that Jesus did in fact locate his own vocation within precisely this complex of biblical and traditional reflection.[7] The visions of Zechariah, so dark and opaque to the twentieth century, seem to have been luminous to him, to have shaped his vocation and choice of action. Daniel's vision of the vindication of "one like a son of man," the symbolic representative of Israel, seems to have provided him with inspiration and cryptic vocabulary.[8] And the poems about the "servant" in Isaiah 40–55 gave particular focus to his sense of call and direction. Other Jews roughly contemporary with him had used them as well. Some interpreted the "servant" figure as a messiah who would inflict suffering on the enemies of Israel; others interpreted it in terms of the (nonmessianic) martyrs of the Maccabean period. The evidence suggests that Jesus, uniquely, so far as we know, combined these two strands, in line with his whole larger agenda. His messianic vocation climaxed in the call to suffer Israel's death, Israel's supreme moment of exile, on Israel's behalf. This is a thoroughly credible first-century Jewish vocation.

More particularly, Jesus thus seems to have believed that it was his vocation to take upon himself, actually and symbolically, the fate which he had announced for the nation as a whole. Despite the protests of some scholars who have doubted how widespread revolutionary tendencies were in Jesus' day, I agree with Horsley, Goodman, and others who have insisted that the desire for, and actions toward, violent revolution against Rome had taken hold of the imagination of the great majority of Jesus' contemporaries.[9] In particular, such aspirations characterized the stricter Pharisaic school, the Shammaites. Jesus had warned, using all the language and imagery of the prophets to make his point, that such action would lead to a devastating debacle in which Rome, like Assyria and Babylon before it, would be the unwitting but effective agent of the wrath of Israel's own God. If Josephus could believe that Israel's God could act through Rome, so could Jesus; except that Josephus's argument was always blatantly self-serving, whereas Jesus' belief led him to a Roman cross. He seems to have construed his vocation in terms familiar in the stories of the martyrs. He would go ahead of the nation to take upon himself the judgment of which he had warned, the wrath of Rome against rebel subjects. That was what his royal vocation demanded. That, I believe, lies at the heart of the New Testament's insistence that Jesus died the death that awaited others, in order that they might not die it.

As a result, as Albert Schweitzer saw a century ago, the best first-century context in which to understand Jesus' own intention as he went to Jerusalem, as he agonized in Gethsemane, and as he faced accusers and governors, torturers and executioners, is the belief, found in many Jewish sources stretching back into the prophets and on into the Christian era, that when Israel's redemption came about it would be born through a period of intense suffering.[10] Israel would pass through the fire and water, and Israel's God would then bring it out into the planned and promised salvation. Jesus seems to have believed that this would occur, uniquely and decisively, in and through his own suffering and death. He would take upon himself the "messianic woes" on behalf of Israel. He would go through the darkest night and lead the way into the dawn of the new day. This was how he would fight the final battle against the real enemy. This was how he would build the true temple. This, in other words, was how he would win the victory that would establish him as Israel's true messiah and transform the kingdom from its current present-and-future state into a fully present reality.

If all of this is anything near the target, someone is bound to ask: does this mean that Jesus' death was actually a complicated form of suicide? Did he simply have a death wish and dress it up in fancy theological language? The answer is emphatically no. As Gethsemane shows (whatever we make of its detail, it is highly unlikely that the entire scene is fictitious), Jesus did not desire to die. Unlike the typical suicide, he had not despaired of life. Rather, he went to Jerusalem determined to announce his particular kingdom message in word and (particularly) in symbolic action, knowing what the inevitable reaction would be, and believing that this reaction would itself be the means of God's will being done. There have been many in the history of the world and the church who, not desiring to die for its own sake, have continued as a matter of integrity and vocation to follow the course on which they were set, knowing that this might, or even would inevitably, result in their deaths, and being ready to interpret that, too, as part of the same integrity and vocation. Did Socrates commit suicide? Did Janani Luwum?

The position I have outlined here has considerable historical strength. It fits closely within the Jewish world of Jesus' day, while offering a fresh construal of that thought-world which, to our knowledge, no other Jew had espoused in quite that form. It also (as we shall see presently) explains the rise of early Christian reflection on Jesus' death without being credibly explicable as a reading back, a spurious historicization, of later atonement-theology. In other words, it possesses the double similarity and double dissimilarity with Jesus' Jewish context, and with the early church, which is a major hallmark of historical plausibility.[11]

This account thus answers simultaneously the standard objections to supposing that Jesus envisaged his own death and gave it a theological interpretation (he couldn't have thought like that; the early church made it up and read it back). Of course late-modern westerners will find such a train of thought strange; that is what historians are always discovering about the way people other than ourselves thought. We may also find it, initially at least, unattractive; but if we are only to accept about Jesus those elements which naturally attract us we shall sail close to the wind of making a Jesus-figure in our own image. In particular, it dovetails completely with the many-sided picture of Jesus the kingdom-prophet I outlined in chapter 3. It belongs, in other words, with an understanding of Jesus according to which he shared the widespread contemporary Jewish belief that world history was focused on Israel's history and that Israel's history was rapidly reaching its great showdown; and it shows how he believed, as did some other Jews of the time about themselves, that this showdown would take place in and through his own work, his own fate.

## THE POLITICAL REASONS

The authorities, blundering about in their eagerness to prevent riots and to save their own political skins, handled the affair in a reasonably predictable manner. The Jewish authorities in question were of course the chief priests, whose power base Jesus had threatened with his action in the temple. They were understandably eager to prevent his apparently antitemple movement gaining any more ground. They needed, however, a charge that they could present to Pilate as a plausible ground for Jesus' removal and, at the same time, a charge that they could offer to the people as a good Jewish reason why Jesus had to die. Their questioning about Jesus' temple action and its significance quickly unearthed what they had already suspected, that he saw himself in messianic terms and believed that Israel's God would vindicate him as such. This completely explains the interchange, much abbreviated, no doubt, that is reported in the Marcan tradition.[12]

This sequence of thought, despite much counterassertion, is hardly likely to be a retrojection of later Christian theology. It could only be that if one were to take it at a broad-brush level, allowing oneself to be dazzled by phrases like "son of the blessed" and "son of man" and assuming them to possess, on their surface, all the meanings they acquired through the next century or three. In fact, there is scarcely any evidence (apart from the Marcan tradition itself, which of course would produce a circular argument) that post-Easter Christians constructed a Christology in which the destruction of the temple was linked to Jesus' messiahship and vice versa, or in which either was linked directly to Daniel 7. Nor is there any other evidence, except perhaps for the Stephen speech in Acts 7, that the political meaning of Jesus' messiahship was regularly combined with Jesus' temple sayings, or that the early Christians were accused of blasphemy for claims about Jesus involving these titles and texts. (I leave out of the reckoning the question of the "second coming," since I do not think that Mark 14.62 refers to it.) In fact, we can only claim that the exchange between Jesus and Caiaphas consists of a retrojection of later Christian theology if we first invent, out of nothing, a later Christian theology that combines these elements and then claim that it has been turned into a fictitious narrative. What has happened, in fact, is that a much later, and rather loose and shallow, scholarly reconstruction of Christian origins has taken over, in which the so-called titles of Jesus, and the dogma of the *parousia* (a Greek word meaning "presence," often used loosely to refer to Jesus' second coming), are all that matter. Seeing a couple of these titles and "the coming of the son of man," it has been assumed that the passage is a retrojected "Christian confession of faith." The problems about a hasty night hearing have been very much overblown; it may not have been an official trial, and regulations drafted in a cool hour two hundred years later (in the Mishnah, our main source) are hardly good evidence for what might have happened in an emergency, at a festival season, under the eagle eye of Rome.

What about Pilate? The idea that the gospels try to whitewash him (which has more to do with a modern desire to make the gospels out to be anti-Jewish than a scholarly desire to understand the political dynamics involved) is very implausible. He appears in all the accounts as at best vacillating and weak, at worst a malevolent petty tyrant. The only reason he tries to free Jesus is because he routinely wanted to snub the chief priests. His arm is twisted, though, because the prisoner before him is portrayed to him as a rebel king. Rome would not be pleased if news leaked out that a "king of the Jews" had been on trial and had been released. The crowds, meanwhile, could be won over by the suggestion that Jesus was after all a blasphemer.

The Jewish hearing was not, then, about later Christian theology, but about the two politically necessary moves the chief priests had to make. They wanted Jesus out of the way because of his challenge to the temple. Pilate could be told that Jesus was a rebel king. The crowds

could be told that he was "leading Israel astray" as a false and blas-
pheming prophet. And so Jesus went to his death, the cruelest and most
brutal that Roman ingenuity and efficiency could devise, the death that
proclaimed, within that symbolic universe, that Caesar was the master
of the world and that the gods of the nations, including Israel, were
powerless before him.

## THE BEGINNINGS OF CHRISTIAN REFLECTION ABOUT JESUS' DEATH

Had the story ended there, there is no reason to suppose that any kind
of Jesus movement would have survived for very long. John the Baptist's movement survived, as we know from Acts (and by implication
from the gospels, not least John), but probably not for more than a
generation. John could still be regarded as a prophet after his death. It
is conceivable that after Jesus' death some of his followers would have
continued to see him in the same way, however much that would have
represented a shrinking of the aspirations and expectations they had
cherished during his lifetime. But the more we recognize the messianic
nature of Jesus' actions and words, and the messianic expectations of
his followers, the more it becomes exceedingly strange to imagine such
a movement, with such a messianic emphasis, continuing after his
death. Nobody in 71 C.E. said that Simon bar Giora was the messiah, or
even a great prophet; nobody in 136 C.E. continued to believe that
Simeon ben Kosiba really was Bar-Kochba, "the son of the star." This
line of thought points us toward the next chapter, on the resurrection.

But, granted the continuation of Jesus' movement, what we have said
so far enables us to understand why, within the very earliest stages of the
Christian movement, we discover that Jesus' death was regarded as
much more than a tragic incident, the cutting short of a promising career. Much more, too, than a martyrdom, though some martyr stories
point forward to the sort of things the early Christians said about Jesus'
death. Embedded within the earliest strands of Christian tradition we
find an already formulaic statement: the messiah died for our sins according to the scriptures.[13] I suggest that this represents, not only an ac-

curate summary of what the earliest Christians believed, but a strand of thought going back to the mind and intention of Jesus himself.

It is important to see what this strand meant at its very beginning. It was not, first and foremost, a way of saying that the moral failures of individuals had been atoned for in some abstract theological transaction. That would come, and quickly; we find it already in Paul's mature thought. But in the beginning it was a claim about what Israel's God had done, in fulfillment of the scriptural prophecies, to bring Israel's long night of exile to its conclusion, to deal with the "sins" that had kept Israel enslaved to the pagan powers of the world, and to bring about the real "return from exile," the dawn of the new day, for which Israel had longed.

This interpretation of Jesus' death was not, in the first instance, a feeling or a doctrine. (Here, as elsewhere, we must beware of false either-or distinctions, of sketching a shallow and simplistic conservative pietism and assuming that its only alternative is liberal skepticism.) It was not, that is, a matter of the early Christians "feeling forgiven," experiencing the divine forgiveness for moral misdemeanors as an inner existential reality. Nor was it a new theory about how "atonement" functioned, supplanting previous Jewish beliefs on the subject. It was the early Christian deduction, from Jesus' resurrection, that his death had been after all effective, as the hinge upon which the door to God's new world had swung open. To say that the messiah had died for sins in fulfillment of the scriptures was to make a claim, not so much about an abstract atonement theology into which individuals could tap to salve their guilty consciences, as about *where Israel and the world now were within God's eschatological timetable.* The sins that had caused Israel's exile had now been dealt with, and the time of forgiveness had arrived.

Hence what might be seen as the earliest statement of atonement theology in the New Testament: "Save yourselves," said Peter to the crowd on the day of Pentecost, "from this corrupt generation."[14] In other words, if the messiah has broken through the barrier of sin that has kept Israel in exile, there is no need for anyone to remain bound any longer within the old agendas. It is this train of thought, I suggest, that led Paul, in one of his earliest letters, to declare that "the Messiah loved me and gave himself for me."[15] Paul knew himself to have been following an agenda, a way of being Israel, that led inexorably to the wrath of Rome, in other words, to crucifixion. He saw in Jesus' death God's judgment on that entire way of being, a judgment borne by the messiah, Israel's representative, on his behalf.

How did this very early, very Jewish atonement theology become transformed into the message for the wider world that we increasingly find in the New Testament ("not for ours only, but for the sins of the whole world")?[16] Here, as elsewhere, the key is to see the place of the Gentiles within the strands of first-century Jewish eschatology that influenced the early church. Israel's God is the creator, the God of the whole world. What, therefore, he does for Israel he does in some sense or other for the whole world. And once it is clear that he has dealt with Israel's "real" exile, its enslavement to evil (and not merely to pagan armies) in and through Jesus, it is not a difficult step to take to suppose that he has also dealt, by the same means, with the exile of the whole world, the enslavement of the nations and peoples of the world to the principalities and powers. That Paul's mind moved in just this direction seems clear from various passages.[17]

I suggest, therefore, that early Christian atonement theology derives ultimately not simply from the fact of Jesus' death together with an interpretation extraneously projected onto the event by the ingenious minds of early Christians, but from Jesus' death seen, as he saw it himself, as the eschatological act whereby, in accordance with scriptural and postscriptural traditions, but making a new amalgamation of them, Israel's God had dealt with the state of exile-because-of-sin in which Israel, and the whole world, had languished. Although the early church developed ways and means of making this point which went beyond anything that Jesus himself had said, that interpretation was indeed a development of, not an evolution away from, his own aim and intention. And—though it would take us too far afield to explore this further—this central emphasis on the unique achievement of Jesus' death as the sin-forgiving, once-for-all liberating act of Israel's God remained at the center of early Christian thought, sustaining but not being replaced by the belief, which became so beloved of theologians and pastors in later years, that the sin of individual sinners had been dealt with on the cross.

## JESUS' DEATH THEN AND NOW

What is the relevance of Jesus' death, seen in this way, to the church, the world, and the individual Christian today?[18]

Traditionally this question has been answered in terms of the remission of sin and guilt, whereby the individual sinner finds peace for a troubled conscience, in the present, and the assurance of ultimate forgiveness from God, in life after death. This answer is, I believe, perfectly true and valid, biblically rooted and pastorally as vital as ever it was. It does not, however, tell the whole story that the New Testament tells about the meaning of Jesus' death. To explore that fuller story in no way detracts from this individual application but rather sets it in its proper context.

The larger story concerns the victory over evil as a whole that was won, according to the New Testament, on the cross. (It is interesting to observe how in the "traditional" readings this central biblical theme is regularly screened out, though making an occasional comeback in such works as the celebrated *Christus Victor* of Gustaf Aulén.)[19] It quickly becomes clear, of course, why this theme is regularly ignored: there is an obvious credibility gap between such a claim and the realities of the world. The now-traditional scheme avoids this problem by projecting the victory on the one hand inward, into the heart and conscience of the believer, and on the other hand forward, into the state of affairs after death or at the end of the world. In neither case is there any outward change in the world, except in that the forgiven sinner will now live in a different manner, out of gratitude for forgiveness and in the power of the Spirit working in his or her life. This, of course, is not to be sneezed at: forgiveness is one of the most powerful things in the world, and when God's forgiveness is then passed on by the grateful recipient, all sorts of new situations can be created, all sorts of new possibilities of healing can open up.

But the New Testament, not least Paul and the book of Revelation, regularly point beyond this to a larger and stranger victory that is to be worked out in the world, a victory beyond what can be measured in terms of the effect of forgiven Christians making their own personal impact. Somehow, the suffering of Christians in the present, as they share Christ's sufferings and groan in awaiting their final redemption, is to become the means by which the Spirit of God prays from within the heart of a world in pain, in order that the world itself might be redeemed.[20] Somehow, the witness of the martyrs, as they live their lives and die their deaths in obedience to the gospel of Jesus, puts into effect the victory of the cross above and beyond the immediate impact that their witness may have on the actual observers. Somehow, "through the church" (particularly, it seems, through the fact that Jews and Gentiles are brought together into one body by the cross) "the many-splendored wisdom of God may be made known to the principalities and powers in the heavenly places"[21] Somehow, "as often as you eat this bread and drink this cup, you proclaim the Lord's death until he comes."[22] These things—suffering, prayer, martyrdom, church unity, the eucharist—all derive their meaning from the death of Jesus, and all make that death effective in strange ways in the world around, beyond what may be calculated in terms of individual humans coming to faith.

In particular, the cross, seen in the way I have outlined it, opens up the possibility of a more deeply rooted political and liberation theology than is normally offered. It is not enough to analyze the causes of oppression and suffering in the world and to encourage people to stand up to them. Darker powers, unseen forces, are involved in these struggles, as Walter Wink and others have eloquently argued; and only the belief that the principalities and powers have in fact been led as a bedraggled and defeated rabble in Christ's triumphant procession will provide the right foundation for a true Christian political activity.[23] Without being rooted in the life, death, and resurrection of Jesus, such activity all too quickly becomes a "religious" version of one or another contemporary ideology.

Granted all this, the cross of Jesus, seen as the place where, because of the election of Israel and the messiahship of Jesus, the pain and guilt of the world were concentrated once for all, becomes rightly the focus of much Christian spirituality and devotion. Meditation on Jesus' suffering and death becomes a vital and central way of celebrating and gaining access to the free, forgiving, healing love of the creator God.

Many will object, of course, that it is morbid to focus on someone's sufferings; that such meditation encourages passivity in the face of evil; or that the cross has become yet another weapon in the armory of those who use the religion of others as a means of gaining or maintaining political control over them. All these can be true. Yet the death of Jesus still draws children, women, and men to the love of the one true God and, holding them in that love, sustains them not only in their personal living but also in their own wrestling with the powers of evil, giving them courage, like Janani Luwum, to stand up to the Caiaphases and Pilates of this world and to take the consequences. The cross of Jesus is thus the Christian symbol par excellence, forming the focal point of Christian spirituality, Christian praying, Christian believing, and Christian action. And the manifold ways in which it is and does all this can trace their roots legitimately to the mind and intention, to the action and passion, of Jesus himself.

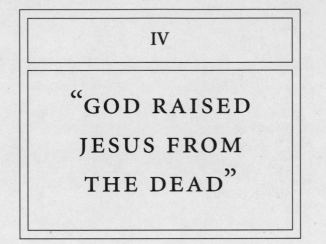

IV

"GOD RAISED
JESUS FROM
THE DEAD"

## CHAPTER 7

# THE TRANSFORMING REALITY OF THE BODILY RESURRECTION   *N. T. Wright*

THE QUESTION, "What happened on Easter Day?" is part of a larger question and cannot properly be considered in isolation from it. The larger question is: "Why did Christianity arise, and why did it take the shape it did?"[1]

Other prophets, other messiahs, came and went in Jesus' day. Routinely, they died violently at the hands of the pagan enemy. Their movements either died with them, sometimes literally, or transformed themselves into a new movement around a new leader. Jesus' movement did neither. Within days of his execution it found a new lease of life; within weeks it was announcing that he was indeed the messiah; within a year or two it was proclaiming him to pagans as their rightful Lord. How can a historian explain this astonishing transformation?

The early Christians themselves, to a man and (particularly) a woman, gave one answer only. They said that after his shameful death God had raised Jesus from the dead. It is vital that we discover what precisely they meant by this, so that we can try both to evaluate what they said and to grapple with the meaning of their claim for today.

## RESURRECTION IN FIRST-CENTURY JUDAISM

When the early Christians spoke of the resurrection of Jesus, they spoke as first-century Jews. What would they have understood by *resurrection*, and why would they use this language to describe what had happened to

Jesus? Many people today, both Christian and non-Christian, use the word loosely, to refer to life after death or reincarnation or something else. Words that have become unspecific and generalized may have carried precise meaning once, and we must find it.[2]

There was a spectrum of belief about life after death in first-century Judaism. The Sadducees, the ruling elite, denied a future life of any sort. This may be because those who believed strongly in the future life were the more ready to risk death in seeking political or religious reform. One can well imagine that existing rulers would not wish to encourage such attitudes.

Many Jews believed in a continuing life after death, but in a disembodied state that neither needed nor expected a future reembodiment. The Alexandrian philosopher Philo took this view—hardly surprising, in view of his blending together of Plato's philosophy and Jewish tradition. So did the book called *Jubilees,* which was popular at Qumran and probably in other circles. The Dead Sea Scrolls may possibly agree; there is only one scroll out of the hundreds now published that speaks about resurrection, and it is by no means clear whether this is to be taken literally or metaphorically. Certainly if the Qumran sectarians believed in the resurrection, it was not among their central tenets. This middle position, then, posits the existence of a soul or spirit after death but does not see this entity as being given a new body. This position believes firmly in the continuing existence of human beings in a nonbodily form after their death but never refers to this continuing existence as resurrection.

At the other end of the spectrum from the Sadducees we find the Pharisees, with their well-known belief in the resurrection of the body. This formed part of the wider Pharisaic agenda of reform or even revolution. Resurrection functioned for them not simply as the assurance of a newly embodied life after death (as opposed to mere immortality), but as part of the larger package in which Israel's God would create a new state of affairs within the space-time world, bringing about justice and peace, overthrowing oppression and wickedness—and raising to life, in order to enjoy this new day, all the righteous dead who had longed for its appearing but had died ahead of time. Resurrection, for Pharisees, was thus part of their belief both in the goodness of the created, physical world and in the ultimate triumph of the justice of God.

Already we see an important point emerging. For the first-century Jew, *resurrection* was not a general term for "life after death." It was one point on a spectrum of beliefs about life after death.

But *resurrection* itself seems to have had different meanings. As far as we can tell, first-century Jewish belief in the rising again of dead bodies looks back to a few passages in the prophetic literature, notably in Isaiah, Ezekiel, and Daniel. In Ezekiel (the passage on the valley of dry bones), the idea of corpses coming back to life is used as a vivid apocalyptic metaphor to denote the renewal of Israel's fortunes, Israel's restoration after exile. It is quite possible that this is in mind in the Isaiah reference as well.[3]

But when we reach the second century B.C.E., what began as metaphor has become literal. The referent, in other words, was no longer the concrete return from exile, but the concrete reembodiment of formerly dead persons. The Maccabean martyrs in the 160s taunted their torturers with the assurance that they, the martyrs, would receive their bodies back again, whole and entire, while their enemies would not. (The hagiographical nature of the stories, in, for instance, 2 Maccabees 7, 12, and 14 is not the point; what matters is that they reflect the beliefs of the writers within the following century or so.) The book of Daniel, after speaking of the suffering and martyrdom of some Israelites,[4] goes on to promise new life for those who "sleep in the dust of the earth,"[5] a new life in which "those who are wise shall shine like the brightness of the sky, and those who lead many to righteousness, like the stars for ever and ever." Daniel thus uses new metaphors to denote the concrete rising to life of dead people and to connote two things: (a) that it will be like waking from sleep, and (b) that it will be to a life of more splendor than before. And the Wisdom of Solomon, reflecting a similar period and set of questions, and quite possibly dependent on this text in Daniel, insists that the righteous who have died will, in the time of their visitation, "shine forth and run like sparks through the stubble; they will govern nations and rule over peoples, and the Lord will reign over them for ever."[6]

This literal meaning of *resurrection*—the concrete reembodiment of those who have died, especially the righteous and wise—continued on to become the mainstream Pharisaic belief, enshrined in subsequent rabbinic Judaism. Daniel 12 became the favorite prooftext for this view.

The concreteness with which the topic was taken is well illustrated by a later rabbinic discussion as to whether, when God gave the dead their new bodies, he would start with the bones and sinews and work up to flesh and skin, as in Ezekiel 37, or whether he would make a new body all over again, the same way as the original one was made, starting with the skin and flesh and "firming it up" with sinews and bones.[7] The discussion is interesting in itself, but the point is this: one would only raise such questions if the concrete physicality of the resurrection body were taken absolutely for granted.

Strictly speaking, this means (as Marcus says) that it was possible for people to believe in resurrection without necessarily believing that something had happened to a corpse. That seems to have been the Hillelite view: God would make a new whole person from scratch. However, the force of the point is blunted by the consideration that it was clearly a new person, bones, sinews, flesh, skin, and all, that the Hillelites, along with the Shammaites, believed would result at the end of the day.

We should remind ourselves, further, that, with all this concentration on the concrete new bodies, the wider meanings were not lost. "The resurrection" still formed part of the long-term Pharisaic and rabbinic hope for a new state of affairs within very much this-worldly life, in which Israel would be redeemed, justice and peace would triumph, and God would at last be King of the world. Thus what began as a metaphor was transformed into metonymy: instead of remaining simply a vivid image for God's new day, it became one element within that final hope, which could be referred to, like the phrases "the messianic age" and "the kingdom of God," as a shorthand for the entire coming time of redemption and justice.

This highlights an important point about Jewish resurrection language. It was never envisaged that *one* person might receive "the resurrection" while the rest of history continued unchecked. To be sure, within popular superstition and imagination it was always conceivable that one of the great prophets of old, or even one of recent days, might return again in the guise of someone else: had not Malachi, after all, promised that Elijah would return to herald the great coming day? Thus when the crowds speculated that Jesus might be Elijah or Jeremiah or John the Baptist returned to life, we should not see this as a belief about "the resurrection" per se, but rather an ad hoc explanation of a remarkable person. "The resurrection" was to be the raising to life of all the righteous dead (and perhaps the unrighteous dead, too, though that varies from text to text) as part of the great final reversal of the world's, and Israel's, fortunes; not the raising to life of one person within otherwise ongoing history and life. When hints of the latter occur—Herod Antipas's speculations about Jesus being John the Baptist *redivivus,* for example—it is noteworthy that the supposedly resurrected individual is a concrete human being, not a disembodied spirit.[8]

This highlights a second key point. If the dead will be raised to newly embodied life, in principle, where are they, and indeed *what* are they, at the present time? One can stick with Ezekiel's metaphor and say that they are simply a set of inanimate physical remains, awaiting reanimation. But the more usual first-century option was to speak of a continuing existence either as a spirit, a soul, or an angel. "The souls of the righteous are in God's hand," declares the Wisdom of Solomon: they are safe from their torturers at last, enjoying a peaceful rest until the time of visitation and resurrection.[9] When the Jerusalem Christians suppose that Peter has been killed in prison, only to be told that Peter's voice is addressing them from behind a shut door, they assume that this is a postmortem disembodied visitation: "It must be his angel," they say.[10] Resurrection was one option among others for how one interpreted what God was going to do with and for those who had died; and resurrection itself could have various interpretations, various ways of putting together the jigsaw of *how* God would accomplish this remarkable reembodiment and of what could be said about the dead in the meantime.[11]

There is no evidence for Jews of our period using the word *resurrection* to denote something essentially nonconcrete. The word retained its metaphorical echoes and acquired new metonymic ones, but without losing the literal reference to the concrete event of dead bodies coming to life. This must be borne in mind throughout what follows.

## EARLY CHRISTIANITY
## WITHIN ITS JEWISH CONTEXT

What then did the earliest Christians mean when they said that Jesus of Nazareth had been raised from the dead?

They cannot have meant that, though his body remained in a tomb, his spirit or soul was now safe in the hands of God, perhaps even given a place of honor. That was a perfectly reasonable Jewish thing to think about someone now dead, particularly a great leader or teacher, particularly one who had died a cruel death. There was normal Jewish language to express such a belief. If that had been what Jesus' first followers believed about him, Jesus would have been on a par, in their eyes, with the Maccabean martyrs or the prophets of old.

Resurrection implies at the very least a coming *back* to something that had been forfeited, that is, bodily life. In the well-developed Jewish language for describing the continuing nonphysical existence of someone who had died there would be no question of "coming back" but only of going *on,* with a spiritual life in unbroken continuity with what had existed before. What the early church insisted about Jesus was that he had been well and truly physically dead and was now well and truly physically alive. If all they had meant was that he was now exalted to a place of honor with God, the language of dying and new life the other side of death would not have been appropriate.

Nor, I submit, would they have used the language of resurrection to describe a sense that Jesus was personally present with them. Such a thing would have been unprecedented, but if it occurred, the natural categories for them would have been angel, spirit, and so forth.[12] In addition, had Jesus' resurrection been simply a matter of people being aware of his presence, there would not have been a sense, as there clearly is in all our evidence, of a sequence of resurrection "appearances" that then *stopped.* Paul knows, and he knows that the Corinthians know, that his seeing of Jesus was the last such event. His churches, not least the Corinthians, had had all kinds of wonderful spiritual experiences; they knew Jesus as their Lord in the power of the Spirit; but they had not seen him as Paul had.[13]

Nor would they have drawn the conclusion that the new age had dawned. When a Jewish leader, teacher, or hero died violently at the hands of Israel's enemies, this was the sign that the old age was still here, that the new age had not yet come. Yet the early Christians not only said that Jesus had been raised from the dead; they concluded from this that God's new age had indeed begun, however paradoxically.

This rules out as well the explanation that has recently been offered, that the early Christians received a ghostly visitation from their recently deceased leader.[14] Such events are well known in the modern, as in the ancient world; the worried church thought they were receiving such a visit from Peter in Acts 11. "It must be his angel," they said; that meant that Peter had been killed by Herod, and they would have to go and collect his body for burial. It would not mean that Peter had been "raised from the dead"; indeed, it would mean that he hadn't been.

So why did the early Christians use the word *resurrection* to describe what they believed had happened to Jesus? The large package of heaven-sent renewal expected by many Jews, including the general resurrection, had not occurred. Pilate, Caiaphas, and Herod were still ruling. Injustice, misery, oppression, and death were still daily features of life for Jews and everyone else. Nor were Abraham, Isaac, Jacob, Moses, David, and the prophets alive again. From that point of view, "the resurrection" expected by Jesus' contemporaries had obviously not occurred.

And yet they said that it had—and proceeded to build a new worldview, a significant variation from within contemporary Judaism, on this belief. "The resurrection," as something that has already happened that must now determine life, faith, prayer, and thought, dominates a good deal of the New Testament: the early Christians really did believe that they were living in the "age to come" for which Israel had longed, the time of forgiveness of sins, the gift of the Spirit, when the Gentiles would be brought in to worship the one God of Israel. The "present age" was still continuing, but the "age to come" had been inaugurated.

We see the same pattern if we ask the vital question: why did the early church believe and declare that Jesus was the messiah? Other would-be messiahs executed by the authorities were thereby forever discredited: a messiah was supposed to lead Israel to liberation from the pagans and to rebuild the temple, not die in pagan hands, leaving the temple still in the grip of Israel's oppressive pseudoaristocrats. Other groups whose messiah was killed faced a choice: either find a new messiah, or give up the revolution. We have evidence of both patterns. Declaring that God had raised one's messiah from the dead was not an option. First-century Jews do not seem to have had time or mental energy to indulge in that peculiar twentieth-century phenomenon, cognitive dissonance, believing that something is still true when events have in fact disproved it. Life was too short and hard for fantasy.

Why, for instance, did the early church not decide that James, the brother of Jesus, was now the messiah? He was the central leader in the early church: holy man, wise teacher, man of prayer, man of God. He was known as the brother of the Lord. Other groups, faced with the death of their would-be messiah and the emergence of his brother as the natural new leader, would have been quick to put two and two together: the brother is the real messiah. But the early church did not. Jesus was the messiah; and the explanation was that God had vindicated him by raising him from the dead. Nor was this belief the mere granting of an honorific title to Jesus, a word with grandeur but little substance. Early Christianity was self-consciously a messianic movement, announcing Jesus as the true Lord of the world even at the risk of offending the existing lords of the world, Caesar included. And this political-religious affirmation grew clearly and visibly out of Jewish messianic beliefs, redefined around the person, agenda, and fate of Jesus of Nazareth.

The early Christians, in other words, affirmed not only that "the resurrection," the great hope of Israel, had happened, but that it had happened in a way that nobody had imagined (a single human being raised within the middle of ongoing history). They reconstructed their worldview, their aims and agendas, around this belief so that it became, not merely an extra oddity, bolted onto the outside of the worldview they already had, but the transforming principle, the string that had pulled back the curtain, revealing God's future as having already arrived in the present.

It is thinkable that Christianity would have continued, as John the Baptist's movement continued, as a Jewish renewal movement looking for a fulfillment of what its prophet had been pointing to. It is thinkable that some of Jesus' followers would have taken some of his sayings and welded them into a new form, shorn of their Jewish context and embodying now a more Hellenistic form of religion or wisdom. The first may have happened in Ebionite Christianity, though we know frustratingly little about it. The second may have happened in the circles that produced and cherished the so-called gospel of Thomas, though it is far from clear that any such developments took place before the middle of the second century. But the great majority of very early Christians known to us really did believe that Jesus of Nazareth had been raised from the dead, in the fully second-temple Jewish sense of attaining a newly embodied existence through and out the other side of physical death; and that, therefore, though the "present age" continued as before, the "new age," the "age to come," had already dawned and that they, Jesus' followers, were both the beneficiaries and the agents of that new age.

## THE EVIDENCE: PAUL

How they expressed this belief of course varied. The first and greatest text to explain what had happened and what it meant is 1 Corinthians 15. Five points stand out.

First, Paul quotes a very early tradition in which the death, burial, and resurrection of Jesus were seen as the decisive events in which the great scriptural story reached its climax. Early Christianity did not consist of a new spirituality or ethic. It consisted of the *announcement* of things that had *happened*, whose significance lay precisely in their happenedness: specifically, the messiah's death, burial, and resurrection. (The mention of burial underlines the fact that, for a Jew like Paul, *resurrection* does not mean "survival" or "nonphysical immortality" but involves the undoing of death and burial alike. The empty tomb, though not mentioned here, is presupposed. It is we, not the early Christians, who have made the empty tomb a major focal point of discussion. For Paul the Pharisee, saying "he was raised, leaving an empty tomb" would have been tautologous.)

Second, Paul stresses that his "seeing" of the risen Jesus was "last of all."[15] This marks off the early "seeings" from subsequent Christian experience. We cannot reduce the former to terms of the latter. Nor, because of the same verse, can we use Paul's dramatic experience of seeing Jesus as a model for what the earlier "seeings" had been like. Paul describes himself at his conversion as "like one ripped suddenly from the womb." There was a violent and dramatic character to the event that the other seeings of Jesus lacked.[16]

Third, Paul constructs a new eschatological time scale. Jesus' resurrection is the beginning of the "end," and the resurrection of all believers is (one feature of) the final end of the "end." The world as a whole has entered the last days, in which Jesus rules as Messiah and Lord. These days will continue until all that opposes or threatens his rule has been dealt with.[17] Finally, death itself—the ultimately dehumanizing and anticreation power—will be destroyed, and God will be all in all.[18] The significance of Jesus' resurrection is not simply that it opens up hope for life after death for individual Christians, but that the new creation has already begun.

Fourth, the resurrection body possesses both continuity and discontinuity with the existing body. The plant grows from the seed yet is a different sort of thing; there are different types of physicality in God's creation, each with its own peculiar splendor.[19] The resurrection body is thus not identical with the original body; it has not, that is, merely been resuscitated; it is, rather, the *transformation* of the existing body into a new mode of physicality.[20] This is underlined by Paul's application in verse 51: we shall not all sleep, he says, but we shall all be *changed*.[21] Paul is not asking whether the resurrection state is physical or nonphysical; that is our late-modern question. His question is, rather, Granted that the resurrection body is of course physical, what sort of physicality is it? It is, he says, a *transformed* physicality, with new properties and attributes but still concrete and physical. "Flesh and blood," which cannot inherit the kingdom,[22] are the present mode of physicality; *flesh* (*sarx* in Greek) is a regular Pauline word, not for what we mean by *flesh* but for "humankind in rebellion against God and subject to corruption and decay."

When Paul describes the new body as a *soma pneumatikon,* often translated "spiritual body,"[23] *he does not mean a "nonphysical body."* Despite one tradition of contemporary translation (the RSV, followed by the NRSV), what Paul contrasts with this "spiritual body" is not a "physical body" (inviting the reader to suppose that Plato has won the game after all), but rather a *soma psychikon,* literally, a "soulish body." The contrast is not so much between physical and nonphysical, but rather between *a body animated by "soul"* (the present natural body, which will, like those of animals, die and decay), and *a body animated by "spirit,"* presumably God's spirit, which will therefore possess a quality of life that transcends the present decaying existence.

This complex argument, so Jewish and yet so unprecedented within Judaism, demands an explanation. What made Paul so clear, far more clear than other Jews of his day, about what the resurrection entailed? The best possible answer is: the resurrection of Jesus himself. It was

Jesus' going through death and out the other side that gave to the Pharisee Paul not only the conviction that "the resurrection" had now occurred, but also a far more detailed picture of what "the resurrection" involved.

Fifth, the resurrection, precisely because it will possess continuity as well as discontinuity with the present life, and will therefore be the reaffirmation of present this-worldly existence, gives not only hope for the future but a sense of purpose and meaning to the present.[24] The final verse of the chapter (58) is most significant: "be steadfast, unmoved, abounding in the Lord's work, because you know that in the Lord your work is not in vain." If the present world is to be abandoned, why work to improve it, to rid it of oppression and dehumanization? The point of the resurrection, for Paul, is that entropy does not have the last word, for humans or for the world as a whole. God has the last word, and it will be lifegiving. Present Christian existence, therefore, with all its pains and struggles, is infinitely worthwhile.

Paul, of course, discusses Jesus' resurrection in many other places, but this chapter is central and vital. For him, what mattered was that the resurrection had happened—not, of course, as an isolated bizarre miracle, but as the messianic focal point and climax of the story of the creator and covenant God with Israel and the world. This was the hinge on which the door of history turned. The resurrection of Jesus did not merely offer new, or more sharply defined, hope for the future. It gave new perspective to the present time, cosmically and personally.

## THE EVIDENCE: THE GOSPELS

Turning to the gospels, we find all the puzzles of which readers have been aware for centuries (not simply with the rise of modern scholarship). The stories of Easter morning in Matthew 28, Mark 16, Luke 24, and John 20 are notoriously difficult to harmonize. We shall never be sure how many women went in what order to the tomb, at what point two or more male disciples went as well, how many angels they all saw, where or in what order the appearances of Jesus took place. But, as many have pointed out, it is precisely this imprecision, coupled with the breathless quality of the narratives, that gives them not only their unique flavor but also their particular value. Despite the scorn of some, lawyers and judges have regularly declared that this is precisely the state of the evidence they find in a great many cases: this is what eyewitness testimony looks and sounds like. And in such cases *the surface discrepancies do not mean that nothing happened; rather, they mean that the witnesses have not been in collusion.*

We must remind ourselves again of how stories functioned in the early communities. A story that carried significance for a person, a family, a village, or a community would not change; it would always be told that way in and for that community. When someone collected such stories and edited them within a larger narrative framework, other factors would, of course, creep in. Thus, for instance, Luke 24 fits well as the conclusion of Luke as a whole, and John 20 as the conclusion of John as a whole, balancing the themes of the prologue.[25] But the editors did not feel free to modify the details of the story so as to make them fit with other resurrection narratives (always supposing they knew them). They let them stand, warts and all: this was how their community had told the story from the very first days.

The underlying story they tell, remarkably enough, is the same as that of 1 Corinthians 15, though Paul's developed theology and biblical exegesis are entirely lacking. It is the story of how the body of Jesus was neither resuscitated nor left to decay in the tomb but was rather *transformed* into a new mode of physicality, shocking and startling to the disciples and to all subsequent readers. This aspect of the story has no precedents in previous Jewish literature and imagination; if we were to put together Ezekiel 37, Daniel 12, 2 Maccabees 7, and similar passages, we would not arrive at a picture like that in the gospels (why, for instance, does Jesus not shine like a star?). They cannot be explained as the wish-fulfilling projection of disappointed but Bible-reading Jesus followers. The stories hold together both (what we would call) the physicality of the risen Jesus (the empty tomb, the fact that Jesus could in principle be touched and felt, his cooking of breakfast, his eating of fish) and his ability to appear and disappear at will, passing through locked doors, and to remain unrecognized on one occasion and puzzling on others ("none of them dared ask him, 'Who are you?,' for they knew it was the Lord"; "when they saw him they worshiped, but some doubted").[26] Without wishing to invoke Tertullian's bracing *credo quia impossibile,* "It's impossible, so I believe it!,"[27] I insist that the sheer odd-ity of these stories, though with the *same* oddity consistent across all the narratives—consistent, too, with Paul's developed resurrection the-ology—counts heavily in their favor as genuine recollection of deeply puzzling events. It is as though the writers are saying, all through, "I know this sounds ridiculous and extraordinary, but this is actually what happened."

This is not to say, of course, that the truth value of the stories con-sists simply in their bare historicity. They are pregnant with so many layers of metaphorical meanings, mythical and eschatological alike, that it is almost impossible to explore them fully. But they are not like the parables (stories whose "truth" is unaffected by whether there was ever an actual "prodigal son"). The deep point of the stories is that the creator God, the God of Israel, has liberated his people and renewed creation. If this is "translated" into a meaning that does not involve events within creation itself, it has deconstructed itself and is halfway to Gnosticism. If these stories were intended to convey the profound truth that Jesus was present with his people, not physically but as a "spiritual" presence, they made a poor job of it. If the answer then is, "Ah, yes, but the more 'physical' stories were invented later, when the early faith was becoming more concrete," are we to say that Luke was so insensitive as to place such a story (Jesus eating fish) right beside his beautifully metaphorical Emmaus Road narrative? Can we not give him credit for knowing what he was talking about? And can we not see that the undoubted, and deeply important, metaphorical dimensions of the stories work, ultimately, only if the basic thing they are describ-ing actually happened?

## HISTORICAL CONCLUSION

These stories, with all their metaphorical layers, are not explicable, I suggest, on the basis of subtle scribes sitting down with biblical texts and transforming a non-resurrection-centered early Christianity into a community that told its own stories in terms of the myth of Jesus' res-urrection. We are, in short, offered a stark choice: either grasp the net-tle, or resign yourself to a long walk round through thorns and thistles.

Grasping the nettle—proposing, as a historical statement, that the tomb of Jesus of Nazareth was empty because his body had been transformed into a new mode of physicality—will of course evoke howls of protest from those for whom the closed world of Enlightenment theory renders any such thing impossible from the start. But if Christianity is only going to be allowed to rent an apartment in the Enlightenment's housing scheme, and on its terms, we are, to borrow Paul's phrase, of all people the most to be pitied—especially as the Enlightenment itself is rumored to be bankrupt and to be facing serious charges of fraud. The lines of historical enquiry point relentlessly inward to the first day of the week after Jesus' crucifixion. Once you allow that something remarkable happened to his body that morning, all the other data fall into place with astonishing ease. Once you insist that nothing so outlandish happened, you are driven to ever more complex and fantastic hypotheses to explain the data. For the historian, as for the scientist, the answer should be clear.

Of course, the historian qua historian cannot compel anyone to assent to anything. The historian can take the argument as far as I have taken it, leaving it clear what the options are: either solve the historical puzzle by agreeing that Jesus' body was transformed into a new sort of life, or leave it in essence unsolved by coming up with flights of fancy, which themselves create far more problems. But at this point the theologian or philosopher can and must step in and ask: do we in fact have good grounds for ruling the straightforward solution out of court a priori? The answer to that will depend, of course, on your worldview: on what you believe about God, the world, yourself, and a host of other things. The question is, whether you are prepared to allow that certain worldviews, including the many skeptical ones that render resurrection out of the question, could and perhaps should be challenged, or whether they are set in stone forever.

It is no good falling back on "science" as having disproved the possibility of resurrection. Any real scientist will tell you that science observes what normally happens; the Christian case is precisely that what happened to Jesus is not what normally happens. For my part, as a historian I prefer the elegant, essentially simple solution rather than the one that fails to include all the data: to say that the early Christians believed that Jesus had been bodily raised from the dead, and to account for this belief by saying that they were telling the truth. Marcus asks, would a video camera have recorded the event? Assuming that a camera would pick up what most human eyes would have seen (by no means a safe assumption), my best guess is that cameras would sometimes have seen Jesus and sometimes not. But that, from early on Easter day, someone in principle could have photographed the empty tomb where he had lain the previous thirty-six hours, I have no doubt.

## THE MEANINGS OF EASTER

I have heard many devout sermons explaining the "meaning" of the resurrection in ways that to me seem inadequate. I have heard, for instance, that Jesus' resurrection proves the existence of life after death. That certainly was not the point for the first Christians: they already believed in life after death, *and in resurrection after "life after death."* For them, Jesus' resurrection meant that the story of God, Israel, and the world had entered its new phase. It was about history and eschatology, not just about personal futures.

I have heard, too, that the resurrection means that Jesus is now alive, and one can enter into relationship with him. That is true so far as it goes, but it is not the specific truth of the resurrection, and it is certainly not the meaning that the evangelists and Paul read from the first Easter. It is, in fact, more the truth of Pentecost, as seen through the Johannine lens: Jesus has not abandoned his people but will come to them by his spirit. The risen Christ is now "with you always, even to the end of the age,"[28] but this is a *further* promise, made possible by the fact of the resurrection, not the inner meaning of the event itself. If the meaning of the stories, with all their apparent embodiedness, is that Jesus is after all a disembodied presence, they do seem to have chosen a rather unfortunate, almost self-contradictory, way of getting their message across.

Rather, the meaning of the resurrection must begin with the validation of Jesus as messiah, as Paul says in Romans 1.4. It means that Israel's God, the creator, has affirmed that Jesus really was, all along, his "son."[29] It means, therefore, the acceptance and validation of his messianic achievement, supremely in his crucifixion: the resurrection declares that the cross was a victory, not a defeat. It is this perspective, of course, that underlies such passages as Colossians 2.14–15 and particularly 1 Corinthians 15.17: if the messiah is not risen, your faith is futile and you are still in your sins. It is the resurrection that declares that sins have indeed been dealt with. Of course, the truth of the Christianity is not just about past events. But take the past events away, and the other layers of truth begin to disintegrate.

The deepest meanings of the resurrection have to do with new creation. If the stories are metaphors for anything, they are metaphors for the belief that God's new world had been brought to birth. When Jesus emerged, transformed, from the tomb on Easter morning, the event was heavy with symbolic significance, to which the evangelists drew attention, without wishing to detract from the historical nature of what they were talking about. It was the first day of God's new week, the moment of sunrise after the long night, the time of new meetings, new meals, of reconciliation and new commissioning. It was the beginning of the new creation.

It was, therefore, the sign of hope for the future, not only for individuals but for the whole world. As Paul saw so clearly in Romans 8, it was the sign that the whole creation would have its exodus, would shake off its corruption and decay, its enslavement to entropy. The New Testament is full of the promise of a world to come in which death itself will be abolished, in which the living God will wipe away all tears from all eyes. The personal hope for resurrection is located within the larger hope for the renewal of all creation, for God's new heavens and new earth. Take away the bodily resurrection, however, and what are you left with? The development of private spirituality, leading to a disembodied life after death: the denial of the goodness of creation, your own body included. If Jesus' resurrection involved the abandoning of his body, it would make exactly the wrong metaphorical point.

Because of this hope, the resurrection of Jesus means that the present time is shot through with great significance. What is done to the glory of God in the present is genuinely building for God's future. Acts of justice and mercy, the creation of beauty and the celebration of truth, deeds of love and the creation of communities of kindness and forgiveness—these all matter, and they matter forever. Take away the resurrection, and these things are important for the present but irrelevant for the future and hence not all that important after all even now. Enfolded in this vocation to build now, with gold, silver, and precious stones, the things that will last into God's new age, is the vocation to holiness: to the fully human life, reflecting the image of God, that is made possible by Jesus' victory on the cross and that is energized by the Spirit of the risen Jesus present within communities and persons. "If then you have been raised with Christ, seek the things that are above"; get rid of all the dehumanizing behavior that destroys God's good creation and the creatures made in his image, all anger and lust, greed and pride.[30] The resurrection thus opens the door to a new world: a new mode of life for the whole cosmos and for all who will dwell in it here and hereafter.

## CHAPTER 8

# THE TRUTH OF EASTER     *Marcus Borg*

---

EASTER STARTLES US. Into the story of Jesus it introduces post-death experiences plus the extraordinary affirmation that a Galilean Jewish peasant is "Lord," claiming our allegiance and participating in the power and being of God. In this chapter, I will treat what I see as the central meanings of Easter, including how I see the historical ground of Easter, and then explore the meanings that early Christianity saw in the combined pattern of Jesus' death and resurrection.

## THE CENTRALITY OF EASTER

---

Easter is utterly central to Christianity. "God raised Jesus from the dead" is the foundational affirmation of the New Testament. About this Tom and I agree. We also agree that the best explanation for the rise of Christianity—indeed, the only adequate explanation—is the resurrection of Jesus. We also agree about its central meanings. Put most compactly, I see the meanings of Easter as twofold: Jesus lives, and Jesus is Lord. Both claims are essential: Easter means that Jesus was experienced after his death, and that he is both Lord and Christ. Though each of us might add further subpoints of meaning, we agree about all of the above.

# THE HISTORICAL GROUND OF EASTER

What we disagree about is the historical ground of those affirmations. What lies behind the Easter traditions of the New Testament? What happened? Specifically, we disagree about whether the truth of Easter depends upon an empty tomb. Did something utterly remarkable happen to the corpse of Jesus so that the tomb was empty? And how much does that matter? Equally basic to our disagreement is how we are to understand the gospel stories of the empty tomb and the appearances of the risen Christ.[1] Are we to understand these stories as reporting the kinds of events that could have been videotaped, if one had been there with a videocamera? That is, are these the kinds of events that disinterested observers could have seen had they been present? And these historical questions lead to an interpretive theological question: does the truth of Easter depend upon the empty tomb and appearance stories being historically factual in this objective sense?

We answer these questions differently. Tom argues vigorously for the historical factuality of the empty tomb and sees it as central to the truth of Easter. He thus affirms what is commonly called a "physical resurrection": something utterly remarkable did happen to the corpse of Jesus, namely, it was transformed into "a new mode of physicality." I see the empty tomb and whatever happened to the corpse of Jesus to be ultimately irrelevant to the truth of Easter. Tom sees the gospel stories of Easter (empty tomb and appearance stories alike) as ultimately going back to multiple eyewitnesses. If I understand him correctly, one could have videotaped what the gospel eyewitnesses saw if one had been there. I see them as the product of a developing tradition and as powerfully true metaphorical narratives.

## THE IRRELEVANCE OF THE EMPTY TOMB

Within the framework of our broader agreement, I will begin with our different views of the historical ground of Easter. My understanding of Easter has changed over the course of my lifetime. Not just deepened (I trust), but changed. My childhood memories include singing the great Easter hymns, their melody lines as triumphant as their words. My fa-

vorite was (and is) "Christ the Lord Is Risen Today." Its glorious, repeating alleluias are as wonderful as ever. Almost as vivid in my memory is "Up from the Grave He Arose," its ascending notes emulating the
rising of Christ himself. As a child, I took it for granted that Easter
meant that Jesus literally rose from the tomb.

I now see Easter very differently. For me, it is irrelevant whether or
not the tomb was empty. Whether Easter involved something remarkable happening to the physical body of Jesus is irrelevant. My argument
is not that we know the tomb was not empty or that nothing happened
to his body, but simply that it doesn't matter. The truth of Easter, as I
see it, is not at stake in this issue.

There are three major reasons.[2] The first is a crucial distinction between two words that are often confused: *resuscitation* and *resurrection*.
The meaning of *resuscitation* is obvious: a person dead or believed to
be dead comes back to life again. Such a person returns to the life she
or he had before, needs to eat and drink and sleep, and will die again
someday. Resuscitation is resumption of previous existence.

Resurrection in a first-century Jewish and Christian context is a
very different notion. Put compactly and somewhat abstractly, resurrection does not mean resumption of previous existence but entry into
a new kind of existence. We cannot say in detail what this new existence
is like, but it is obviously an existence very different from what we
presently experience. In a sense, it is beyond the categories of life and
death, for a resurrected person will not die again. There is a sense in
which it is also beyond the categories of space and time; the resurrected
Christ can appear anywhere and presumably can appear in more than
one place at the same time. Thus, whatever happened on Easter, it was
not resuscitation.[3]

To apply this distinction: resuscitation intrinsically involves something happening to a corpse; resurrection need not. Resurrection does
not refer to the resumption of protoplasmic or corpuscular existence.
To be sure, resurrection could involve something happening to a
corpse, namely the transformation of a corpse; but it need not. Thus, as
a Christian, I am very comfortable not knowing whether or not the
tomb was empty. Indeed, the discovery of Jesus' skeletal remains would
not be a problem. It doesn't matter, because Easter is about resurrection, not resuscitation.

*mincing words?*

My second reason for affirming that the truth of Easter does not depend upon something having happened to Jesus' corpse flows out of the earliest discussion of his resurrection in the New Testament, that provided by Paul in 1 Corinthians 15.[4]

Three features of that complex chapter are important for the current point. Two are found near the beginning of the chapter, in Paul's summary of the tradition that he had received:

> For I handed on to you as of first importance what I in turn had received: that Christ died for our sins in accordance with the scriptures, and that he was buried, and that he was raised on the third day in accordance with the scriptures, and that he appeared to Cephas (Peter), then to the twelve. Then he appeared to more than five hundred brothers and sisters at one time, most of whom are still alive, though some have died. Then he appeared to James, then to all the apostles. Last of all, as to one untimely born, he appeared also to me.[5]

The first point to note is that Paul does not mention an empty tomb. The absence may or may not be significant. Perhaps, as some argue, the reference to "buried" implicitly points to an empty tomb, though it could also be a way of saying, "He was really dead." In any case, Paul does not say, "And on the third day, they found the tomb empty."[6]

The second point concerns the list of people to whom the risen Christ "appeared," a verb used four times in this text. In the Bible, the verb *appeared* is often (though not always) used in connection with "apparitions," a particular kind of vision. Like a vision, an apparition is a paranormal kind of experience, not visible to everybody who happens to be there, and not the kind of experience that could have been videotaped.

That Paul thinks of the resurrection appearances as apparitions is further suggested by his inclusion of himself in the list of people to whom the risen Christ appeared: "Last of all, as to one untimely born, he appeared also to me."[7] Implicitly, he regards his own experience of the risen Christ as similar to the others. His own experience on the Damascus Road, as we know from its threefold narration in Acts 9, 22, and 26, was a vision. The people traveling with him did not experience what he did. Importantly, I think visions and apparitions can be true, by which I mean truthful disclosures of the way things are. I do not put them in the category of hallucinations. Equally importantly, apparitions do not involve a physical body, even though what is seen often includes seeing a person in bodily form.

The third feature of 1 Corinthians 15 is found in the last half of the chapter. There Paul addresses the question of what the resurrection body is like: "How are the dead raised? With what kind of body do they come?"[8] It is, of course, our question: how physically are we to think of the resurrection?

As Paul responds to that question, he uses an analogy that points to both continuity and discontinuity. The physical body is to the resurrection body as a seed is to a full-grown plant. Continuity: the seed becomes the plant. Discontinuity: a full-grown plant looks radically different from the seed.

Then Paul distinguishes between two kinds of bodies.[9] As Tom correctly points out, scholars disagree about how to translate the Greek phrases for these two kinds of bodies.[10] Tom also correctly points out that the translation "physical body" and "spiritual body" goes beyond what the Greek says; the Greek phrase behind "physical body" means literally "a body animated by soul," and the second phrase means "a body animated by spirit." Yet the context suggests to me that the contrast "physical body" and "spiritual body" does express what Paul means. According to other things Paul says in the immediate context, the "body animated by soul" is "flesh and blood," "perishable," "of the earth," "of dust." This is what we typically mean by a physical body. The "body animated by spirit," on the other hand, is none of these things.

Thus Paul affirms a bodily resurrection, even as he radically distinguishes the resurrection body from a flesh-and-blood (that is, physical) body. The two bodies are as different as a plant is from a seed. Whether Paul's language points to a new mode of physicality (as Tom suggests) is indeterminate, it seems to me. Perhaps we need to take seriously that Paul thought there are spiritual bodies that are not physical.

Before I leave 1 Corinthians 15, I want to note an irony. Verse 14 is often quoted by our conservative and fundamentalist Christian brothers and sisters in support of the absolute centrality of a physical resurrection: "If Christ has not been raised, then our preaching has been in vain and your faith has been in vain." But the verse is found in a chapter that strongly suggests that the resurrection body is not a physical body.[11]

My third reason for saying that the empty tomb is irrelevant has to do with the nature of the resurrection stories in the gospels. We are back to the question of literal or metaphorical interpretation. Are we to think of these stories as reporting the kinds of events that anybody could have witnessed if they had been there, that is, videocam kinds of events?

I use my favorite Easter story as a way of inviting reflection on this question: the story of the risen Christ appearing to two of his followers on the Emmaus Road.[12] According to the story, it is the day we know as Easter Sunday. Two followers of Jesus are journeying from Jerusalem to a village named Emmaus. They are joined by a stranger, whom we as the readers know to be the risen Christ. But they don't recognize him. He asks them what they are talking about. They say to him, "Are you the only stranger in Jerusalem who does not know the things that have taken place there in these days?" A rather odd thing to say to the central figure in the whole drama. They journey together for some time, conversing about various matters, including the meaning of scripture. As they reach Emmaus, the stranger is about to leave them, but they say to him, in wonderfully evocative words, "Stay with us, for it is evening, and the day is far spent." Stay with us, for the night is coming on. Or, as the famous hymn has it, "Abide with me, fast falls the eventide." The stranger agrees to do so. They sit down at a table together, and the stranger takes bread, blesses it, breaks it, and gives it to them—and then, Luke tells us, *they recognized him.* And then what happened? "He vanished from their sight."

How much of the content of this story could we have captured on a videotape? Would we have been able to record the risen Christ joining them, walking with them, conversing with them, and finally vanishing from the room as they received bread from him? For me, one has only to ask these questions in order to begin to wonder, "Maybe it's not that kind of story." Rather, the story looks to me to be a metaphorical narrative with rich resonances of meaning. Most centrally, the story makes the claim that the risen Christ journeys with us, whether we know that or not, realize that or not, even as it also affirms that there are moments of recognition in which we do realize that. Thus I do not see the Emmaus Road story as reporting a particular event on a particular day, visible to anybody who happened to be there, but as a story about how the risen Christ comes to his followers again and again and again.[13]

The truth of the Emmaus story is grounded in that kind of experience, not in its being a report ultimately going back to eyewitnesses. I would extend this same principle to all of the Easter stories. Their truth, and the truth of Easter itself, does not depend upon their being literally and historically factual. It does not depend upon the tomb being empty or on something happening to the corpse of Jesus.

For me, the historical ground of Easter is very simple: the followers of Jesus, both then and now, continued to experience Jesus as a living reality after his death. In the early Christian community, these experiences included visions or apparitions of Jesus. I think Paul and others (including the author of the book of Revelation) had them. I think the community experienced the power of the Spirit they had known in Jesus continuing to be and to operate. I think there were experiences of the same presence they had known in Jesus during his historical lifetime. Indeed, I think such experiences were the reason they said, "Jesus is still here, but in a radically new way." Continuity and discontinuity are both affirmed.

Thus I see the post-Easter Jesus as an experiential reality. I take the phenomenology of Christian religious experience very seriously. Christians throughout the centuries have continued to experience Jesus as a living spiritual reality, a figure of the present, not simply a memory from the past. Those experiences (then and now) have taken a variety of forms. They include dramatic forms such as visions and mystical experiences, and less dramatic forms such as a sense of the presence of Jesus—whether in prayer, worship, or the eucharist, in other people, or in the dailiness of our lives. The truth of Easter is grounded in these experiences, not in what happened (or didn't happen) on a particular Sunday almost two thousand years ago.[14]

## THE TWO CENTRAL MEANINGS OF EASTER

The first of the central meanings of Easter has just been stated: Jesus lives. He continued to be experienced after his death. But the meaning is not simply "Jesus lives," as if Easter were primarily about the conquest of death and the promise of an afterlife.

There is a second equally important meaning in the New Testament: Jesus is Lord. A lord, of course, is a master, one to whom one gives one's allegiance. In the gospels and the Bible as a whole, it is sometimes used in this sense. But it can also have a further meaning. Namely, *lord* is one of the words used for God, and thus it also sometimes has resonances of divinity. It is used in both of these senses to refer to the post-Easter Jesus. Already in the New Testament itself, prayers and hymns were addressed to Jesus as if to God.

The affirmation "Jesus is Lord" suggests something further about early Christian experiences of the risen Christ. These experiences were not in the same category as having an experience of one's deceased parent or spouse. From such an experience, we would not draw the inference that our parent or spouse is Lord. But the followers of Jesus did. I think the affirmation is grounded in part in their experience of Jesus before his death. I think they experienced him as quite extraordinary even during his lifetime. The other ingredient was their experience of him after his death as having the qualities of God: like God, he was a spiritual reality; like God, he could be experienced anywhere. Hence, "Jesus is Lord."

The classic New Testament metaphor associated with "Jesus is Lord" is the phrase "raised to God's right hand." Indeed, I see "raised to God's right hand" as the central meaning of being "raised from the dead." Jesus not only lives but is Lord. The right hand of God is a position of honor, authority, and participation in the power and being of God. To say "Jesus has been raised to God's right hand" and "Jesus is Lord" is to say the same thing: Jesus has become one with God and functions as Lord in the lives of his followers. The exclamation of Thomas in the story of his experience of the risen Christ expresses this concisely: "My Lord and my God!"[15]

Easter thus means "Jesus is Lord." The phrase has depths of meaning not always seen in a tradition in which the affirmation has become a commonplace. Jesus is Lord. Rome is not. The domination system is not. The lord of conventional wisdom is not. If Jesus is Lord, then all the would-be lords of our lives are not.

To summarize how I see the difference between Tom and me as this section draws to a close: we both affirm the resurrection of Jesus and see it as central to the New Testament. But we understand the historical events or ground behind this affirmation differently. My position is that experiences of the risen Christ as a continuing presence generated the claim that "Jesus lives and is Lord" and that the statement "God raised Jesus from the dead" and the story of the empty tomb may well have been generated by those experiences.[16] Tom's position is that the fact of the empty tomb and the appearances generated the claim "Jesus lives and is Lord." But we both affirm the claim. This is who Jesus is for us as Christians.

## THE COMPLETED PATTERN OF GOOD FRIDAY AND EASTER

From the time of the New Testament onward, the death and resurrection of Jesus have commonly been seen together, not in isolation from each other. The combined pattern of death and resurrection has meaning. Good Friday and Easter belong together, historically and theologically.

In the concluding section of this chapter, I will briefly describe five meanings of the completed pattern of death and resurrection found in the New Testament itself. All of them are post-Easter retrospective interpretations generated within the community. All speak powerfully of the meaning of Good Friday and Easter as the climax of Jesus' life and as the center of the Christian community's life.

### Rejection/Vindication

Seeing Good Friday and Easter as a pattern of rejection and vindication is very simple and very early. It may well be the earliest interpretation. The execution of Jesus was the rejection of Jesus by the religious and political authorities of the day. The domination system killed him. The resurrection of Jesus is God's vindication of Jesus. It is a simple no-yes pattern: Jesus' death was the domination system's no to what he was doing; Jesus' resurrection was God's yes to Jesus. It is therefore also God's no to the rulers of this world.

The pattern is found in passages such as, "This Jesus whom you crucified God has made both Lord and Christ."[17] Emphasizing that Jesus is Lord, it often uses the language of "raised (or exalted) to God's right hand." Its central meaning is both religious and political: the lords of this world crucified Jesus, but Jesus is Lord, and they aren't. The pattern is thus part of a larger story, namely the story of the age-old conflict between the domination system and the God of Israel, beginning with Moses and continuing through the social prophets of the Hebrew Bible. It is the continuation and climax of the conflict between the lordship of God and the lordship of Pharaoh.

## Defeat of the Powers

A second primary way in which the death and resurrection of Jesus were understood is an extension of the first: here they signify the defeat of "the powers."[18] It is the story of Pharaoh and the Exodus projected onto a cosmic screen. For this understanding, those who crucified Jesus are not simply the political and religious authorities in Jerusalem, but the powers that rule this age. The New Testament names these powers in several ways: the principalities and powers, the elemental spirits of the universe, the prince of the power of the air, Satan, the dragon, the beast from the abyss. Within the New Testament worldview, these are spiritual powers. Because they become embodied in earthly institutions, they include political powers, but they include also discarnate spiritual powers.[19]

These powers hold us in bondage. The truth of this language is that we are, individually and collectively, in bondage to many things. We live under the powers, and our bondage is not simply political. Our struggle is not just with flesh and blood, but with principalities and powers. As in the Exodus story, which this understanding resembles, bondage has become a comprehensive metaphor for the human condition.

The central claim of this interpretation: Good Friday and Easter are the defeat of the powers. God in Christ "disarmed the principalities and powers and made a public example of them, triumphing over them in the cross."[20] The internal logic is clear: Jesus got swallowed up by the powers; the powers got him. As in the first understanding, the resurrection is God's yes to Jesus and no to the powers. Good Friday and Easter are about our liberation from the powers. The Lordship of Christ is the path of personal and existential liberation from the lords of this world.

## Revelation of the Way

A third understanding of the death and resurrection of Jesus is as the revelation or disclosure of the way or path of transformation to new life. Here death and resurrection become a metaphor for the internal spiritual process that lies at the heart of the Christian path.

The metaphor is early. Paul, our earliest New Testament author, uses it to speak of the transformation that he has undergone. He refers to himself as having died, and crucifixion is a metaphor for his own internal death: "I have been crucified with Christ." The result of that internal death is a new identity: "It is no longer I who live, but Christ who lives in me."[21] This metaphorical understanding of the cross is also widespread. It is the meaning of the famous saying about bearing one's cross: "If any want to become my followers, let them deny themselves and take up their cross and follow me."[22] Following Jesus means following him on the path of death and resurrection. Good Friday and Easter embody the path that Jesus taught: the path of dying to an old way of being and being born into a new way of being. The remarkable congruence between the way that he taught and the way his life ended means that he himself becomes the incarnation of the Way. "Jesus is the way"—and the way that Jesus is is the path of death and resurrection.

## Revelation of the Love of God

Good Friday and Easter are also seen in the New Testament as a revelation of the depth of God's love for us. This interpretation depends upon the completed Christian story already being in place, in which Jesus is seen as God's only and beloved son. Within this framework, the death of Jesus is not the execution of a prophet or the rejection of Jesus by the rulers of this world; it is rather God's giving up of that which is most precious to God—namely, Jesus as God's only son. This is the central meaning of John 3.16: God so loved the world that God gave Jesus, the only begotten Son of God, for us.

How much does God love us? That much. This understanding is part of a larger story running throughout the biblical tradition: the story of God the divine lover. As the gospel in the Hebrew Bible puts it, "You are precious in my eyes, and I love you."[23] Good Friday as the death of God's only son for us is the incarnation of the depth of the divine love.

## Sacrifice for Sin

"Jesus died for our sins" was central to my childhood understanding of Christianity. It is found in many Christian hymns, and it lies at the center of most eucharistic liturgies. Indeed, this interpretation is so widespread that it is often seen as the "real" meaning of Jesus' death. And so I will unpack it at somewhat greater length.

When I am asked, "Do you believe Jesus died for your sins?," my answer is no and yes. If they mean, "Do you think Jesus saw his own death as a sacrifice for sin?" or "Do you think that God can forgive sins only because of Jesus' sacrifice?," my answer is no. But if they mean, "Is the statement a powerfully true metaphor of the grace of God?," then my answer is yes. Let me explain.

I begin with a reminder that I do not see this as Jesus' own purpose but as a post-Easter metaphorical interpretation of his death using sacrificial imagery. Sacrifice as a way of dealing with sin was central to the world of Jesus. Moreover, both the timing and location of Jesus' death meant that such imagery was close at hand. He died at Passover, when the Passover lambs were sacrificed; and he died in Jerusalem, the location of the temple and sacrifice.[24] The temple and temple sacrifice are the linguistic home of the metaphor "Jesus died for our sins."

To understand how the metaphor works, we need to ask what it would have meant in a first-century Jewish context to say, "Jesus is the sacrifice for sin." The statement has both a negative and a positive meaning, and both meanings are strikingly radical.

To see the negative meaning, we need to realize that in temple theology, the temple claimed an institutional monopoly on the forgiveness of sins. There were certain kinds of sins and impurities that could be atoned for only by sacrifice. By extension, the temple claimed an institutional monopoly on access to God, for reconciliation with God depended on appropriate sacrifice. In that setting, to say "Jesus is the sacrifice for sin" negated the temple's claim to have an institutional monopoly on forgiveness and access to God. The metaphor thus radically subverted the role of the temple. In effect, to say "Jesus is the sacrifice" means "You don't need the temple; you have access to God apart from the temple." It is thus an antitemple statement.

Positively, "Jesus is the sacrifice" is a metaphorical proclamation of the radical grace of God and of our unconditional acceptance. To say, as the letter to the Hebrews does, that Jesus is "the once for all"[25] sacrifice for sin means that God has already taken care of whatever it is that we think separates us from God. If our own sense of sin and guilt, or unworthiness or failure, makes us feel unacceptable by God, then we simply have not understood that God has already taken care of it. As Paul put it, "Christ is the end of the law," meaning the end of the system of requirements and failing to measure up.[26] Of course, if we don't see this, nothing in our life changes. But if we do see this, then our sense of ourselves in relationship to God changes dramatically.

There is a striking congruency between this understanding of Jesus' death and Jesus' own wisdom teaching. As a wisdom teacher, Jesus taught the immediacy of access to God apart from convention, tradition, and institution. Proclaiming his death as the once for all sacrifice for sin makes the same affirmation: God is accessible apart from institutional mediation.

I conclude this section by commenting on two very different ways "Jesus died for our sins" has been understood. Among some Christians, it is seen as an essential doctrinal element in the Christian belief system. Seen this way, it becomes a doctrinal requirement: we are made right with God by believing that Jesus is the sacrifice. The system of requirements remains, and believing in Jesus is the new requirement. Seeing it as a metaphorical proclamation of the radical grace of God leads to a very different understanding. "Jesus died for our sins" means the abolition of the system of requirements, not the establishment of a new system of requirements.

Thus we have five primary understandings of the death and resurrection of Jesus in the New Testament. Each makes affirmations about

Jesus. The first two emphasize that Jesus is Lord, and the domination system and the powers are not.

The third sees the end of Jesus' life as the embodiment of the path of transformation. The fourth affirms that the death of Jesus as God's only son is the incarnation of God's love for us. The fifth sees him as the once-for-all sacrifice who brings an end to the law as the basis of the divine-human relationship.

Each also expresses central claims of major importance to the Christian life. Domination systems and Jesus are antithetical to each other. God makes possible our liberation from the powers that rule this world and our lives. The path of transformation is the path of an internal dying and being reborn. God is in love with us. God is immediately accessible and accepts us just as we are. All provide rich understandings for mediating the Christian life today.

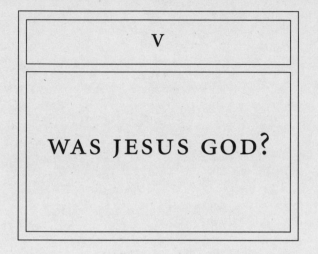

V

WAS JESUS GOD?

## CHAPTER 9

# JESUS AND GOD                    *Marcus Borg*

---

As CHRISTIANS, we live in a tradition that affirms the most extraordinary things about Jesus. In our worship services, we regularly speak of him as divine. In the words of the Nicene Creed, he is "very God of very God," "of one substance with the Father," as well as the second person of the Trinity. In our hymns, we praise him as "Lord" and "king." At Christmas we sing about him: "Veiled in flesh, the Godhead see; hail, incarnate deity"; and "Of the Father's love begotten, ere the worlds began to be; he is Alpha and Omega, he the source, the ending he." In our prayers, we pray to him as to God. Indeed, for many Christians, Jesus is one of the names of God.

It is therefore not surprising that most Christians think of Jesus as divine, and most non-Christians think this is what Christians believe. Some Christians see agreement with this claim as a primary test of orthodoxy. I am sometimes asked, usually by a hostile questioner, "Do you believe Jesus was God?" Typically the question includes a demand for "a simple yes-or-no answer." My response to this question is the same as my response to the question "Do you believe Jesus died for our sins?": no, and yes.

Though the response sounds evasive, what I mean is quite precise. Do I think Jesus thought of himself as divine? No. Do I think he had the mind of God—that is, did he know more than his contemporaries (and anybody who has ever lived) because, in addition to having a human mind, he had a divine mind? No. Do I think he had the power of God? That he could, for example, have called down twelve legions of angels to protect himself, as Matthew 26.53 reports he said? No. But if we make the distinction between the pre-Easter Jesus and the post-Easter Jesus, then my answer would be, "Yes, the post-Easter Jesus is a divine reality—is indeed one with God." And about the pre-Easter Jesus, I would say, "He is the embodiment or incarnation of God."

In this chapter, I will explain more fully what I mean by the above. I will describe how I see both the pre-Easter Jesus and post-Easter Jesus in relationship to God.[1] Doing so will involve treating the emergence of christological images in the early Christian movement and their conceptual development in the Nicene Creed of the fourth century.

## THE PRE-EASTER JESUS AND GOD

As I argued in chapter 4 of this book, I do not think that Jesus proclaimed himself with any of the exalted titles by which he is known in the Christian tradition. I grant that it is possible that Jesus thought of himself as the messiah, as Tom argues, but I am not at all confident about such a claim. If by *messiah*, one means something as modest as believing oneself to have been anointed by God, I could accept that Jesus thought that, in which case *messiah* and *prophet* would be closely-related terms (though I still don't think Jesus spoke of himself as messiah). But if by *messiah* one means much more than this, as Tom does, namely, one anointed by God to be the climactic figure in Israel's history who would lead the final and decisive battle against evil, then I have misgivings like those I have about Jesus seeing his own death as central to the God-Israel relationship.

Let me put the misgiving in extreme and provocative form: if you think you are the light of the world, you're not. That is, perceiving oneself in such grand terms is a fairly good indicator that you're off base. The parallel statement, of course, is: if you think you are the messiah, you're not. I am not proposing this as a law of the universe; perhaps you can think you are the messiah and really be the messiah.

But as the New Testament scholar John Knox argued a generation ago, thinking that Jesus thought of himself in such grand terms raises serious questions about the mental health of Jesus.[2] And though saints and Spirit persons are a bit crazy, when judged by conventional standards, they typically do not think of themselves in grandiose terms. I don't think people like Jesus have an exalted perception of themselves.

What I am confident about is that Jesus as a Jewish mystic knew God. Moreover, as a Spirit person and healer, he would have experienced himself as one "anointed by the Spirit," whether he used this particular phrase or not.[3] This claim is the starting point for how I think of the historical Jesus in relationship to God.

## As Incarnation of God

Christians commonly speak of the relationship between Jesus and God using incarnational language: Jesus is the incarnation of God. *Incarnation* means "embodiment": in Jesus, God became embodied, the Word became flesh. But there are two quite different ways of understanding this, connected to the two different ways of thinking about God described earlier.[4]

The first understanding of Jesus as the incarnation of God sees the meaning of this claim within the framework of supernatural theism. Common in popular-level Christianity throughout the centuries, it flows out of taking biblical and creedal language quite literally. Supernatural theism sees God as a being "out there" and not "here." Within this framework, God's relationship to the world is seen in interventionist terms. From "out there," God intervened by sending Jesus as the only Son of God into the world to live and die for us. For thirty years or so, more or less, God was here, incarnate in Jesus. But normally God isn't here.[5] This view sees Jesus as the unique incarnation of an absent interventionist God, an unparalleled divine insertion into the natural order.

A second way of understanding Jesus as the incarnation of God is to do so within the framework of panentheism or dialectical theism. Namely, God is not "out there" but "right here" as well as *more* than right here, both transcendent and immanent. God is the encompassing Spirit in whom we live and move and have our being. Within this view, Jesus as a Spirit person was open to the presence of God. Writers on spirituality sometimes speak of "emptiness" as a condition of the psyche that makes possible being filled by God. For whatever combination of reasons (genetic inheritance, socialization, spiritual practices, and so forth), we may imagine that Jesus was so "empty" in this sense that he could be filled with the Spirit. Thus I see Jesus as the embodiment and incarnation of the God who is everywhere present. But he is not a visitor from elsewhere, sent to the world by a god "out there." He is not different in kind from us but as completely human as we are.[6] In the fully human life of this utterly remarkable Spirit person, we see the incarnation of God.

## THE POST-EASTER CHRISTOLOGICAL IMAGES

In the decades after his death, a host of striking images for speaking about Jesus emerged within the early Christian community. All of them have their roots in the Jewish tradition, even though some later came to have additional nuances of meaning in the larger Mediterranean world. Many of them have become christological "titles" or designations within the Christian tradition.

The list is impressive: messiah, Son of God, Lord, Word of God, Wisdom (Sophia) of God, lamb of God, true light, Light of the World, bread of life, the way, great high priest and sacrifice, servant of God, good shepherd, true vine, and so forth. Jesus was spoken of in the most exalted language known in his tradition.

### *The Origin of the Images*

Why did this happen? In my judgment, there were two primary factors. One was the Easter experience. As I said in my previous chapter, I do not mean a specific experience on a particular day or a set of such experiences over a period of forty days (to use Luke's time frame). Rather, I mean experiences (which continue to this day) of Jesus as a living reality with the qualities of God, a figure of the present and not of the past.

But it was not only the Easter experience that accounts for the application of exalted language to Jesus. The high estimate of him expressed by these metaphors also flows out of what his followers experienced in the pre-Easter Jesus. I think they sometimes experienced him as an epiphany of the Spirit, as one in whom the Spirit was present. I think they found his healing ability to be remarkable, even as I think they were struck by his wisdom teaching and awed by his courage and determination. I do not think they experienced him as ordinary. Thus, ultimately, the exalted language is grounded in what he was like as a historical person, even though I am skeptical that he or his followers used this language during his lifetime.

## The Christological Images as the Voice of the Community

I begin with a comment building on my claim that explicitly christological language is the voice of the community after Easter and not the voice of Jesus. I will do so by using the remarkable collection of "I am" sayings attributed to Jesus in the gospel of John:

> I am the light of the world.
> I am the bread of life.
> I am the way, truth, and life.
> I am the true vine.
> I am the resurrection and the life.
> I am the door.
> I am the good shepherd.
> Before Abraham was, I am.

Jesus also makes other grand statements about himself in John's gospel:

> I and the Father are one.
> Whoever has seen me has seen God.

As already mentioned, I and most mainline scholars do not think Jesus said these things. He did not speak like this.

To some Christians, this statement comes as a bit of a shock and seems to devalue the "I am" sayings and the other christological sayings in John. But I find these statements to be far more powerful as the voice of the community than if I were to think of them as claims of Jesus about himself.

To explain, what would we think of a person who solemnly said about himself, "I am the light of the world" or "Whoever has seen me has seen God"? Or, to expand one of the statements with more language from John: "I am the bread of life; unless you eat the flesh of the Son of Man and drink his blood, you have no life in you."[7] As self-statements, these are highly problematic. Indeed, we have categories of psychological diagnosis for people who talk like this about themselves.

But if we think of these not as self-statements of Jesus but as the voice of the community, they become very powerful. If a community says about someone, "We have found in this person the light of the world who has shown us the way out of darkness," "We have found in this person the way that leads from death to life," "We have found in this person the spiritual food that feeds us in the midst of our journey even now," that is very impressive indeed. In short, I find the christo-logical language of the New Testament much more compelling when I hear it as the testimony of the community rather than as the self-proclamation of a Galilean Jewish peasant. It is worth taking seriously.

Finally, though the exalted christological images are the post-Easter voice of the community, they are not simply statements about the com-munity's experience. They are also affirmations about the pre-Easter Jesus. The community says, in effect, "This one who was among us as Jesus of Nazareth is also the Word of God, the Son of God, and the Wisdom of God." In him, we see what God is like.

## The Christological Images as Metaphors

The christological affirmations of the New Testament are metaphors. When one thinks about it, this is quite obvious: Jesus was not literally a door, a vine, a light, or a loaf of bread. Moreover, the multiplicity of images points to their metaphoricity. Putting the images into a single sentence makes the point: Jesus is the Word of God, Wisdom of God, Son of God, lamb of God, light of the world, great high priest, and so forth. He was all of this. That is, it is not that one of these is literally true and the rest "only" metaphors. Rather, all are metaphors. Metaphors can, of course, be true, but their truth is not literal.

The essential meaning of metaphor is "to see as."

Thus, to say "Jesus is the true vine" is to *see him as* the true vine, and to say "Jesus is the Son of God" is to *see him as* the Son of God. The point is not to believe *that* Jesus is the true vine or the Son of God, as if these were facts about him. But to see him *as* the true vine implies tak-ing him very seriously as the one upon whom we as the branches de-pend for life, and as one whose life flows through us.

I will further illustrate the meaning of metaphor as "to see as" with two of the most important christological images in the New Testament:

Jesus as Son of God, and Jesus as Wisdom of God. The first uses male imagery to speak about Jesus, the second uses female imagery.

"Son of God" is perhaps the single most familiar christological title. Indeed, it is so familiar that many people think it is the "real" one, with the others perhaps being metaphorical. Tracing its development illuminates the meaning of the phrase. It has a history in the Hebrew Bible and the Jewish tradition.

"Son of God" could refer to Israel. In the story of the Exodus, Moses is told to say to Pharaoh: "Thus says the Lord: Israel is my firstborn son. . . . Let my son go that he may worship you." Hosea says in the name of God, "When Israel was a child, I loved him, and out of Egypt I called my son."[8]

"Son of God" could also refer to the king of Israel. Speaking in the name of God, Nathan the prophet said about the king, "I will be a father to him, and he shall be a son to me."[9] In a psalm probably used in a coronation liturgy in ancient Israel, the divine voice addresses the king and says, "You are my son; today I have begotten you."[10]

In the book of Job, angels or perhaps members of the divine council are referred to as sons of God: "One day the sons of God came to present themselves before the Lord, and Satan also was among them."[11]

One further use of the metaphor in the Jewish tradition is also worth noting. Near the time of Jesus, other Jewish Spirit persons were sometimes called "son" of God.[12]

What do Israel, the king, angels, and Jewish religious ecstatics have in common? All have a close relationship with God. That is, "Son of God" is a relational metaphor, pointing to an intimate relationship with God, like that of beloved child to parent.

This seems to be its initial meaning as applied to Jesus: an affirmation that Jesus stood in an intimate relationship with God. Moreover, in the world of Jesus, a son could also represent his father: he could speak for his father, and act on behalf of his father. Sonship has resonances of agency. Then it became a biological metaphor in the birth stories: Jesus as Son of God was conceived by the Spirit of God, not by a human father. Ultimately, it became a metaphysical or ontological claim: Jesus as the only begotten Son of God is of one substance with God. But initially, to see Jesus as the Son of God points to a relationship of special intimacy and agency.

A second important christological image is female: Jesus as the wisdom of God.[13] Because the Greek word for *wisdom* is *sophia,* it is now common to speak of a Sophia Christology. Wisdom/Sophia in the Jewish tradition is often personified as a woman. Sophia was with God at creation, and the world was created with her aid. She is also spoken of as a Spirit that pervades everything and is everywhere present. She speaks through prophets and invites people to her banquet of bread and wine. And, of course, she invites people to follow her way, which is the way of wisdom rather than folly.[14]

The use of Sophia imagery to speak of Jesus is early and widespread in the New Testament.[15] In the synoptics, Paul, and John, Jesus is spoken of as the child, prophet, and incarnation of divine Sophia. Presumably the historical ground for this is Jesus' roles as a wisdom teacher and prophet who was also known for inviting all and sundry to banquet with him.

Thus to say Jesus is the Son of God is to see Jesus *as* the Son of God, just as to say Jesus is the Sophia of God is to see Jesus *as* the Sophia of God. What it means to see him *as* Son and Sophia is illuminated by the resonances the metaphors have in the tradition from which they came. But it is not the case that Jesus is literally the Son of God and only metaphorically the Sophia of God. Both are metaphors.

### *The Christological Images as Confessional Language*

The christological metaphors are confessional. That is, they are confessions of faith, not statements of verifiable fact. To say "Jesus is the messiah" or "Jesus is the Wisdom of God" is not a fact about Jesus in the sense that "He was five feet three inches tall and weighed 125 pounds" (or whatever size he was) is a fact about Jesus. The latter statement was open to verification by anybody with a tape measure and a scale. The former statements involve conviction and commitment. To see Jesus as "the Wisdom of God" and "Son of God" and "messiah" means to take very seriously what we see in him as a disclosure of God.

As I end this section on the christological metaphors, I want to emphasize that as a Christian I think these affirmations about Jesus are true. But they are true as metaphors. The recognition that this is metaphorical language is crucial. When we do not see this, we take the language literally. Unfortunately, this has often happened within the

Christian tradition. Very early on, we metaphorized our history, and since then we have often historicized our metaphors. When we literalize metaphors, we get nonsense. We also lose the metaphors, with their rich resonances of meaning.

## THE CREED AND THE TRINITY

As early Christianity developed, the post-Easter Jesus increasingly functioned as a divine reality within the community. Even before the gospels were written, prayers were addressed to Jesus as if to God, and hymns praised Jesus as divine. By the early second century, Ignatius could speak of "our God, Jesus Christ."

This created a conundrum of sorts. How could early Christians reconcile their experience of and devotion to the post-Easter Jesus as a divine reality with their commitment to monotheism? The solution to the conundrum was ultimately the Trinity, expressed in the trinitarian pattern of the Nicene Creed.

To continue with a personal comment: I have no difficulty saying and affirming the Nicene Creed. I see it as both the crystallization and indigenization of early Christian theological development. It crystallizes the developing tradition at a particular point in time, even as it also indigenizes it in a particular culture by combining biblical language with categories drawn from Hellenistic philosophy.

By indigenization, I mean that the creed is the product of adapting the essentially biblical language of earliest Christianity into the cultural categories of the larger Mediterranean world of the fourth century. For example, the terms *substance* and *persons,* as they are used in the creed and the doctrine of the Trinity, are both derived from Hellenistic thought. They are culturally relative terms, as is the language of the Bible, for that matter.

The cultural relativity of biblical and creedal language struck me with considerable force when I was in South Africa on a lecture trip a few years ago, soon after the official end of apartheid. My schedule included lecturing at a black theological seminary, an interesting learning experience. On the drive back to Pretoria with my white host, I was told that the black church was being encouraged to develop its own creed. The reason? Because the status of "only son" was not a very high status in that particular black culture. One has no access to an "only son"; he is socially isolated. A much higher status was that of "oldest brother." Thus, if one were to speak of Jesus with the highest status known in that culture, one would speak of him as "our oldest brother" and not as an "only son." The cultural relativity of creedal and biblical language hit home. To say the obvious, if the creed had been formulated in a different culture, its language would have been very different.

This awareness relativizes the creed and the Trinity, even as it helps us to understand it. The meaning of its language is to be understood in the fourth-century context in which it was framed. As I have thus far been able to understand what the creed and the Trinity affirm about Jesus, I see it as having three functions.

First, it affirms what Christian experience and devotion already knew and still know: that the living risen Christ is a divine reality. Though the claim that Jesus is "of one substance" with God uses metaphysical language, it is ultimately not simply the product of philosophical speculation but is grounded in early Christian experience of the risen Christ.

Second, it reconciles the above with monotheism by speaking of one God in three *personae*. This means something quite different from "persons" in modern English, where *person* commonly means a separate center of personality. Thus popular notions of the Trinity commonly imagine God as a committee of three somewhat separate divine beings. But in both Greek and Latin, the word translated "person" means a mask, such as that worn by an actor in the theater—not as a means of concealment, but as a way of playing different roles. Applying this to the notion of God, the one God is known in three primary ways: as the God of Israel, as the Word and Wisdom of God in Jesus, and as the abiding Spirit.

The risen living Christ is thus not a second God but is one with God. And though I am aware that some theologians emphasize that the Trinity means more than this, it seems to me to mean at least this much.

Third, like the christological metaphors of the New Testament, the creed also makes an affirmation about the historical Jesus. At first glance, it appears not to: the creed moves from Jesus' birth to death with nothing at all about his historical life. I once saw this as a defect, as if it implied no interest in the historical Jesus. I now see it as a clue to the function of the creed: namely, by framing the life of Jesus within conception by the Spirit and resurrection to God's right hand, it affirms that what happened in Jesus was "of God."

Aware of all of the above, I can say the creed without misgivings. I do not see it as a set of literally true doctrinal statements to which I am supposed to give my intellectual assent, but as a culturally relative product of the ancient church. Were we to try to write a creed today, we would not use their language, not because we have become unfaithful, but simply because it is not our language. But I do see it as affirming the reality of God, known to us in creation and in the abiding Spirit and preeminently in Jesus.

When I say the creed, I understand myself to be identifying with the community that says these words together. For those of us in creedal churches, doing so is part of our identity. Moreover, I identify not only with the community in the present, but also with generations of long-dead Christians who said these same ancient words as they stood in the presence of sacred mystery. I experience a momentary participation in the communion of saints. Given all of the above, I think we would understand the purpose of the creed better if we sang it or chanted it.

## THE CUMULATIVE CHRISTOLOGICAL CLAIM

As I move toward a concluding crystallization, I begin by emphasizing the riches of the multiple christological metaphors of the New Testament. Each metaphor has its own nuances, and it is important and illuminating to explore them individually. Jesus as "the light of the world" invites us to explore the multiple resonances of "light" and "darkness" as images of the human condition, just as Jesus as "the bread of life" invites us to tease out the resonances of "hunger" and "being filled" as metaphors of yearning and satisfaction. Thus I do not want my somewhat abstract crystallization to detract in any way from the richness of the individual metaphors.

The christological metaphors and the more conceptual language of the Nicene Creed make a cumulative claim about the significance of Jesus. Taken together, and put very compactly, they claim that Jesus is the decisive revelation of God. The word *revelation* has a number of synonyms: *disclosure, manifestation, epiphany.* Jesus discloses what God is like. Jesus is the epiphany of God, a word that means the manifestation on the surface of something from the depths. He is, to return to the metaphors, the Word of God, Wisdom of God, Son of God, and Light of the World.

To affirm that Jesus is the decisive revelation of God does not require affirming that he is the only, or only adequate, revelation of God. Christians have sometimes thought so. Indeed, a few passages in the New Testament suggest as much. The Jesus of John's gospel says, "I am the Way, the Truth and the Life; no one comes to God except through me." In the book of Acts, Peter is reported to have said about Jesus, "There is salvation in no one else, for there is no other name under heaven by which we must be saved."[16]

However, whatever these passages may have meant in their first-century contexts, they need not be understood to mean that Jesus (or Christianity) is the only way of salvation. Instead, we might understand them (and similar Christian statements about Jesus being "the only way") as reflecting the joy of having found one's salvation through Jesus, and the intensity of Christian devotion to Jesus. They should be understood as exclamations, not doctrines, and as "the poetry of devotion and the hyperbole of the heart."[17] So *decisive* need not mean "only."

But the claim does mean that for us, *as Christians,* Jesus is the decisive revelation of God, and of what a life full of God is like. Indeed, I see this as the defining characteristic that makes us Christian rather than something else. If we found the decisive revelation of God in the Torah or in the Koran, then we would be Jews or Muslims. But to be Christian is to affirm, "Here, in Jesus, I see more clearly than anywhere else what God is like." This affirmation can be made with one's whole heart while still affirming that God is also known in other traditions.

The New Testament itself contains an exceedingly compact christological crystallization: "Jesus is the image of the invisible God."[18] Jesus is the image of God: in him, we see what God is like. The Greek word behind *image* is *icon,* which suggestively adds another nuance of meaning. An icon is a sacred image; further, its purpose is to mediate the sacred. Jesus as image and icon of God not only shows us what God is like but also mediates the sacred. The one who was and is Word of God, Wisdom of God, and Son of God is also the sacrament of God.

○ CHAPTER 10

# THE DIVINITY OF JESUS       *N. T. Wright*

WHEN PEOPLE ASK "Was Jesus God?," they usually think they
know what the word *God* means and are asking whether we can
fit Jesus into that. I regard this as deeply misleading.

For seven years I was college chaplain at Worcester College, Oxford.
Each year I used to see the first-year undergraduates individually for a
few minutes, to welcome them to the college and make a first acquaintance. Most were happy to meet me, but many commented, often with
slight embarrassment, "You won't be seeing much of me; you see, I
don't believe in God."

I developed a stock response: "Oh, that's interesting. Which god is
it you don't believe in?" This used to surprise them; they mostly regarded the word *God* as univocal, always meaning the same thing. So
they would stumble out a few phrases about the god they didn't believe in: a being who lived up in the sky, looking down disapprovingly
at the world, occasionally intervening to do miracles, sending bad
people to hell while allowing good people to share his heaven. Again, I
had a stock response for this very common "spy-in-the-sky" theology:
"Well, I'm not surprised you don't believe in that god. I don't believe
in that god either."

At this point the undergraduate would look startled. Then, perhaps,
a faint look of recognition; it was sometimes rumored that half the college chaplains at Oxford were atheists. "No," I would say, "I believe in
the god I see revealed in Jesus of Nazareth." What most people mean by

*god* in late-modern Western culture simply isn't the mainstream Christian meaning.

The same is true for meanings of *god* within postmodernity. We are starting to be more aware that many people give allegiance to "gods" and "goddesses" which are personifications of forces of nature and life. An obvious example is the earth goddess, Gaia, revered by some within the new age movement.[1] Following the long winter of secularism, in which most people gave up believing in anything religious or spiritual, the current revival of spiritualities of all sorts is an inevitable swing of the pendulum, a cultural shift in which people have been able once more to celebrate dimensions of human existence that the Enlightenment had marginalized. But one cannot assume that what people mean by *god* or *spirit, religion* or *spirituality* within these movements bears very much relation to Christianity. I even heard, not long ago, an Italian justifying the pornography that featured his high-profile wife on the grounds that its portrayal of sexuality was deeply "religious." The pope, he thought, should have welcomed it.

Eros has of course been well known to students of divinities time out of mind. But only when a culture has forgotten, through long disuse, how god language actually works can someone assume that the deeply "religious" feelings, evoking a sense of wonder and transcendence, that serious eroticism (and lots of other things) can produce can be straightforwardly identified with anything in the Judeo-Christian tradition. Did they never hear of paganism?

## *GOD* IN FIRST-CENTURY JUDAISM

What did first-century Jews, including Jesus and his first followers, mean by *god?* This is obviously the place to start. Their belief can be summed up in a single phrase: *creational and covenantal monotheism.*[2] This needs spelling out.

Adherents of some theologies, for example ancient Epicureanism and modern Deism, believe in a god or gods but think they have nothing much to do with the world we live in. Others, as in Stoicism, believe that god, or "the divine" or "the sacred," is simply a dimension of the world we live in, so that god and the world end up being pretty much the same thing. Both of these can give birth to practical or theoretical atheism. The first can let its god get so far away that he disappears; this is what happened with Marx and Feuerbach in the nineteenth century, allowing the "absentee landlord" of eighteenth-century Deism to become simply an absentee. The second can get so used to various gods around the place that it ceases to care much about them; this is what happened with a good deal of ancient paganism in Greece and Rome, until, as Pliny wryly remarks, the arrival of Christianity stirred up pagans to a fresh devotion to their gods.[3]

The Jews believed in a quite different god. This god, YHWH, "the One Who Is," the Sovereign One, was not simply the objectification of forces and drives within the world but was the maker of all that exists. Several biblical books, or parts thereof, are devoted to exploring the difference between YHWH and the pagan idols: Daniel, Isaiah 40–55, and a good many psalms spring obviously to mind. The theme is summed up in the Jewish daily prayer: "YHWH our God, YHWH is one!"[4]

Classic Jewish monotheism, then, believed, first, that there was one God, who created heaven and earth and who remained in close and dynamic relation with his creation; and, second, that this God had called Israel to be his special people. This twin belief, tested to the limit and beyond through Israel's checkered career, was characteristically expressed through a particular narrative: the chosen people were also the *rescued* people, liberated from slavery in Egypt, marked out by the gift of Torah, established in their land, exiled because of disobedience, but promised a glorious return and final settlement. Jewish-style monotheism meant living in this story, trusting in this one true God, the God of creation and covenant, of exodus and return.

This God was utterly different from the pantheist's "one god." Utterly different, too, from the faraway ultratranscendent gods of the Epicureans. Always active within his world—did he not feed the young ravens when they called upon him?[5]—he could be trusted to act more specifically on behalf of Israel. His eventual overthrow of pagan power at the political level would be the revelation of his overthrow of the false gods of the nations. His vindication of his people, liberating them finally from all their oppressors, would also be the vindication of his own name, his reputation.

This monotheism was never, in our period, an inner analysis of the being of the one God. It was always a way of saying, frequently at great risk: our God is the true God, and your gods are worthless idols. It was a way of holding onto hope.[6]

Precisely because this God was both other than the world and continually active within it (the words *transcendent* and *immanent* are pointers to this belief but do not clarify it much), Jews of Jesus' day had developed several ways of speaking about the activity of this God in which they attempted to hold together what they dared not separate. Emboldened by deep-rooted traditions, they explored what appears to us a strange, swirling rhythm of mutual relations within the very being of the one God: a to-and-fro, a give-and-take, a command-and-obey, a sense of love poured out and love received. God's Spirit broods over the waters, God's Word goes forth to produce new life, God's Law guides his people, God's Presence or Glory dwells with them in fiery cloud, in tabernacle and temple. These four ways of speaking moved to-and-fro from metaphor to trembling reality claim and back again. They enabled Jews to speak simultaneously of God's sovereign supremacy and his intimate presence, of his unapproachable holiness and his self-giving compassionate love.

Best known of all is perhaps a fifth. God's Wisdom is his handmaid in creation, the firstborn of his works, his chief of staff, his delight. Through the Lady Wisdom of Proverbs 1–8, the creator has fashioned everything, especially the human race. To embrace Wisdom is therefore to discover the secret of being truly human, of reflecting God's image.[7]

## MONOTHEISM AND EARLY CHRISTOLOGY

This rich seam of Jewish thought is where the early Christians went quarrying for language to deal with the phenomena before them. Some have suggested that it was only when the early church started to lose its grip on its Jewish roots and began to compromise with pagan philosophy that it could think of Jesus in the same breath as the one God. Jewish polemic has often suggested that the Trinity and the incarnation, those great pillars of patristic theology, are sheer paganization.

Whatever we say of later theology, this is certainly not true of the New Testament. Long before secular philosophy was invoked to describe the inner being of the one God (and the relation of this God to Jesus and to the Spirit), a vigorous and very Jewish tradition took the language and imagery of Spirit, Word, Law, Presence (and/or Glory), and Wisdom and developed them in relation to Jesus of Nazareth and the Spirit. One might think that a sixth was also explored, namely God's Love; except that, for them, God's Love was already no mere personification, a figure of speech for the loving God at work, but a person, the crucified and risen Jesus.

Several of these Jewish themes come together in the famous Johannine prologue.[8] Jesus is here the Word of God; the passage as a whole is closely dependent on the Wisdom tradition and is thereby closely linked with the Law and the Presence, or Glory, of God. "The Word became flesh, and tabernacled in our midst; we saw his glory, glory as of God's only son."[9] However much the spreading branches of Johannine theology might hang over the wall, offering fruit to the pagan world around, the roots of the tree are firmly embedded in Jewish soil.

John is usually regarded as late. What about the early material? Paul is our earliest Christian writer, and the earliest parts of his letters may be those that embody or reflect pre-Pauline Christian tradition.

Within that strand of material, three passages stand out.[10] In 1 Corinthians 8.6, within a specifically Jewish-style monotheistic argument, he adapts the *Shema* itself, placing Jesus within it: "For us there is one God—the Father, from whom are all things and we to him; and one Lord, Jesus Christ, through whom are all things and we through him." In Philippians 2.5–11,[11] he draws on the fiercely monotheistic theology of Isaiah 40–55 to celebrate Christ's universal lordship: "At the name of Jesus," he declares, "every knee shall bow." Isaiah has YHWH defeating the pagan idols and being enthroned over them; Paul has Jesus exalted to a position of equality with "the Father" because he has done what, in Jewish tradition, only the one God can do. Colossians 1.15–20, with its clear poetic structure, is a Wisdom poem, exploring the classic Jewish theme that the world's creator is also its redeemer, and vice versa. But at every point of creation and redemption we discover, not Wisdom, but Jesus.

So, too, in Galatians 4.1–11, Paul tells the story of the world as the story of God's freeing of slaves and his making them his children, his heirs. As in the Exodus, the true God reveals himself as who he is, putting the idols to shame.[12] But the God who has now revealed himself in this way is the God who "sends the son" and then "sends the Spirit of the Son."[13] In these passages we have, within thirty years of Jesus' death, what would later be called a very high Christology. It is very early and very Jewish.

Within these passages and others like them,[14] Paul, like other New Testament writers, uses the phrase "son of God" to denote Jesus. Later theologians, forgetting their Jewish roots, would of course read this as straightforwardly Nicene Christology: Jesus was the second person of the Trinity. Paul's usage, though, is much subtler and offers further clues not only as to what the earliest Christians believed, but also why. "Son of God" in Jewish thought was used occasionally for angels, sometimes for Israel,[15] and sometimes for the king. These latter uses[16] were influential both in sectarian Judaism ("son of God" is found as a messianic title at Qumran)[17] and in early Christianity. Since the early Christians all regarded Jesus as the messiah of Israel, the one in whom Israel's destiny had been summed up, it is not surprising, whatever language Jesus had or had not used of himself, that they exploited this phrase (to call it a "title" is perhaps too formal, and too redolent of the wrong way of doing New Testament Christology), which was available both in their Bible and in their surrounding culture, to denote Jesus and to connote his messiahship.[18]

But already by Paul's day something more was in fact going on. "Son of God" came quickly to be used as a further way, in addition to the five Jewish ways already available and exploited by the early Christians, of saying that what had happened in Jesus was the unique and personal action of the one God of Israel. It became another way of speaking about the one God present, personal, active, saving, and rescuing, while still being able to speak of the one God sovereign, creating, sustaining, sending, remaining beyond. Another way, in fact, of doing what neither Stoicism nor Epicureanism needed to do and paganism in general could not do: holding together the majesty and compassion of God, the transcendence and immanence of God, creation and covenant, sovereignty and presence.

Similar exegetical points could be made, were there more space, from other New Testament writings, not least those very Jewish books, the letter to the Hebrews and the book of Revelation. But I have said enough to indicate, or at least point in the direction of, the remarkable phenomenon at the heart of earliest Christianity. Long before anyone talked about "nature" and "substance," "person" and "Trinity," the early Christians had quietly but definitely discovered that they could say what they felt obliged to say about Jesus (and the Spirit) by telling the Jewish story of God, Israel, and the world in the Jewish language of Spirit, Word, Torah, Presence/Glory, Wisdom, and now Messiah/Son. It is as though they discovered Jesus within the Jewish monotheistic categories they already had. The categories seemed to have been made for him. They fitted him like a glove.

## THE ORIGIN OF CHRISTOLOGY

This, of course, raises in an acute form the question: why did they tell it like this?

At this point we need to ward off a frequent misunderstanding. It is often supposed that the resurrection (whatever we mean by that) somehow "proves" Jesus' "divinity."

This seems to me to short-circuit the reasoning that in fact took place. Suppose one of the two brigands crucified alongside Jesus had been raised from the dead. People would have said the world was a very odd place; they would not have said that the brigand was therefore divine. No: the basic meaning of Jesus' resurrection, as Paul says in Romans 1.4, was that Jesus was indeed the messiah. As we saw in chapter 6, this led quickly, within earliest Christianity, to the belief that his death was therefore not a defeat but a victory, the conquest of the powers of evil and the liberation, the Exodus, of God's people and, in principle, of the world. In Jesus, in other words, Israel's God, the world's creator, had accomplished at last the plan he had been forming ever since the covenant was forged in the first place. In Jesus God had rescued Israel from its suffering and exile. And then the final step: in Jesus God had done what, in the Bible, God had said he would do himself. He had heard the people's cry and had come to help them.

Ultimately, then, it is true that Jesus' resurrection led the early church to speak of him within the language of Jewish monotheism. But there was no easy equation. Resurrection pointed to messiahship; messiahship, to the task performed on the cross; that task, to the God who had promised to accomplish it himself. From there on it was a matter of rethinking, still very Jewishly, how these things could be.

Does any of this train of thought go back to Jesus himself? I have argued that it does.[19] This is not the same as Jesus' messianic vocation. It cannot be read off from the usage of any "titles" such as "son of God" or "son of man." It grows out of Jesus' basic kingdom proclamation and from Jesus' conviction that it was his task and role, his vocation, not only to speak of this kingdom, but also to enact and embody it.

As I said in chapter 3, a central feature of Jewish expectation, and kingdom expectation at that, in Jesus' time was the hope that YHWH would return in person to Zion. Having abandoned Jerusalem at the time of the exile, his return was delayed, but he would come back at last. Within this context, someone who told cryptic stories about a king, or a master, who went away, left his servants tasks to perform, and then returned to see how they were getting on must—not "might," *must*—point to this controlling, overarching metanarrative. Of course, the later church, forgetting the first-century Jewish context, read such stories as though they were originally about Jesus himself going away and then returning in a "second coming" (on which, see chapters 13 and 14 below). Of course, cautious scholars, noticing this, deny that Jesus would have said such things. I propose that here, at the heart of Jesus' work, and at the moment of its climax, Jesus not only told stories about the king who came back to Zion to judge and to save, he also acted as though he thought the stories were coming true in what he was himself accomplishing. This is the context, at last, in which I think it best to approach the question with which this chapter began.

It is of course a huge and difficult matter. Caricatures abound: the Jesus who wanders around with a faraway look, listening to the music of the angels, remembering the time when he was sitting up in heaven with the other members of the Trinity, having angels bring him bananas on golden dishes. (I do not wish to caricature the caricatures; but you would be surprised what devout people sometimes believe.)

Equally, scholars sometimes throw up the Jesus who wandered around totally unreflectively, telling stories without perceiving how they would be heard, announcing God's kingdom, speaking of bringing it about, yet failing to ruminate on his own role within the drama. We must not lose our nerve and start asking the sort of questions (for example, "what sort of a person would think he was divine?") that depend for their rhetorical force on the implied assumption "within our culture." We must hold onto the question: how would a first-century Jew have approached this matter?

There is some evidence—cryptic, difficult to interpret, but evidence nonetheless—that some first-century Jews had already started to explore the meaning of certain texts, not least Daniel 7, that spoke of Israel's God sharing his throne with another (something expressly denied, of course, in Isaiah 42.8).[20] These were not simply bits of speculative theology. They belonged, as more or less everything did at that period, to the whirling world of politics and pressure groups, of agendas and ambitions, all bent on discovering how Israel's God would bring in the kingdom and how best to speed the process on its way. To say that someone would share God's throne was to say that, through this one, Israel's God would win the great decisive victory. This is what, after all, the great Rabbi Akiba seems to have believed about Bar-Kochba.

And Jesus seems to have believed it about himself. The language was deeply coded, but the symbolic action was not. He was coming to Zion, doing what YHWH had promised to do. He explained his action with riddles all pointing in the same direction. Recognize this, and you start to see it all over the place, in parables and actions whose other layers have preoccupied us. Why, after all, does Jesus tell a story about a yearning father in order to account for his own behavior?[21] This also accounts for his sovereign attitude to Torah; his speaking on behalf of Wisdom; his announcement of forgiveness of sins. By themselves, none of these would be conclusive. Even if they are allowed to stand as words and actions of Jesus, they remain cryptic. But predicate them of the same young man who is then on his way to Jerusalem to confront the powers that be with the message, and the action, of the kingdom of God, and who tells stories as he does so that are best interpreted as stories of YHWH returning to Zion; and you have reached, I believe, the deep heart of Jesus' own sense of vocation. He believed himself called to do and be what, in the scriptures, only Israel's God did and was.

His actions during the last week focused on the temple. Judaism had two great incarnational symbols, temple and Torah: Jesus seems to have believed it was his vocation to upstage the one and outflank the other. Judaism spoke of the presence of its God in its midst, in the pillar of cloud and fire, in the Presence ("Shekinah") in the temple. Jesus acted and spoke as if he thought he were a one-man countertemple movement. So, too, Judaism believed in a God who was not only high and mighty but also compassionate and caring, tending his flock like a shepherd, gathering the lambs in his arms. Jesus used just that God image, more than once, to explain his own actions. Judaism believed that its God would triumph over the powers of evil, within Israel as well as outside. Jesus spoke of his own coming vindication, after his meeting the Beast in mortal combat. Jesus, too, used the language of the Father sending the Son. The so-called parable of the Wicked Tenants could just as well be the parable of the Son Sent at Last. His awareness, in faith, of the one he called Abba, Father, sustained him in his messianic vocation to Israel, acting as his Father's personal agent to Israel.[22] So we could go on. Approach the incarnation from this angle, and it is no category mistake but the appropriate climax of creation. Wisdom, God's blueprint for humans, at last herself becomes human.

I do not think Jesus "knew he was God" in the same sense that one knows one is tired or happy, male or female. He did not sit back and say to himself ,"Well I never! I'm the second person of the Trinity!" Rather, "as part of his human vocation, grasped in faith, sustained in prayer, tested in confrontation, agonized over in further prayer and doubt, and implemented in action, he believed he had to do and be, for Israel and the world, that which according to scripture only YHWH himself could do and be."[23] The question is often raised as to whether such a position compromises Jesus' modesty or his sanity. These objections gain their force from anachronistic assumptions about the way normal people behave; but in any case Jesus was frequently challenged on both grounds, and we have no reason to suppose the early church made this material up.[24] The Jesus I have described is both thoroughly credible as

a first-century Jew and thoroughly comprehensible as the one to whom
early, high, Jewish Christology looked back.

## JESUS AND CHRISTOLOGY TODAY

What are the implications of all this for how we approach questions of
Christology today?

Thinking and speaking of God and Jesus in the same breath are not,
as often has been suggested, a category mistake. Of course, if you start
with the deist god and the reductionists' Jesus, they will never fit, but
then they were designed not to. Likewise, if you start with the new age
gods-from-below, or for that matter the gods of ancient paganism, and
ask what would happen if such a god were to become human, you
would end up with a figure very different from the one in the gospels.
But if you start with the God of the Exodus, of Isaiah, of creation and
covenant, and of the psalms, and ask what that God might look like
were he to become human, you will find that he might look very much
like Jesus of Nazareth, and perhaps never more so than when he dies on
a Roman cross.

Anyone can, of course, declare that this picture was read back by the
early church into Jesus' mind. The evidence for this is not good. The
early church did not make much use of these themes; there is, of
course, some overlap, but also quite substantial discontinuity. (This,
ironically, may be why this latent Christology has often gone unnoticed;
scholar and pietist alike have preferred the early church's christological
formulations to Jesus' christological vocation, the pietist reading them
back into Jesus' mind, the scholar declaring this impossible.) As with
Jesus' messiahship and his vocation to suffer and die, the key sayings
remain cryptic, coming into focus only when grouped around the central symbolic actions. Such riddles make sense, find a natural life setting, only within Jesus' own ministry. The early church was not reticent
about saying that Jesus was messiah, that his death was God's saving
act, and that he and his Father belonged together within the Jewish picture of the one God.

I see no reason why the contemporary church should be reticent about this, either. Using incarnational language about Jesus, and trinitarian language about God, is of course self-involving: it entails a commitment of faith, love, trust, and obedience. But there is a difference between self-involving language and self-referring language. I do not think that when I use language like this about Jesus and God I am merely talking about the state of my own devotion. I think I am talking, self-involvingly of course, about Jesus and God.

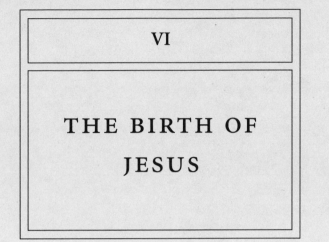

VI

# THE BIRTH OF JESUS

## CHAPTER 11

# BORN OF A VIRGIN? *N. T. Wright*

---

J ESUS' BIRTH USUALLY gets far more attention than its role in the New Testament warrants. Christmas looms large in our culture, outshining even Easter in the popular mind. Yet without Matthew 1–2 and Luke 1–2 we would know nothing about it. Paul's gospel includes Jesus' Davidic descent, but apart from that could exist without mention of his birth.[1] One can be justified by faith with no knowledge of it. Likewise, John's wonderful theological edifice has no need of it: God's glory is revealed, not in the manger, but on the cross.[2] Yet try to express any New Testament theology without Jesus' death and resurrection, and you will find it cannot be done. "Man shall live for evermore," says the song, "because of Christmas Day." No, replies the New Testament. Because of Calvary, Easter, and Pentecost.

Nevertheless, the birth stories have become a test case in various controversies. If you believe in miracles, you believe in Jesus' miraculous birth; if you don't, you don't. Both sides turn the question into a shibboleth, not for its own sake but to find out who's in and who's out. The problem is that *miracle,* as used in these controversies, is not a biblical category. The God of the Bible is not a normally absent God who sometimes intervenes. This God is always present and active, often surprisingly so.

Likewise, if you believe the Bible is true, you will believe the birth stories; if you don't, you won't. Again, the birth stories are insignificant in themselves; they function as a test for beliefs about the Bible.

Again, the birth stories have functioned as a test case for views of sexuality. Some believers in the virginal conception align this with a low view of sexuality and a high view of perpetual virginity. They believe the story not because of what it says about Jesus, but because of what it says about sex—namely, that it's something God wouldn't want to get mixed up in. This, too, has its mirror image: those who cannot imagine anything good about abstinence insist that Mary must have been sexually active.

More significantly, the birth stories have played a role within different views of the incarnation. Those who have emphasized Jesus' divinity have sometimes made the virginal conception central. Those who have emphasized Jesus' humanity have often felt that the virginal conception would mark him off from the rest of us.

None of these arguments bears much relation to what either Matthew or Luke actually say. But before we turn to them, two more preliminary remarks.

First, we are of course speaking of the virginal *conception* of Jesus, not, strictly, of the "virgin birth." Even if I come to believe in the former, the latter would remain a different sort of thing altogether. Neither, of course, should be confused with the "immaculate conception," a Roman Catholic dogma about the conception, not of Jesus, but of Mary.

Second, some things must be put in a "suspense account," in Marcus's happy phrase, while others are sorted out. The birth narratives have no impact on my reconstruction of Jesus' public agendas and his mind-set as he went to the cross. There might just be a case for saying that *if* his birth was as Matthew and Luke describe it, and *if* Mary had told him about it, my argument about Jesus' vocation to do and be what in scripture YHWH does and is might look slightly different. But as a historian I cannot use the birth stories within an argument about the rest of the gospel narratives.

I can, however, run the process the other way. Because I am convinced that the creator God raised Jesus bodily from the dead, and because I am convinced that Jesus was and is the embodiment of this God, Israel's God, my worldview is forced to reactivate various things in the suspense account, the birth narratives included. There are indeed more things in heaven and earth than are dreamed of in post-Enlightenment metaphysics. The "closed continuum" of cause and effect is a modernist myth. The God who does not intervene from outside but is always present and active within the world, sometimes shockingly, may well have been thus active on this occasion. It is all very well to get on one's high metaphysical horse and insist that God cannot behave like this, but we do not know that ahead of time. Nor will the high moral horse do any better, insisting that God *ought* not to do things like this, because they send the wrong message about sexuality or because divine parentage gave Jesus an unfair start over the rest of us. Such positions produce a cartoon picture: the mouse draws itself up to its full height, puts its paws on its hips, and gives the elephant a good dressing down.

## THE BIRTH NARRATIVES

The stories in question are complex and controversial. I simply highlight certain features.

Matthew's story, told from Joseph's point of view, reminds one of various biblical birth stories, such as that of Samson in Judges 13. Matthew's whole book is about the scriptures being fulfilled in Jesus. The angel, the dream, the command not to be afraid, the righteous couple doing what they are told—all is familiar. Like Samson, the promised and provided child has a dangerous public future: here, the true king of the Jews is born under the nose of the wicked king, Herod. This is a major theme in Matthew's gospel. His picture of Jesus' messiahship has both feet on the ground of first-century *realpolitik*.[3]

Matthew tells us that Jesus fulfills at least three biblical themes. He brings Israel into the promised land; *Jesus* is the Greek for *Joshua*. As Immanuel, he embodies God's presence with his people.[4] As the new David, he is the messiah born at Bethlehem.[5] In the genealogy, Jesus is the point toward which Israel's long covenant history has been leading, particularly its puzzling and tragic latter phase. Matthew agrees with his Jewish contemporaries that the exile was the last significant event before Jesus; when the angel says that Jesus will "save his people from their sins,"[6] liberation from exile is in view. Jesus, David's true descendant, will fulfill the Abrahamic covenant by undoing the exile and all that it means.

Well-known problems abound. Why does the genealogy finish with Joseph if Matthew is going to say that he wasn't after all Jesus' father? This cannot have been a problem for Matthew, or he would hardly have followed the genealogy so closely with the story of the virginal conception. It was enough that Jesus was born into the Davidic family; adoption brought legitimation. Further, anyone can say that Matthew made it all up to fulfill Isaiah 7.14 ("the virgin shall conceive").[7] Since Luke doesn't quote the same passage, though, the argument looks thin. Is Bethlehem only mentioned, perhaps, because of Micah 5.2–4? Again, Luke doesn't quote the same passage but still gets Mary to Bethlehem for the birth. Some have questioned whether Herod would really have behaved in the way described in Matthew 2; the answer, from any reader of Josephus, would be a firm yes. One can investigate, as many have, whether there was really a star. One can challenge the flight into Egypt as simply a back-projection from a fanciful reading of Hosea 11.1.

These are the natural probing questions of the historian. As with most ancient history, of course, we cannot verify independently what is reported in only one source. If that gives grounds for ruling it out, however, most of ancient history goes with it. Let us by all means be suspicious, but let us not be paranoid. Just because I've had a nightmare, that doesn't mean there aren't burglars in the house. The fact that Matthew says something fulfilled by scripture doesn't mean it didn't happen.

What then about his central claim, the virginal conception itself, dropped almost casually into the narrative with no flourish of trumpets? Some have argued, of course, that there is instead a flourish of strumpets: Matthew has taken care to draw our attention to the peculiarities (to put it no stronger) of Tamar, Rahab, Ruth, and Bathsheba, presumably in order to warn us that something even stranger is coming, or perhaps to enable us, when the news is announced, to connect it with God's strange way of operating in the past. He is hardly likely on this occasion, however, to have made up the story of Mary's being with child by the Holy Spirit in order to "fulfill" this theme.

What about Luke, who tells the story from Mary's point of view? His setting is just as Jewish as Matthew's, with verbal and narratival allusions to and echoes of the Septuagint. Like Matthew, he insists that with this story Israel's history is reaching its god-ordained climax. But his emphasis, unlike Matthew's, is on the very Jewish point that this birth is a direct challenge to the pagan power: in other words, to Caesar.

This fits with Luke's whole emphasis: the (very Jewish) gospel is for the whole world, of which Jesus is now the Lord. Israel's god is the king of the world; now, Jesus is the king of the world. Attention has focused on the census in Luke 2.2, whether it took place and could have involved people traveling to their ancestral homes, but Luke's point has been missed. The census was the time of the great revolt—the rebellion of Judas the Galilean, which Luke not only knows about but allows Gamaliel to compare with Jesus and his movement.[8] Luke is deliberately aligning Jesus with the Jewish kingdom movements, the revolutions that declared that there would be "no king but god."

The census is not, of course, the only query that people have raised about Luke's birth stories. Jesus' birth at Bethlehem seems to have been a puzzle to Luke (which he explains by the census), rather than something he has invented to make some other point. The fact that Luke does not mention the wise men, or Matthew the shepherds, is not a reason for doubting either; this sort of thing crops up in ancient historical sources all the time. Of course, legends surround the birth and childhood of many figures who afterward become important. As historians, we have no reason to say that this did not happen in the case of Jesus and some reasons to say that it did. But by comparison with other legends about other figures, Matthew and Luke look after all quite restrained.

## THE VIRGINAL CONCEPTION

Except, of course, in the matter where the real interest centers. Matthew and Luke declare unambiguously that Mary was a virgin when Jesus was conceived. What are we to make of this?[9]

It will not do to say that we know the laws of nature and that Joseph, Mary, the early church, and the evangelists did not. Mary and Joseph hadn't seen diagrams of Fallopian tubes, but that doesn't mean they didn't know where babies came from. Hence Mary's question to Gabriel (in Luke) and Joseph's determination to break the engagement (in Matthew).

Nor can we say that if we believe this story we should believe all the other similar ones in the ancient world as well. Of course, the argument "miracles are possible, therefore virginal conception is possible, therefore Jesus' virginal conception may well be true," also commits one to saying, "therefore Augustus's virginal conception may well be true."[10] But that is not my argument.

My argument, rather, works in three stages.

First, the position I have reached about the resurrection and incarnation of Jesus opens the door to reconsidering what we would otherwise probably dismiss. Miracle, in the sense of divine intervention "from outside," is not in question. What matters is the powerful, mysterious presence of the God of Israel, the creator God, bringing Israel's story to its climax by doing a new thing, bringing the story of creation to its height by a new creation from the womb of the old. Whether or not it happened, this is what it would mean if it did.

Second, there is no pre-Christian Jewish tradition suggesting that the messiah would be born of a virgin. No one used Isaiah 7.14 this way before Matthew did. Even assuming that Matthew or Luke regularly invented material to fit Jesus into earlier templates, why would they have invented something like this? The only conceivable parallels are pagan ones, and these fiercely Jewish stories have certainly not been modeled on them. Luke at least must have known that telling this story ran the risk of making Jesus out to be a pagan demigod. Why, for the sake of an exalted metaphor, would they take this risk—unless they at least believed them to be literally true?

Third, if the evangelists believed them to be true, when and by whom were they invented, if by the time of Matthew and Luke two such different, yet so compatible, stories were in circulation? Did whoever started this hare running mean it in a nonliteral sense, using virginal conception as a metaphor for something else? What was that something else? An embroidered border, presumably, around the belief that Jesus was divine. But that belief, as I argued earlier, was a *Jewish* belief, expressed in classic Jewish god language, while the only models for virginal conception are the nakedly pagan stories of Alexander, Augustus, and others. We would have to suppose that, within the first fifty years of Christianity, a double move took place: from an early, very Jewish, high Christology, to a sudden paganization, and back to very

Jewish storytelling again. The evangelists would then have thoroughly deconstructed their own deep intentions, suggesting that the climax of YHWH's purpose for Israel took place through none other than a pagan-style miraculous birth.

To put it another way. What would have to have happened, granted the skeptic's position, for the story to have taken the shape it did? To answer this, I must indulge in some speculative tradition history. Bear with me in a little foolishness. Are they tradition critics? So am I. Are they ancient historians? So am I. Are they reconstructors of early communities? So am I. Are they determined to think the argument through to the end? I speak as a fool—I am more so. This is how it would look. (a) Christians came to believe that Jesus was in some sense divine. (b) Someone who shared this faith broke thoroughly with Jewish precedents and invented the story of a pagan-style virginal conception. (c) Some Christians failed to realize that this was historicized metaphor and retold it as though it were historical. (d) Matthew and Luke, assuming historicity, drew independently upon this astonishing fabrication, set it (though in quite different ways) within a thoroughly Jewish context, and wove it in quite different ways into their respective narratives. And all this happened within, more or less, fifty years. Possible? Yes, of course. Most things are possible in history. Likely? No. Smoke without fire does, of course, happen quite often in the real world. But *this* smoke, in *that* world, without fire? This theory asks us to believe in *intellectual* parthenogenesis: the birth of an idea without visible parentage. Difficult. Unless, of course, you believe in miracles, which most people who disbelieve the virginal conception don't.

Maybe, after all, it is the theory of the contemporary skeptic that is metaphor historicized. The modernist belief that history is a closed continuum of cause and effect is projected onto the screen of the early church, producing a myth (specifically, a tradition-historical reconstruction) that sustains and legitimates the original belief so strongly that its proponents come to believe it actually happened.

This foolishness is, of course, a way of saying that no proof is possible either way. No one can prove, historically, that Mary was a virgin when Jesus was conceived. No one can prove, historically, that she wasn't. Science studies the repeatable; history bumps its nose against the unrepeatable. If the first two chapters of Matthew and the first two of Luke had never existed, I do not suppose that my own Christian faith, or that of the church to which I belong, would have been very different. But since they do, and since for quite other reasons I have come to believe that the God of Israel, the world's creator, was personally and fully revealed in and as Jesus of Nazareth, I hold open my historical judgment and say: if that's what God deemed appropriate, who am I to object?

# THE MEANING OF
# THE BIRTH STORIES        *Marcus Borg*

---

TOGETHER WITH THE stories of his death and resurrection, the stories of Jesus' birth have been most instrumental in shaping Christian and cultural images of Jesus.[1] They are very familiar stories, in part because Christmas is the major holiday of the year in modern Western culture. Indeed, for many people, they are more familiar than the stories of Good Friday and Easter. They are also powerful stories. Part of their power comes from their familiarity; they take many of us back into the magical world of Christmas in childhood. But they are powerful for other reasons as well, as I will suggest in this chapter.

Tom and I see the birth stories quite differently. To state my conclusion in advance, I do not think they are historically factual, but I think they are profoundly true in another and more important sense. For reasons I will soon explain, I do not think the virginal conception is historical, and I do not think there was a special star or wise men or shepherds or birth in a stable in Bethlehem. Thus I do not see these stories as historical reports but as literary creations. As the latter, they are not history remembered but rather metaphorical narratives using ancient religious imagery to express central truths about Jesus' significance.

## WHY NOT HISTORICAL

---

There are three primary reasons why I (and most mainline scholars) do not see these stories as historically factual. First, the tradition that Jesus had a remarkable birth is relatively late. The stories of his birth are found only in the first two chapters of Matthew and Luke, both written near the end of the first century. Earlier writers (as well as the rest of the New Testament) do not refer to a special birth. Paul, our earliest writer, does not. Neither does Mark, our earliest gospel.[2] Moreover, though the gospel of John is probably later than Matthew and Luke, John does not include it, either.

At the very least, this indicates that it was possible to write a gospel without mentioning the birth of Jesus. There are two possible explanations. The tradition of a special birth was old, but these authors either didn't know about it or didn't consider it important enough to include. Or the tradition didn't develop until quite late, and the reason most New Testament authors do not mention it is because the stories did not yet exist. The second option seems more likely to me, to a considerable extent because of the next two reasons.

The second reason is the striking differences between Matthew's birth story and Luke's birth story. Without being comprehensive, I note the following differences.

1. The genealogy of Jesus. Both Matthew and Luke trace the genealogy of Jesus back through Joseph to King David and beyond.[3] But the genealogies differ significantly. Matthew takes Jesus' ancestry back to Abraham, the father of Israel; Luke takes it back to Adam, the father of the human race. Moreover, the genealogies differ even when they are covering the same period of time. From David forward, Solomon and the kings of Judah are the ancestors of Jesus in Matthew; in Luke, the lineage goes through the prophet Nathan, not King Solomon.

2. The home of Mary and Joseph. In Luke, Mary and Joseph live in Nazareth but because of the census travel to Bethlehem, where the birth occurs in a stable. They go back home to Nazareth after the birth. In Matthew, Mary and Joseph live in Bethlehem and the birth occurs at home (not in a stable). The family then moves to Nazareth after spending time in Egypt. Matthew has no trip to Bethlehem.

3. Birth visitors. In Matthew, "wise men from the East" follow a special star to the place of Jesus' birth. Luke has neither wise men

nor star but instead angels singing in the night sky to shepherds who then come to the manger.

4. Herod's plot. In Matthew, Herod the Great orders the killing of all male infants under the age of two in Bethlehem. The family of Jesus escapes by fleeing to Egypt. Luke's story has neither Herod's plot nor a trip to Egypt.

5. Use of the Hebrew Bible. Both Matthew and Luke use the Hebrew Bible extensively, but they use it differently. Matthew uses a prediction-fulfillment formula five times in his birth story: "This took place to fulfill that which was spoken by the prophet."[4] Luke, on the other hand, echoes language from the Hebrew Bible without treating it as fulfillment of prophecy, especially in the great hymns that he attributes to Mary (the "Magnificat") and Zechariah (the "Benedictus").[5]

There are other differences as well. But these are enough to make the point that we have two very different stories. Though some of the differences can perhaps be harmonized, some seem irreconcilable.

Third, the stories look like they have been composed to be overtures to each gospel. That is, the central themes of each birth story reflect the central themes of the gospel of which they are a part. For example, for Matthew Jesus is "the king of the Jews," and so his ancestry is traced through the kings of Judah. For Luke, Jesus is a Spirit-anointed social prophet, and so his ancestry includes prophets. For Matthew, Jesus is "one like unto Moses," and the story of Herod's plot calls to mind the story of Pharaoh ordering the death of all newborn Hebrew boys in the time of Moses. Luke emphasizes the spread of the gospel into the Gentile world (especially in the book of Acts), and so the ancestry of Jesus is traced back not simply to Abraham the father of the Jewish people, but to Adam, the father of Jew and Gentile alike. In short, the stories look like the literary creation of each author.

Among these differences, there are some similarities. These include the names of Jesus' parents, his birth while Herod the Great was still king, and the tradition of Jesus growing up in Nazareth. Beyond these details, there are two major similarities: conception by the Spirit, and birth in Bethlehem. I will leave the first until later in this chapter and comment about the second now. How does one account for the common emphasis upon Bethlehem? One possibility, of course, is that Jesus really was born in Bethlehem, even though the two stories disagree about why Mary and Joseph were there.

A second possibility is that Jesus was born in Nazareth, but the story of his birth in Bethlehem arose because of Bethlehem's significance in the Hebrew Bible. It was the ancestral home of King David, and there was a tradition that the great and future king of Israel would be descended from David. This is the point of the famous passage in Micah 5.2: "But you, O Bethlehem . . . from you shall come forth one who is to rule in Israel, whose origin is from of old, from ancient days." By the time of Jesus, many thought of the great and future Davidic king as the messiah. On this view, the early Christian conviction that Jesus was the messiah and Son of David created the story of Jesus being born in "the city of David." Certainty is impossible, but I think the second option is more likely.

What then is left historically from these stories? Jesus was born before the death of Herod the Great, and thus probably not later than 4 B.C.E.[6] His parents were Mary and Joseph.[7] He was probably born in Nazareth, not Bethlehem. He was born into a marginalized peasant class.

## THE TRUTH OF THE BIRTH STORIES

Thus I do not see the basis of the birth stories as history remembered. Yet, though I do not think the birth of Jesus happened this way, I think these stories are true. To use by now familiar terminology, I see these stories as history metaphorized, that is, as metaphorical narratives. And the history that is being metaphorized is not the birth itself, but the Jesus story as a whole. With beauty and power, these symbolic narratives express central early Christian convictions about the significance of Jesus.

### Light in the Darkness

Light shining in the darkness is a central image in the birth stories. It is most obvious in the star of Matthew's gospel, shining in the night sky and leading the wise men of the Gentiles to the place of Jesus' birth. Luke uses the imagery in his story of "shepherds keeping watch over their flocks by night." The "glory of the Lord shone around them" as an angel told them of the birth of Jesus, and then "a multitude of the heavenly host" filled the night sky, singing "Glory to God!"

The symbolism of light and darkness is ancient, archetypal, and cross-cultural. It has many rich resonances of meaning. Darkness is associated with blindness, night, sleep, cold, gloom, despair, lostness, chaos, death, danger, and yearning for the dawn. It is a striking image of the human condition. Light is seen as the antidote to the above and is thus an image of salvation. In the light, one is awake, able to see and find one's way; light is associated with relief and rejoicing that the night is over; in the light one is safe and warm. In the light there is life.

Many texts in the Hebrew Bible use this symbolism. Light is associated with creation: "Let there be light" is the first of God's creative acts in the book of Genesis.

Light is a metaphor for God's illumination of the path: "Your word is a lamp to my feet and a light to my path."[8]

In texts from the Hebrew Bible often read in churches during the season of Advent, light is associated with God's acts of deliverance:

> The people who walked in darkness have seen a great light; those who lived in a land of deep darkness—on them has light shined.[9]
>
> Arise, shine; for your light has come, and the glory of the Lord has risen upon you. For darkness shall cover the earth, and thick darkness the peoples; but the Lord will arise upon you, and God's glory will appear over you. Nations shall come to your light, and kings to the brightness of your dawn.[10]

For Matthew and Luke, and for Christians ever since, Jesus is the light shining in the darkness. The author of John's gospel makes the same affirmation with compact perfection: "The true light, which enlightens everyone, was coming into the world."[11] Jesus is the light who brings enlightenment; indeed, he is "the light of the world."[12] This is the truth of this theme of the birth stories. And it is true independent of their historical factuality.

## A Tale of Two Lordships

The conflict between two lordships runs through the birth stories. In Matthew, the conflict is between rival claims to be "king of the Jews."

Herod the Great saw himself as the king of the Jews and indeed was the reigning king. But for Matthew, Jesus is "the king of the Jews." Moreover, by portraying Herod as acting like Pharaoh, Matthew calls to mind Israel's story of the ancient conflict between the lordship of Pharaoh and the lordship of God. Jesus, not the Herods and Pharaohs of this world, is the true king and lord.

Luke does this differently. For Luke, the conflict is between the lordship of Caesar and the lordship of Christ. Luke signals this most clearly in the words spoken by the angel to the shepherds and in the chorus sung by the heavenly host:

> I bring you good news of great joy for all the people: to you is born this day in the city of David a Savior, who is the Messiah the Lord. . . .
>
> Glory to God in the highest heaven, and on earth peace among those whom God favors.[13]

Much of this language was also used about Caesar, the emperor of Rome. In an inscription from 9 C.E. found in Asia Minor, Caesar is spoken of as "our God" and as a "Savior" who brought "peace" throughout the earth, and whose birth was "good news" to the world. In other texts, he is also spoken of as divine and as descended from a divine-human conception. By echoing language used about the Roman emperor, Luke affirms that Jesus, not Caesar, is the good news, the true savior and Son of God who brings peace.

The theme of two lordships is powerful and central to the biblical tradition as a whole. Explicitly, the birth stories affirm that Jesus is the true lord. Implicitly, they leave us with a question: where are you going to see your lord? In the power and wealth of Herod and Caesar, of kingship and empire? Or in this Galilean Jewish peasant who saw things very differently? Where are you going to see the decisive manifestation of God? In the domination system? Or in Jesus who was executed by the domination system?[14]

Thus, like Easter itself, the birth stories affirm the lordship of Christ. His lordship has both existential and political dimensions. Existentially, we are in bondage to many things, and the lordship of Christ is the path of personal liberation. Politically, the lordship of Christ challenges systems of domination in the name of God's passion for justice. It is no accident that the rulers of this world, both at the beginning of Jesus' life and at the end, seek to destroy him.

## Virginal Conception

What is the truth of the story of a virginal conception? Two related claims seem most important.

First, the theme of remarkable births is part of the tradition of Israel. According to the book of Genesis, Abraham the father of Israel was given the promise that he would have many descendants. Yet he and his immediate descendants (the patriarchs of Israel) all have difficulty having children. Sarah and Abraham, we are told, were ninety and one hundred years old when they finally conceived Isaac. Isaac married Rebekah, and they also were infertile until their old age, when they conceived twins, Esau and Jacob. Jacob became the child of promise, but he and his beloved wife Rachel also had difficulty conceiving. The theme continues in the stories of the conception of Gideon and Samuel. Both were deliverers of Israel in a time of crisis, and both were born to barren women. This repeating theme suggests that the people of God come into existence and are sustained in their existence by the grace of God. Humanly speaking, it was impossible that God's promise would be fulfilled, but by God it was.

Matthew and Luke are both playing this theme. Just as God had acted in the history of Israel to create and sustain the people of God through remarkable births, so also God had now acted in the birth of Jesus. Just as Israel came into existence through the grace of God when humanly speaking it was impossible, so the early Christian community as the continuation of Israel came into existence through the grace of God. This is one dimension of meaning in the story of the virginal conception of Jesus.

There is a second nuance as well. Namely, the story of Jesus being conceived by the Spirit affirms that what happened in Jesus was "of God." The activity of the Spirit of God in his life was projected back to the beginning of his life. What happened in Jesus was not "of the flesh" but "of the Spirit." The story of Jesus' virginal conception affirms that Jesus was "born not of blood or the will of the flesh or of the will of man, but of God."[15] It is a metaphorical affirmation of Jesus' identity and significance. Like the voice in the transfiguration story, it affirms, "This is my beloved son; listen to him."[16]

Thus I do not see the story of the virginal conception as a marvel of biology that, if true, proves that Jesus *really* was the Son of God. Rather, it is an early Christian narrative confession of faith and affirmation of allegiance to Jesus. To say "What happened in Jesus was of the Spirit" is not a factual claim dependent upon a biological miracle, but a way of seeing Jesus that immediately involves seeing him as the decisive disclosure of God. He was not possessed by another spirit, as some of his critics said, but was animated by God's Spirit. This is the truth claim in the story of Jesus' conception by the Spirit of God.

The truly important questions about the birth stories are not whether Jesus was born of a virgin or whether there was an empire-wide census that took Mary and Joseph to Bethlehem or whether there was a special star leading wise men from the East. The important questions are, "Is Jesus the light of the world? Is he the true Lord? Is what happened in him 'of God'?" Answering these questions affirmatively lays claim to our whole lives.

Much more could be said about the meanings of these stories for Christians. Like all good stories, their resonances are many. But I will conclude by noting one more dimension of meaning, which I owe to Meister Eckhart, a Christian mystic, theologian, and preacher from the thirteenth century. In one of his Christmas sermons, Eckhart spoke of the virgin birth as something that happens *within us*. That is, the story of the virgin birth is the story of Christ being born within us through the union of the Spirit of God with our flesh. Ultimately, the story of Jesus' birth is not just about the past but about the internal birth in us in the present.

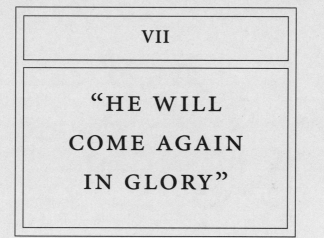

VII

"HE WILL
COME AGAIN
IN GLORY"

# THE SECOND COMING
# THEN AND NOW                          *Marcus Borg*

---

"HE WILL COME again in glory" is central to Christian beliefs about Jesus. The expectation of the second coming of Jesus has been part of the Christian tradition since its beginnings. Of the twenty-seven books in the New Testament, twenty-one refer to it. It is also included in the church's creeds recited by many Christians each Sunday. Jesus "ascended into heaven and is seated at the right hand of the Father. *He will come again in glory to judge the living and the dead,* and his kingdom will have no end."[1]

The coming again in glory of the one who is now Lord, seated at God's right hand, will involve the judging of all who have lived and the establishing of the everlasting kingdom. In short, the second coming is associated with what we commonly think of as "the end of the world," the subject matter of eschatology.[2]

Through the centuries, some Christians have expected the second coming (or *parousia*) of Jesus in their own time.[3] Many in the first century did, as we shall see. Though the belief that the parousia was near waned among some Christians as time went by, some, like the theologian Tertullian in the early 200s, still argued vigorously for it. Waves of imminent expectation of the parousia surfaced several times in succeeding centuries: as the year 1000 approached, in the 1200s with the teaching of Joachim of Fiore, in the 1500s at the time of the Protestant Reformation, and in the 1800s among a number of Christian movements. Many expect it in our own day: according to one survey, approximately one-third of Americans think it will be soon.[4]

How might we understand the second coming of Jesus? What is the origin of this belief? Does it go back to Jesus himself, or is it a development within the early Christian movement? And what should this belief mean to Christians in our time? Does Christian faithfulness entail expecting a future visible return of Jesus? Or are other understandings of this notion both possible and faithful? In this chapter, I will first describe the expectation of the second coming in the New Testament and then turn to the question of what it might mean for us today.

## THE SECOND COMING IN EARLY CHRISTIANITY

The expectation of the second coming of Jesus is widely attested in the New Testament, and from its earliest to latest documents. Moreover, many texts suggest that it was expected to happen in the near future.

Paul seems to have expected the second coming of Jesus while some of his contemporaries were still alive, including perhaps himself. In his earliest letter (and also the earliest document in the New Testament), sent to a Christian community in Thessalonica in northern Greece around the year 50, Paul wrote,

> For since we believe that Jesus died and rose again, even so, through Jesus, God will bring with him those who have died. For this we declare to you by the word of the Lord, that *we who are alive, who are left until the coming of the Lord,* will by no means precede those who have died. For the Lord himself, with the cry of command, with the archangel's call and with the sound of God's trumpet, will descend from heaven, and the dead in Christ will rise first. Then *we who are alive, who are left,* will be caught up in the clouds together with them to meet the Lord in the air; and so we will be with the Lord forever.[5]

"Lord" in this passage is Jesus. Paul speaks of him descending from heaven, accompanied by the blast of the eschatological trumpet and the cry of the archangel, the raising of "the dead in Christ," and the gathering of Christians who are still alive, so that together they will be "caught up in the clouds" to "meet the Lord in the air."[6] Paul's distinction between those who have died and "we who are alive" is most naturally understood to mean some of those then alive.[7] Paul apparently thought Jesus would come soon.[8]

Expectation of the imminent second coming of Jesus is also found in the gospels. The thirteenth chapter of Mark, often called "the little apocalypse," speaks of "signs" that will precede the coming of "the Son of Man." The chapter reaches its climax in these words attributed to Jesus:

> But in those days, after that suffering, the sun will be darkened, and the moon will not give its light; and the stars will be falling from heaven, and the powers in the heavens will be shaken. Then they will see "the Son of Man coming in clouds" with great power and glory. Then he will send out the angels, and gather his elect from the four winds, from the ends of the earth to the ends of heaven.[9]

A few verses later, the Jesus of Mark says, "Truly I tell you, this generation will not pass away until all these things have taken place."[10] Mark, like Paul, seems to have thought the second coming was near. Several other passages in the gospels are most naturally read the same way.[11]

The author of Revelation also expected the second coming of Jesus in his time. Written near the end of the first century, this apocalyptic letter to seven churches in Asia Minor uses symbolic language to speak of the coming destruction of the Roman Empire and the return of Christ.[12] Its visions reach their climax in the battle of Armageddon, the defeat of the armies of the beast by the warrior Christ, the binding of Satan, the last judgment, and the vision of the New Jerusalem descending from the sky. This "must soon take place," the author wrote at the beginning of his letter, "for the time is near." At the end of the letter, the assurance is twice put into words attributed to the risen Christ: "See, I am coming soon." "Surely I am coming soon."[13]

Finally, the second letter of Peter, seen by many scholars as the latest document in the New Testament, acknowledges that the second coming had not happened as soon as expected.[14] Scoffers, we are told, were saying. "Where is the promise of his coming? For ever since our ancestors died, all things continue as they were from the beginning of creation." The author defends continuing belief in the second coming by expanding the time span indefinitely: "But do not ignore this one fact, beloved, that with the Lord one day is like a thousand years, and a thousand years are like one day."[15] His words are evidence of a hope disappointed: Jesus did not return as many had expected.

## THE ORIGIN OF THE BELIEF

Thus many Christians in the New Testament period believed that the second coming would be soon. A common scholarly shorthand phrase for this kind of expectation is *apocalyptic eschatology:* the expectation of imminent dramatic divine intervention in a public and objectively unmistakable way, resulting in a radically new state of affairs, including the vindication of God's people, whether on a renewed earth or in another world. Apocalyptic eschatology was relatively strong within Judaism near the time of Jesus. For early Christians, it was associated with the expected imminent return of Jesus.

Where did this widespread early Christian belief come from? There are two possibilities. Either the expectation of a second coming goes back to Jesus himself, or it is the product of the early Christian movement after Jesus' death.

*From Jesus himself.* Most Christians throughout the centuries have thought that the belief originated with Jesus, simply because texts in the gospels attribute it to Jesus. However, mainline scholars generally do not think Jesus spoke specifically about his own second coming. What could such language have meant to Jesus' followers while he was still with them, and at a time when, according to the gospels, they had not really comprehended that his life would end in crucifixion and resurrection? Could they make any sense of his speaking of a second coming when they hadn't understood that his "first coming" would soon come to an end?

But many scholars in this century have thought that the early movement's expectation of Jesus' imminent second coming was grounded in things Jesus did say and believe, namely in an apocalyptic eschatology that they trace back to Jesus himself. According to this view, Jesus did not speak of his own second coming, but he did expect a dramatic divine intervention in the near future: God would act soon to establish the messianic kingdom.[16]

Two lines of argument are used to support this view. The first is based on two categories of sayings attributed to Jesus: imminent kingdom of God sayings, and coming Son of Man sayings. An example of the former: "Truly, I say to you, there are some standing here who will not taste death before they see the Kingdom of God come with power."[17] An example of the latter: to his disciples, Jesus said, "When they persecute you in one town, flee to the next; for truly I say to you, you will not have gone through all the towns of Israel before the Son of Man comes."[18] Both—the coming of the kingdom and the coming of the "Son of Man"—were to happen soon.

The second line of argument points out that John the Baptizer was a prophet of apocalyptic eschatology and that Paul and much of the rest of the New Testament affirm an apocalyptic eschatology. Given that Jesus' immediate predecessor as well as his immediate successors had an apocalyptic eschatology, it therefore makes sense to think that Jesus did, too.

Together, these two lines of argument lead to the following understanding: Jesus did not speak of his own second coming, but he did expect the imminent coming of the kingdom of God and the Son of Man. After his death, this expectation got transferred to the expectation of his imminent return as king of the kingdom that he had proclaimed. Put most simply: Jesus expected the kingdom of God; the early church expected Jesus. Thus, according to this view, the notion of a second coming of Jesus is based on Jesus' own apocalyptic eschatology.

*From the community.* A second way of understanding the origin of belief in a second coming denies that Jesus had an apocalyptic eschatology. A recent development in scholarship, this view is a reversal of what had been a strong majority position for much of this century.[19] For this view, the apocalyptic eschatology of early Christianity and the expectation of the second coming of Jesus emerge within the early Christian community after Easter.

This is my own position.[20] I see more than one factor contributing to the expectation of Jesus' return. To a considerable extent, it was an inference flowing out of the Easter experience. Within Judaism, resurrection was seen as an "end-time" event. Thus the conviction that Jesus had been resurrected led to the inference that the end time (including the general resurrection) was near. A second factor was the conviction that Jesus was Lord: the one who had been executed by the rulers of this world would soon return as the judge of the world. Yet a third factor was the tumult of Jewish history in the first century, including especially the destruction of Jerusalem and the temple in the year 70. Within a Jewish framework, events like this could easily lead to a sense that "the end" was at hand.[21]

This view also emphasizes that the coming Son of Man sayings are in fact second coming of Jesus sayings. That is, I do not think that Jesus spoke of the imminent coming of the Son of Man and that the community later saw these as referring to Jesus. Rather, I see them as a product of the community, created after Easter to express the conviction that Jesus would soon return as the Son of Man.

## THE SECOND COMING TODAY

Whichever understanding of the origin of belief in the second coming is found to be more persuasive, we are left with the same question: what are we to make of the widespread early Christian expectation that Jesus would return soon? In particular, what are we to think of this belief in our time? As mentioned in the introduction to this chapter, a significant percentage of Christians in North America think the second coming may be near. Moreover, many Christians who are not persuaded that it is near nevertheless think that they should believe that it will happen someday.

As we ponder the question of its meaning today, candor requires that we acknowledge that the early Christians (and Jesus himself, if he had an apocalyptic eschatology) were wrong about the end being near. Are we to say, "They got the belief right—Jesus really will come again; but their timing was off"? To use a specific example, does Christian faithfulness entail retaining the expectation of the author of Revelation and transferring it to our time or to some distant future, even though he expected it in his time and was mistaken? Or do we say that his expectation was mistaken not only in its timing, but also in its content? His symbolic language refers to the Roman Empire in his own time; why should we think it refers to some still future scenario? And when

Paul refers to "meeting the Lord in the air," an event that he thought was near, should we think that is still going to happen?

I do not myself think there will be a future visible return of Christ. One reason is the historical approach to this material that we have just reviewed. I see the belief in an imminent and manifestly public return of Christ to be a mistaken belief of the early community. A second reason is that I literally cannot imagine a future return of Jesus (or of Christ—I am using the words interchangeably here). To explain, I can imagine the end of the world. I can imagine a final judgment. But I cannot imagine a return of Christ. If we try to imagine that, we have to imagine him returning to *some place*. To be very elementary, we who know the earth to be round cannot imagine Jesus returning to the whole earth at once. And the notion of a localized second coming boggles the imagination.[22] I do not think it will happen.

Yet I also think there are important meanings in the theme of the second coming in the New Testament. The notion of a second coming affirms what is already affirmed by Easter: Jesus is Lord. It adds to that claim the recognition that his lordship is not yet apparent, even as it affirms that the dream of God is the lordship of Christ throughout all of creation.

The book of Revelation, despite its being mistaken about the end being near, makes the strong affirmation that Christ is Lord and Rome is not. Indeed, that's the central theme of the book: the conflict between the lordship of Christ and the lordship of empire, a conflict that continues to this day. Its central message is that the lords of this world do not have the final word: therefore, take heart, have courage, be faithful.

Moreover, the theme of a last judgment in the New Testament makes the point that how we act within history does matter. Matthew does this in a particularly arresting way with his parable of the sheep and goats. In Matthew's context, it is a second coming parable: "When the Son of Man comes in his glory, and all the angels with him, then he shall sit on the throne of his glory, and all the nations will be gathered before him."[23] What is striking is the criterion by which the judgment is made: have you fed the hungry, welcomed the stranger, clothed the naked, cared for the sick, visited the prisoners? The point of the parable is clear: the most important ethical issue is, "Have we lived compassionately?"

There is one more meaning to be noted, suggested by the season of Advent in the liturgical year. The theme of Advent is the two comings of Christ. During Advent, we remember the first coming of Jesus, even as we prepare for his second coming. And the second coming occurs each year at Christmas, with the birth of Christ within us, the coming of Christ into our lives. Christ comes again and again and again, and in many ways. In a symbolic and spiritual sense, the second coming of Christ is about the coming of the Christ who is already here.

No doubt there is more. But this is what I have thus far been able to see.

# THE FUTURE OF JESUS          N. T. Wright

---

J ESUS AND THE *Victory of God* has evoked anxious questions from conservative Christian friends. Do I, they ask, believe in the "second coming"? After all, I argue that "the son of man coming on the clouds" denotes exaltation, not return. It is apocalyptic metaphor, signifying the vindication of God's people after their suffering.

I can answer the question only in the light of a larger one: what do I believe about the plans of the creator God for creation as a whole? This chapter will therefore be more sketchy, more confessional, and less historically grounded than the previous ones.

## THE FUTURE OF THE GOOD CREATION

---

To understand the end, begin with the beginning. If God is the maker and redeemer of heaven and earth, the created world is the first stage and vital sign of God's eventual design. This rules out much vague and sub-Christian language about hope. Dualists think of abandoning the present world and entering a disembodied, timeless eternity. Materialists hope to build the kingdom here and now. Try singing "Till in the ocean of thy love, we lose ourselves in heaven above" immediately after singing (as some English people still do) "Till we have built Jerusalem in England's green and pleasant land."

Neither approaches the New Testament's more subtle and consistent picture. God intends to create new heavens and a new earth, married together, in dynamic and perhaps even material continuity with the present creation. The new will be to the old as the flower is to the seed, as the butterfly is to the chrysalis. Analogies like this, inevitable if we are to speak of realities beyond present experience, point into the bright cloud of God's future. Birth, so central to the original creation, points to the final one: the new emerges from the womb of the old, an idea as difficult for puzzled modernists to grasp as it was for Nicodemus.[1] The new reality corresponds to our present one as the baby to the mother. Regular devout language about leaving "earth" and going to "heaven" needs to be challenged by Revelation's picture (chapter 21) of new heavens and new earth, and by Paul's great image, in Romans 8, of the whole creation groaning in birth pangs, longing for liberation, sharing the freedom and glory of the children of God in the world that is yet to be.

Confusion has been caused by John the Seer being told, in Revelation 4, "Come up here, and you will be shown what must happen hereafter." Revelation 4 itself is not a picture of the future. It is a symbolic picture of the heavenly throne room *within which* the secrets of the future are revealed. The animal kingdom and the people of God, seen in the vision adoring God as the creator, are hardly preparing us to hear that the created order is destined to be scrapped. Creation is good and will be reaffirmed at the last.

But creation needs more than mere completion or fulfillment. God's act of new creation must also deal with the problems of the old. The path to life is blocked by evil, corruption, and death. The world needs rescue, redemption.

## THE FUTURE FOR A REBELLIOUS WORLD

Classical theology insists that evil is an intruder into God's good world. This holds together two other affirmations: the created order is good and God given; evil is real and potent. Soft-pedal the first, and you end with dualism (creation itself is evil). Soft-pedal the other, and you end with pantheism (creation is divine; nothing is really wrong). Avoiding these is difficult. We find it remarkably hard simultaneously to affirm the goodness of God's world and to use it appropriately. But we mustn't abandon the basic claim. Evil, though powerful, is not a necessary part of creation. God does not love evil, but "God so loved the world."

This affects profoundly how we think about the end. The dualist supposes that, to escape evil, one must escape the created, physical universe. Lots of casual Christian talk (and song) about our future destiny slips unthinkingly into this mode. The pantheist looks forward to being absorbed into the great all-divine cosmos or supposes, with the ancient Stoics, that history will simply repeat itself endlessly. The dualist will be uncomfortable with talk of bodily resurrection. The pantheist may be anxious that if (what is thought of as) evil is removed from the world all the fun will disappear, too. Descriptions of "eternal life" sometimes sound incredibly boring.

Eternal life, however, in first-century Jewish terms, means "the life of the age to come." This should give us, so to speak, real hope about hope. The New Testament envisages a world enhanced, made more joyful, by the removal of evil. Creation will be free to be itself at last, and we with it. In particular, death, the shadow that falls across all our dreams, will be abolished. The question of whether death was part of God's original creation or whether it, too, is an intruder is another difficult one. Maybe God's original design, that creatures would sleep at the end of their labor, has been changed, because of rebellion, into a threat. Darkness, part of the original creation, has become a symbol of creation's malaise. What was once, perhaps, a kind and wise friend is now a malevolent enemy. The promise that death will be abolished assures us both that God will be true to creation and that all our present griefs will at last be healed.

## THE FUTURE FOR HUMANS

How are we to envisage the renewed life promised, within God's new creation, to all those in Christ? Many assume that *resurrection* simply means "life after death." Put this together with the prevailing dualism of much Western (and sometimes would-be Christian) culture, and "the resurrection of the body" comes to mean the opposite of what it says. One caller on an Easter phone-in program insisted that he would be going to heaven when he died and wouldn't be taking his body with him, so he couldn't see why Jesus hadn't done the same.

If the goodness of God's present creation, though, is to be reaffirmed at the last, this applies to humans, too. Most Jews of Jesus' day believed strongly in bodily resurrection, as we saw, and devised ways of talking about the state of continuing existence between death and reembodiment. This was thoroughly in line with their belief, shared by early Christianity, that the redeemer God was also the creator.

Low-level puzzles beset these discussions today. Resurrection doesn't mean resuscitation: we share, swap, and pass on our molecules, so there aren't nearly enough for everyone to have their own ones back. Resurrection demands, and the New Testament envisages, a great act of new creation, not the reassembling of identical sets of atoms. As Paul insists in 1 Corinthians 15 and 2 Corinthians 5, the future embodiedness of God's people will involve a new mode of physicality, over and above the present one.

Regular talk of "going to heaven" and the reference to "heaven and hell" as final destinies can therefore be misleading, encouraging visions of a disembodied future existence. Paradise (as in Jesus' words to the dying brigand[2]) was not, for the Jews, a final destiny but a temporary rest before the final glorious new world. When the Wisdom of Solomon says that "the souls of the righteous are in the hand of God," it goes on quickly to speak of their future glorious embodied life.[3] The classic Christian hope and prayer for the faithful departed is that they may rest in peace *and rise with Christ in glory.*

The "heavenly country" for which we long, according to Hebrews 11.16, is not, then, a disembodied existence. It is the new world in which heaven and earth are joined at last, in which what God is currently preparing in heaven is brought to birth in a world that we will recognize as physical.[4] "Thy kingdom come," we pray, "*on earth as it is in heaven,*" not "in heaven once we've escaped earth."

All this depends, of course, on a particular meaning of *heaven.* In biblical language heaven is usually neither a location within our cosmos (say, a place several miles up in the sky) nor a destination within our time sequence (say, the state of affairs at the very end). It is God's dimension of day-to-day reality.[5] It is normally veiled from our sight, but "seers" are granted glimpses into it, such as when Elisha's servant saw the horses and chariots surrounding his master[6] or when a great door swung open and John the Seer found himself looking straight into God's throne room.[7] Once we grasp this, we are ready to inquire about the place of Jesus within this final unveiling.

## THE FUTURE OF JESUS

The second coming of Jesus has puzzled theologians as much as the first. The question demands linguistic humility. Language describing God's future, as I said, is a set of signposts pointing into a mist. The signposts may tell the truth but shouldn't be mistaken for the reality.

The first signpost is God's promise to renew heaven and earth. This has already happened in the person of Jesus: he has united God and humanity, and his resurrection body already enjoys God's new mode of physicality. When we enter that renewed existence, we will find Jesus there as its prototype and pioneer. It will be we who "come" to him, arriving in God's new world, where he has gone before.

The second signpost is the belief that Jesus is the messiah, the true Lord of the world. At his name every knee shall bow, as he brings justice, peace, holiness, and life to the world and judges injustice, oppression, wickedness, and death itself. It is misleading to see this in terms of Jesus "returning" to our world as a kind of space invader coming to sort out a rebel planet. Rather, when God finally ushers in his new creation, Jesus will be, in person, both the standard and the instrument of that just and deeply welcome judgment and restoration.

The third signpost is the Jewish expectation of the return of YHWH to Zion, reapplied in some early Christian writings to Jesus himself. The Jews had longed for their God to return in judgment and mercy. The Christians believed he had already done so in Jesus, but as the first part of a two-stage process. They therefore reused the language and imagery of return to express their belief that Jesus himself would be personally present as the loving and redeeming center and agent of God's new creation.

The New Testament often uses the Greek word *parousia*, frequently translated "coming," to express this "presence" of Jesus within God's future recreation of the cosmos. Of course, someone who is present after a time of absence must have "come," "arrived," or "appeared." But the root meaning remains "presence"; the word was often used of the "royal presence" of kings and rulers. If we spoke of Jesus' royal presence within God's new creation, rather than thinking of his "coming" as an invasion from outside, our talk about the future might make more sense. It would also be a lot more biblical.

## THE EARLY CHURCH AND THE FUTURE

By what stages, then, did the early church arrive at the new belief that the royal presence of Jesus would be the central feature in a cosmic denouement that could occur at any time?[8]

In 1 Corinthians 15 Paul describes his belief about the future and hints at why he holds it. The closing paragraph[9] declares that "we shall all be changed"; that is the heart of the matter. The eschatological trumpet will sound; the dead will be raised; "we" (those still alive at the time) will be transformed, putting on the new deathless body on top of the present one.[10] Thus death will be swallowed up in God's victory.[11]

The origins of this belief are exposed in verses 12–28. Paul had expected the kingdom to be ushered in all in one. The resurrection of Jesus, however, has forced him to divide the "end" into two "moments," with the church living in between, grounded on the first and longing for the second. The first (Jesus' resurrection) gives the content of the second (the final resolution) in a nutshell, expressing as it does God's victory over death and the transformation of the physical world. It also guarantees the second, since the risen Lord is now already ruling the world.[12]

Certainty about the development of traditions in the dark period between Pentecost and Paul's letters is impossible. But if Paul gives us a satisfactory account of how and why the very early Christians came to this revolution from within the Jewish apocalyptic expectation, we should not trouble too much about searching elsewhere. I propose that what we call the second coming, which is actually a metonym for the larger picture which includes cosmic renewal, human resurrection, the royal presence of Jesus, and the sovereign rule of God, was a very early Christian development of Jewish apocalyptic eschatology, both necessitated and facilitated by the unexpected resurrection of the messiah. What had been expected as a large-scale event at the end of time had happened as a small-scale, though explosive, event in the middle of time. The end had come, the end was still to come.[13]

In this light we can make sense of the notorious 1 Thessalonians 4.13–18, which, through the literalistic reading of its apocalyptic imagery, has spawned many a fanciful eschatological scheme among fundamentalists in particular. This has generated, in turn, a similar literalism among scholars (including, ironically, several who are eager to read the historical narratives in the gospels as nonliterally as possible), who have supposed that this literal meaning is what all early Christians believed. Since they have declared that meaning incredible, they then proceed to belittle early Christian eschatology.

The passage shares many features with 1 Corinthians 15. The trumpet will sound, the Lord will appear from the heavenly dimension ("will descend from heaven," typical apocalyptic language for this "appearing"), the dead in Christ will rise.[14] Where 1 Corinthians has "we shall be changed," though, 1 Thessalonians has "we shall be snatched up in clouds to meet the Lord in the air." "Snatched up in clouds" echoes the language that in Daniel 7 denotes the vindication of God's people after their suffering.[15] Paul almost certainly means the phrase to be taken metaphorically in this Danielic sense, denoting the changing of the "natural" body into the "spirit-animated" body, which believers will receive as vindication after the apparent victory of death. And the point of "meeting the Lord in the air" is not to stay there forever; the word *meeting* is borrowed from civic life, with citizens going out to "meet" royal dignitaries in order to escort them back into the city.

Thus, Paul, straining at the borders of language, piles metaphor upon metaphor to express the complex truth: when the heavenly dimension is finally unveiled, so that the royal presence of Jesus is visibly and tangibly with us at last, the dead will be raised and the living transformed, to share his new humanity within a transformed world. This will be the fulfillment of the new world, which began in Jesus' resurrection.[16]

When will these things happen?[17] A long tradition, both scholarly and popular, has assumed on the basis of Mark 13.30 and similar passages ("this generation shall not pass away until all is fulfilled") that the early church believed the end was bound to come within a generation. But these passages do not refer to the full end of which Paul was speaking; only to the fall of Jerusalem, seen not least as the vindication of Jesus against the city that had opposed him.[18] Paul himself believed, when writing 1 Thessalonians and 1 Corinthians, that he might well be among those "left alive"; by the time he wrote 2 Corinthians he had recognized that he might well die ahead of that time.[19] But it was not a matter of the final events being bound to occur within a stated period of time; rather, they might occur at *any* time.[20] Ignatius, Justin, Tertullian, and others, to the end of the second century and beyond, still believed this and showed no sign of anxiety or embarrassment that the first generation had all died off without the world coming to an end. It is time that the old scholars' myth of "the delay of the *parousia*" was given a decent burial. Metaphorically, of course.

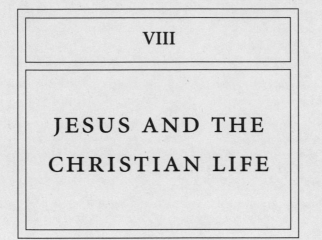

VIII

JESUS AND THE
CHRISTIAN LIFE

# THE TRUTH OF THE GOSPEL AND CHRISTIAN LIVING *N. T. Wright*

I F WHAT I HAVE said about Jesus is on the right lines, then all sorts of things follow for the question of what Christian living consists of. A good many of these I have explored elsewhere in another genre.[1] In this chapter I shall examine some themes that seem to me important within the context of this book in particular.

## THE CONTEXT: WORSHIP AND MISSION

I have come (not very originally) to envisage the two poles of Christian living in terms of worship and mission. The two flow into each other: worship without mission becomes self-indulgence (and might even imply worship of a god other than the one revealed in Jesus); mission without worship degenerates into various kinds of do-goodery, following agendas that may be deeply felt but are by no means necessarily connected with Jesus.

The link between worship and mission is so close that many prefer to speak of them in terms of each other. Glad, rich worship of the God revealed in Jesus invites outsiders to come in, welcomes them, nourishes them, and challenges them. Mission can be conceived, particularly with Matthew 25 in mind, in terms of worshiping and serving the hidden Jesus one meets in the poor and needy. Thus, though I continue to speak of worship and mission as separate activities, I also insist on integrating them.

Worship and mission together create a context for the development of Christian living which holds together, within the person and the community, four different areas of Christian experience. I summarize these areas under the following headings: spirituality, theology, politics, and healing. I need to say something about each of these, showing where and how it relates to the Jesus I have described.

## SPIRITUALITY

The word *spirituality* has recently become fashionable. When I was younger, Christians I knew spoke in different ways of prayer, of knowing God, of a sense of God's presence. The being we called "God" was essentially other, living in a different sphere altogether. Jesus had bridged the gulf between this God and us, his creatures; the Holy Spirit now enabled us to continue bridging the gulf; but a sense of a gulf remained nonetheless, and prayer remained a communication across it. Prayer was thus an activity set apart from the rest of life.

Contemporary use of the word *spirituality,* however, has signaled a very different view: that the presence of the true God can be known and experienced in the midst of, and mediated through, all sorts of ordinary and extraordinary happenings and environments. This use of the word accompanies a shift in belief about, and experience of, God. No longer remote or detached, the true God is strangely present, knowable, and lovable. The word *spirituality* itself has acquired not just descriptive meaning, but a sense of invitation, of welcoming mystery, of meanings just out of sight but perhaps within reach, of worlds unimagined by the increasingly barren secularism of the Western Enlightenment but now accessible, beckoning and perhaps challenging. Offer a lecture course with the word *spirituality* in the title, and you will most likely fill the hall.

I find it impossible to conceive of a Christianity without some form of meaningful spirituality. That begs the question, of course: what counts as meaningful? Initially, at least, "meaningful to the person concerned": I cannot, in other words, imagine a Christianity in which the would-be Christian has no sense, and never has had a sense, of the presence and love of God, of the reality of prayer, of their everyday, this-worldly life being somehow addressed, interpenetrated, confronted, or embraced by a personal being understood as the God we know through Jesus. I did once meet a man—a clergyman, actually—who said at a conference that language like that had never held any meaning for him, but I confess with sorrow that I do not know in what sense the word *Christian* could describe such a person. Of course, most Christians report times when God seems absent or distant, but this is regularly perceived as a break in normality, an interruption to the way things should be, rather than regular or ordinary Christian experience. Equally, many Christians eagerly engage in other activities of Christian life, such as theology, politics, or healing, but if they lose this home base—of personal relationship with the personal God—I believe they are in danger of ending up like the prodigal son, spending half the Father's property in a far country, away from the Father's face.

By *spirituality*, then, I wish to include the various practices of prayer, meditation, contemplation, spiritual reading, and the like that have characterized Christians from the very beginning. Christian spirituality is rooted in Judaism, is focused on Jesus, is shaped by the God known in Jesus and the Spirit. It embraces the whole person, and looks outward in love at the world. Again, a word about each of these is necessary.

Christian spirituality is rooted in Judaism. Its devotion goes back through the psalms and through the rich and often puzzling god-consciousness of the prophets to the *Shema:* "Hear, O Israel, YHWH our god, YHWH is one." It is thus not so much "creation spirituality" (though that phrase has many fine and important overtones) as "creator spirituality": devotion to the creator. And creator spirituality includes not only looking away from creation to the God who made it, but also, simultaneously, celebrating the goodness and god givenness of creation and grieving over its twistedness and brokenness. Creator spirituality is thus *sacramental* while firmly rejecting the *magical:* creation can be the bearer of God's presence, holiness, love, and grace, but this remains God's gift and can never be manipulated. When the Israelites, embattled against the Philistines, tried to use the Ark of the Covenant as a talisman, a good luck charm, they were defeated and the ark was captured. But when the Philistines put it in the temple of

Dagon, their god, Dagon fell on his face before it.[2] The ark and the temple that eventually housed it really were effective symbols of the presence of YHWH with his people. Judaism literally carried the symbol of incarnation in the midst of its national life.

Christian spirituality is focused on Jesus, the messiah of Israel. It isn't just that Jesus is hailed as messiah by Christians and that he happens to have been Jewish. When the early Christians used the word *messiah* of Jesus they were indicating their belief, without which there would not have been a Christianity at all, that the long story of the creator God's dealings with Israel had reached its climax, its great if paradoxical fulfillment, in and through him, his kingdom announcement, his mighty works, his death and his resurrection. There is no split Christology in the New Testament, no Jesus of history played off against a Christ of faith. The scandal at the heart of Christian faith is that Christians are committed to worshiping a first-century Jew, believing that in him the living God, the God of Israel, the creator of the world, was and is personally present, bringing the temple theme in Judaism to a new and surprising conclusion. The true temple, the true dwelling of Israel's God, was to consist not of bricks and mortar but of a human being. "In him," wrote Paul, "the whole fullness of deity dwells bodily."[3]

While I can just about conceive of all this being true of Jesus without Jesus being aware of it, I do not think this was in fact the case. For reasons I have set out in chapter 10, I regard the standard objection (that Jesus' sanity would be called in question if he supposed himself in any sense divine) as beside the point. More important, we are imagining what we would think of a contemporary person within the modern Western world who thought himself or herself divine. When we think within the first-century Jewish categories I set out earlier, it is perfectly conceivable that Jesus might have come to think of himself, in the course of becoming aware of his vocation, in the way I have described. Christian spirituality thus classically meditates not simply on the Christ of faith but also on the Jesus of history, believing them to be one and the same person and discovering, through getting to know this person as living, active, present, loving, and grieving, that they are recognizing in him the human face of the one true God.

Christian spirituality is therefore shaped by this God, the God we know in Jesus and by the Spirit of Jesus. It is never a matter of shouting across a void. Insofar as God and humans inhabit different spheres, Jesus inhabits both, and by the Spirit enables and invites us to do the same. Christian prayer is not a matter of petitioning a distant bureaucrat but of coming in trust before a deeply loving parent. Nor is Christian prayer conceived of in terms of humans coming in their own strength, ability, or cleverness to address their maker; it is always a matter of the Spirit being secretly and subtly at work. One characteristic Christian experience is of being, so to speak, "prayed in," aware of being fully alert, with all faculties in operation, wrestling with issues and with the words to express them, and yet simultaneously also being enabled to do so by the operation of another, of the Spirit of Jesus present within. For all the analogies that exist between Christian prayer and other prayer, therefore, there is thus an essentially trinitarian shape to classical Christian praying. Just as knowledge is shaped by its object, so prayer is shaped by the one to whom it is addressed.

Christian spirituality embraces the whole person. There is no separate "spiritual" sphere, which leaves out of consideration what one does with one's mind or one's body. Indeed, some of the earliest Christian restatements of the *Shema* include the command to love God with heart, mind, soul, and strength; and one of Paul's great summary statements of Christian obligation focuses on presenting one's body as a living sacrifice.[4] Spirituality does not, therefore, imply the splitting or disintegration of the personality, leaving people so heavenly minded that they are of no earthly use. It points, rather, toward integration, enabling exactly that rehumanization to take place that one would expect if one is indeed worshiping, and so coming to resemble, the God in whose image human beings are made. (One of the great spiritual laws is that one comes to resemble what one worships.) A Christian spirituality, therefore, that makes no demands on the mind, to think through the implications of its faith, or on the body (*body* in the New Testament usually means something like what we mean by *person*), to obedience and holiness, has forgotten what it is about. Cultivating "my spirituality" may be important for people whose culture or upbringing has taught them a path of negative self-obliteration, but if it leads to enjoying a kind of spiritual awareness that leaves mind and body out of the reckoning, it has called into question its very nature as Christian.

Christian spirituality, finally, looks out in love at the world. It is not self-centered, regarding its own spiritual progress or development as the be-all and end-all. Precisely because it is rooted in Judaism (where Israel was called for the sake of the world), is focused on Jesus (who gave himself for the world), is shaped by the true God (who made the world)—and because it embraces the whole person, who is constituted not least by her or his vocation to serve the world—Christian spirituality must, like a well-pruned rosebush, encourage those shoots that move outward and discourage those that become intertwined with one another. Thus, though Christian spirituality generates and sustains a self-awareness in God's presence, it can never be content with navel gazing. The self of which one is aware, if it stands in the presence of the God we know in Jesus, must always be turned outward toward God's world.

When this happens, the result is love, taking the forms of both joy and grief. The New Testament warns against being in love with the world but equally tells us that the God whom we worship "so loved the world." The problem is that the world as it now stands, though full of God's glory, is also full of sorrow and shame, of wickedness and violence, of injustice and oppression. One cannot fall uncritically in love with this world without colluding with evil. Rather, the Christian is called to love the world as God loves the world, joyfully celebrating its beauty, its majesty, its curious detail, its flashes of divine glory—*and* bitterly grieving over its wounds, its horror, its tragedy, its crucifixions. Christian spirituality, focused on and shaped by Jesus, looks at the glory and the shame of it all and brings both, in prayer and liturgy, before the presence of God. It thus holds together worship and mission, looking at God in adoration and, precisely because it is this God it looks at, looking out at the world in joyful and grieving prayer. Christian spirituality, at its heart, reflects Christian theology. The God revealed in Jesus and by the Spirit is neither the pantheist's god, identified with creation (and hence unable to provide a critique of, or a solution to, the problem of evil), nor the dualist's god, separate from the wicked world (and hence unable to celebrate its goodness or remake it in resurrection). It is the God of creation and covenant, of psalms and prophets, of gospel and letter and apocalypse. But this already points us to the next theme.

## THEOLOGY

If spirituality is an essential ingredient in a Christianity focused on Jesus, theology is not far behind. Indeed, for many traditions, spirituality and theology have been the two main focal points of Christian experience, sustaining and reinforcing each other.

From its first decades, Christianity showed a remarkable aptitude for thinking through and creatively reexpressing its beliefs, articulating them in a way that was integrated with its spirituality but was never simply an intellectualization of an experience. Christian theology from the first was oriented toward both worship and mission: the true God was to be worshiped truly (to avoid idolatry and its accompanying dehumanization), and the news of what this God had just accomplished was to be communicated accurately and precisely to the whole world. Paul's fiercest, and perhaps earliest, letter insists upon "the truth of the gospel."[5]

The very words send a shiver down our postmodern spines. "Come on," we want to say to Paul, "you mean the truth *as you see it.* Other people see it differently. There are as many 'truths' as there are observers. All this banging on about 'truth' is simply boosting your own insecurities, advancing your own power games." This argument is of course ultimately self-defeating. If all claims to truth are suspect, so is the claim that all claims to truth are suspect. By what right does the postmodernist claim to be standing still, observing the rest of the world going round and round in its biased circles? Our discussions of Christian theology, of the Bible, of Jesus, and indeed of knowledge itself are caught up in the midst of these swirling and highly emotive cultural battlegrounds.

Christian theology is called to walk the tightrope: to claim to be speaking the truth while making it clear in the manner of the claim that this is not after all a covert power play. In fact, I believe that the picture of Jesus as I have articulated it enables Christian theology to do exactly that. Talk about Jesus enables Christian theology to speak, self-involvingly and self-sacrificially, of the God whose self-giving love has truly been revealed. Such speech sustains an appropriate reading of the relevant texts, within an appropriate view of knowledge itself, enabling us to provide a critique of alternate theories.

The key issue in all theology is how to speak truly of God. If we are to speak of something that transcends space and time, that is beyond our ordinary world, how do we know what we are talking about? How can we know whether we are talking sense, let alone true sense? How can we be sure that we are not (as Feuerbach, Freud, and others have suggested) merely projecting our own self-image or our authority-figure fantasies on to the cosmic stage and calling them "god"? The mainstream Christian answer has always been that, though the one true God is in various ways beyond our imagination, let alone our knowledge, and though even such knowledge as we may have is beyond our own unaided power to attain, this God has not left us to speculate, imagine, or project our own fantasies onto the screen of transcendence; this God instead, through self-revelation, has given us such knowledge as is possible and appropriate for us. And the same mainstream Christian answer has gone on to say that this self-revelation has taken place supremely in Jesus, the crucified and risen messiah of Israel.

The whole point of such a claim is, of course, that the one true God is known in Jesus himself, the human being who lived, worked, and died in first-century Palestine. Take that away, or split the historical Jesus off from the Christ known in faith, as some have tried to do, and you are left without a revelation of the one true God within our own world, the world of physicality and history. That is the move regularly made by writers within the Enlightenment tradition, opening up the possibility that Christianity is after all just another distorted perception of "the sacred" and that its absolute claims, so offensive to both modern and postmodern minds, are yet another projection. This is not, of course, Marcus's position; yet I have sometimes wondered if he has offered one or two hostages to it. It might after all, of course, turn out to be the case that this critique is on target. But this is not what is suggested by the picture I have sketched in my earlier chapters. There, a quite shocking claim is proposed: not that we know what the word *God* means and can discover the extent to which this "God" was present in, or revealed through, Jesus; rather that, by close attention to Jesus himself, we are invited to discover, perhaps for the first time, just who the creator and covenant God was and is all along. And when we discover that, we discover that the claim to truth is not a power play. It is a love ploy—something that postmodernity and the hermeneutic of suspicion cannot recognize but cannot ultimately deconstruct.

If this claim can be sustained, it means that we cannot treat the gospels as containing, along with "history remembered," a measure of what Marcus calls "history metaphorized"—by which I take it he means narratives that look now like historical accounts but which originally carried their full meaning at the level of metaphor. (The parables are good examples of narratives of this sort.) I have argued elsewhere that the gospels are what they are precisely because their authors thought the events they were recording—all of them, not just some— actually happened. Of course, we may as historians judge that in some cases they were mistaken; but, if this is so, they were to that extent failing to convey the most important meaning they had in mind, which was precisely that in these events *as historical events* Israel's God, the world's creator, had acted decisively and climactically within creation, within Israel's history. These stories were never designed to express or embody a dehistoricized spirituality, or to convey truths about the post-Easter Jesus which were not anchored in the life of the pre-Easter Jesus. This is not because the gospels were written by "fact fundamentalists," but because they were written, and the pre-gospels stories were told, by Jews.

This is confirmed by the study of the materials themselves. The gospels, viewed in the light of ancient biography, belong firmly within that genre; viewed in the light of Jewish literature, they belong firmly within the genre of Jewish stories of what Israel's God was doing *in actual history.*[6] For us to declare that they contain major segments (along with actual historical material) which express in apparently historical language truths that are not dependent on history is not just to accuse them of incompetence—writing stories which look like history but aren't—but also to say that they have systematically undermined their own deepest theological point. They have spoken eloquently and Jewishly of God's action in history, in order to stress that, though God may sometimes have acted within history, ultimate truth lies in a different sphere altogether.

Marcus does not, of course, hold an extreme position at this point. He insists that the gospels contain a solid measure of historical memory, and is happy to affirm that the God of Israel, and of Jesus, was indeed active within this history. At this point we stand shoulder to shoulder against all attempts to reduce the gospels to a set of theologically inspired fictions. In one of our many discussions before this book took final shape, Marcus expressed the issue between us as follows: Can metaphorical narratives be meaningful and true, apart from their reporting particular events which really happened?

At one level, the answer is obviously "yes." There never was a "prodigal son" or a "good Samaritan," but the stories in which those two characters feature are among the truest ever told. Discerning the nature of these stories, though, is a matter of recognizing the genre involved, not of doing historical research to discover whether these characters really existed. My point remains that the genre of the gospels, and of the individual stories in which Jesus figures, lies along the continuum of history and biography, not of parable.

Nor is this a matter of literary theory only. I cannot, of course, prove that the stories "really happened;" such proof is always difficult in ancient history, just as is proving that they didn't. I stress the importance of the historicity of the Jesus-stories because the whole point of the exercise, as far as the writers (and pre-literary story-tellers) were concerned, was that these things *had* really happened. They were the place where the God of Israel, the God of history, the God of creation, had acted climactically within Israel, within history, within creation. Whether the stories really did happen is another (and very difficult) matter; but everyone who told them thought that they did.

The issue, then, is not whether non-historical stories can have true theological meaning, nor whether historical stories can have metaphorical as well as historical meaning. We agree on both of these points. The issue is whether the metaphorical meaning of stories ostensibly about Jesus is dependent upon the story's reporting a particular historical occurrence. We have often discussed the Emmaus Road story in Luke 24 as a good example. We agree that it carries rich layers of meaning for the ongoing life of the early church. Luke's narrative brings together the exposition of scripture and the breaking of bread in a way that surely points to the regular worshiping life of the church, as in, for instance, Acts 2.42. The story resonates with all those who have felt their hearts burning within them at sudden fresh understanding of scripture and who have then known the Lord in the breaking of the bread. Are these meanings dependent upon some such incident having taken place?

Marcus, following a long line of interpreters, says "no." The burning of the heart and the meeting with the Lord take place in Christian experience whether or not Emmaus really happened. In one sense, of course, I agree. People did and do have these experiences, and this would be true even if Luke's gospel never existed. But would the Emmaus Road story be "true" if it never happened? My answer is "no," for reasons I gave in chapter 7. The foundation meaning of the story is that the risen Jesus truly met two disciples on the road, explained the scriptures to them, and was recognized when he broke the bread. The other meanings are like the waves and ripples caused by a large stone being dropped in a pond. It is because Jesus was truly raised from the dead that these things are now true. Take away the stone, and you wouldn't have any waves, not even a ripple.

When once you open up this issue, of course, there are many layers and subtleties to be investigated for which this is not the place. And the debate between Marcus and myself is not the only discussion to be had on these topics. The main point I have wanted to make in the present discussion, recognizing that in making it my disagreement with Marcus is often more oblique than head on, is that for the first-century Jewish worldview within which we can most credibly situate both Jesus and his first followers, *rich symbolic meanings were to be found precisely within actual events.* I do not think we can take even a small step away from this point without calling into question the actual Jewish context in which all our historical discourse about Jesus ought to take place.

The richest of symbolic meanings were, of course, those that spoke of the presence of God. This brings us back to the task of theology itself and the way in which the things I have said about Jesus open this task up in new ways. Theology is all about learning to think, speak, and write on two levels at once and to do so with such appropriate discipline and balance as may enable one to speak the truth about the true God. If what I have said about Jesus is anywhere near the mark, it is here above all that we need, not an either-or, but a both-and: *both* a language that will draw together speech about things that actually happened *and* speech about the God who operates in and through things that actually happen. That is what, I believe, speech about Jesus is struggling to attain. This both-and propels us forward from spirituality and theology into the turbulent world where people seek justice and peace: the world of politics.

## POLITICS

Western Christianity since the Enlightenment has routinely colluded with its own privatization. Following the post-Reformation European wars in which religious allegiance played a major role, the Enlightenment offered a way of peace, though at a cost: make religion a matter of private opinion, and we will sort out the world without reference to God. The fact that one of the great monuments to the Enlightenment, the French Revolution, had to kill so many people to make the point gives one pause in accepting the Enlightenment's rhetoric at face value. One might also observe that post-Enlightenment Europe and America have been involved in just as many wars as before, even without an official religious reason (and indeed, often enough, with both sides officially embracing the same religion). This suggests, of course, that the religions were all along just an excuse, another bit of surface noise on top of a dispute about other matters; and it seems likely that the Enlightenment's rhetoric about the danger of religion was actually an excuse, an official reason for banishing religion "upstairs," out of harm's way, leaving the powerful, the politicians, the imperialists, and the industrialists to carve up the world how they wanted. But the rhetoric persists, being invoked by right-wingers in the United Kingdom every time a church representative speaks out on political issues and by left-wingers in the United States every time a fundamentalist speaks out on family values. Keep your religion as a matter of private spirituality, they say, and we shall continue to steer the world by other lights.

The Jesus of whom I have written stands over against all such split-level universes. I come back full circle to my opening chapter: within Jesus' world, and his message and ministry, God's sphere and the human sphere belong inseparably together. Thy kingdom come, he taught us to pray, thy will be done, *on earth as it is in heaven.* Not "in heaven, when we eventually get there" or "in heaven, where we enjoy our private spiritualities," but on earth, in the here and now. And that kingdom, that will of God, concerned—for a first-century Jew speaking to first-century Jews—God's becoming king, and Caesar, Herod, and all other claimants being demoted. That language, both then and now, enters the arena known as politics, and any attempt to remove it from that arena falsifies and belittles it.

Nor did this emphasis of Jesus die out in the early church. Calling Jesus "Lord" meant denying that title to Caesar, as Paul and his converts knew very well. Luke, of all people (he is often thought to have been politically quietist), tells us that Paul was accused in Thessalonica of heralding "another king, namely Jesus."[7] The persecution suffered by the early church, at the hands of pagans and Jews alike, did not take place because the Christians carried strange ideas around in their heads; people seldom get persecuted for thinking strange thoughts. Persecution happens when people find their symbolic and political universe challenged by other people whose beliefs commit them to a different set of symbols, to a different political allegiance. The worship and mission of the early church were both inescapably "political": to worship the God revealed in Jesus meant giving him an allegiance that was then denied to all others. To announce the lordship of this Jesus, and to summon people to trust and obey him, was to command them to leave the worship of all other gods. And the god whose stock was on the increase most dramatically in the early Roman Empire was Caesar himself.[8] The church has struggled ever since to work out the implications of its own deeply subversive message.

The perception is widespread today that after the first generation, which had been truly radical, the church went rapidly downhill, seeking political power, or at least an accommodation with the powers that be, until finally this goal was attained, and the nadir of Christian radicalism reached, in the conversion of Constantine. In recent studies of Jesus and the gospels it has become almost commonplace to read that, while the Gnostic gospels and the hypothetical "Early Q" are truly radical, this radicalism was muted, squelched, or lost altogether in the synoptic gospels as we have them. Orthodoxy, it is supposed, was already rearing its ugly head, stifling the rich and exciting variety of early

Christian experience and seeking to curry favor with its social and political masters and rulers. This view, in my opinion, flies in the face of the actual history of the church during its first three centuries. Generation after generation of Christians was persecuted fiercely by officials and authorities, culminating with the ruthless Diocletian, emperor from 284 to 305. When, around 550, an obscure monk called Dionysius Exiguus proposed a new calendar, dating (supposedly) from the conception of Jesus, he was replacing the calendar that Diocletian had instituted, based on his own accession. It was a way of saying, one more time, that Jesus was Lord and Caesar was not.

But this calendar, adopted within the post-Constantinian church, raises in itself the question: what should the church have done when Constantine proposed, not long after becoming emperor in 306, not only to convert to Christianity but to unite the Christian church to the secular state by the closest possible ties? Eusebius's glowing account of the bishops sitting down to dinner with the emperor sticks in our throats today, but what should the bishops have done instead? Begged Constantine not to convert, not to seek to apply the rule of Christ in his empire (whether this was what Constantine actually wanted to do or not is another matter), because it was so much more authentic for Christians to be in the position of being a beleaguered minority, a persecuted radical group? If one really believes that Jesus Christ is the Lord of the world and that his way of life is the truly human and humanizing one, ought one not to rejoice if those in power declare themselves in favor of following it and encourage others to do so, too? (Again, I leave aside the question of whether this was actually what Constantine wanted to do.) After all, if the ruler is serious about allegiance to Jesus Christ, the church will retain the right to tell the ruler in no uncertain terms when he (or she) is failing in this basic duty. The current anti-Constantinian mood in New Testament scholarship fails to take account of the fact that church leaders for centuries after Constantine often did exactly that. Clear thinking is not well served at this point by oversimplifications and broad-brush polemics.[9]

A Christianity that looks back to Jesus himself, then, seen as the messiah of Israel and the Lord of the world, will not shrink from bringing together (a) the spirituality that acknowledges him as lord of one's life, taking precedence over all other claimants, worshiped and adored in prayer, sacrament, meditation, and contemplation, (b) the theology that articulates his lordship and divinity and seeks to express these as truly and clearly as possible for today's world, and (c) the politics that acknowledges him as Lord of the world and seeks to implement that lordship by all appropriate means.

What might this look like in practice? I write these lines tired after a day in which I have taken part in hosting, and speaking at, an all-day seminar held in the cathedral of which I have the honor to be dean. Today speakers from Africa and Europe, including politicians and bishops, addressed the urgent issue of debt in the two-thirds world and the hope for a jubilee in the year 2000. I said there, and have no hesitation in saying here, that if Jesus is lord and Caesar isn't, it is also true that Jesus is lord and mammon isn't. The idea of debt remission is anathema to those who worship mammon; they think up all kinds of excuses to stop the proposal being taken seriously. But it has been done before (Germany's huge debt was remitted in 1953, giving that country a fresh start); it is perfectly possible; and, more important, it is exactly in line with the program articulated by Jesus in Luke 4. I mention this, partly to show that my thinking on the question of Jesus and politics has not been purely at the theoretical level, partly to demonstrate that an established church can be used as a base to launch new and radical political ideas, and more particularly to indicate, by one example, the way in which following the Jesus about whom I have written leads one into direct political action. (We went from the seminar into a typically Anglican service of choral evensong, where the Magnificat, Mary's wonderful liberation anthem, sounded more appropriate than ever before.)

Political action is often costly. It is not known as widely as it should be that, despite the collapse of communism (which many Western Christians had supposed to be the main persecutor of Christians in the contemporary world), Christians even today are being persecuted for their faith. Violence, torture, rape, murder, and major discrimination are daily realities in at least sixty countries around the world.[10] Because we in the West assume that religion and politics belong in different spheres, we forget that there are many today for whom naming the name of Jesus Christ brings direct conflict with the powers that be. Christians in the West, one fears, would turn back and compromise under these circumstances. Many elsewhere do not, and they suffer the consequences. The early Christians, including those who wrote the gospels, would have recognized them as brothers and sisters.

The politics of following Jesus, then, is a vital question to be addressed in our day. I believe (and I think Marcus would agree) that the Jesus whom I have described, the figure who dominates the gospel accounts, has far more to say to these questions than the Jesus shakily sketched by radical criticism or reconstructed out of Q and Thomas. (One wonders, indeed, if the powers that be would have felt very threatened by that Jesus; little groups practicing asceticism or proto-Gnosticism do not trouble rulers half so much as people writing or telling stories about the true messiah who is now the Lord of the world.) And, as I have indicated, this political aspect of discipleship needs to be integrated with the other elements of the picture. Of course, some people are attracted into Christianity because of its political stance, just as some come in because of its offer of a mode of spirituality. But to remain with only one of the elements is to be greatly impoverished. Just as spirituality and theology need politics, so politics needs spirituality and theology. The resulting mixture has not been seen often in Western churches, where the disastrous legacy of the Enlightenment has meant that the two are usually thought of as antithetical. But it is well known in most other parts of the world, not least the places where the churches, supposedly in decline in the West, are at their strongest. Most African Christians have no difficulty in putting together what many Westerners insist on keeping in separate compartments.

## HEALING

The fourth element in the picture can be summarized with the word *healing*. Healing formed a major part of Jesus' public work, and, though in my own writing about Jesus I am aware that I have not provided a very full treatment of the subject, it remains central and important.

By *healing* I mean a wide range of phenomena. Physical healing, certainly; but also psychological healing, inner healing, healing of memories, and the like; and also the healing of societies and institutions. There has been a growth industry in the practice of, and the writing of books about, such things in the last two decades, and I have personally profited enormously from the ministry of those skilled in them. I cannot doubt that the God I worship heals people physically: I have friends, and at least one close relative, who owe their very lives to healings that came swiftly and directly in answer to widespread prayer after the medical profession had given up. I cannot doubt that God also heals people emotionally, dealing with bruised memories, hidden angers, psychological scars. These things are difficult to demonstrate and easy to explain away; but they are real, lasting, and lifegiving to those who have experienced them.

Equally, I know that there are charlatans who manipulate people in private and public, on television and stage, claiming healings that are no such thing, urging people to greater "faith" when the only appropriate stance is silence before the mystery of God. I know also that there are many people for whom confident, believing prayers were said who did not get better. I know that there are appalling tragedies in our world, from the Holocaust to the wasting of little children through famine, that all the prayer in the world seems to have been powerless to combat. I refuse to allow my awareness of all these things to bully or browbeat me into denying other things I also know: that the God who healed through Jesus in his lifetime heals through the Spirit of Jesus today. I do not myself regularly exercise a healing ministry and am secretly jealous of those who do. It is not, or not at the moment, my calling. But that there are people who do have such ministries, overlapping and integrating with those of the medical professionals and sometimes going beyond them, I have no doubt.

But there is also a deeper healing that is, I believe, effected in the church and the world through the presence of the Spirit of the Jesus of whom I have written. I wish to focus on that in particular and to show how it integrates with the other three elements I have described.[11] Paul writes in several of his letters about his own suffering, and that of other Christians, being used in the economy of God to bring about life and healing for others. 2 Corinthians as a whole reflects this belief: there, Paul's suffering as an apostle (directly caused by his challenging the principalities and powers with the news that the crucified Jesus is the Lord of the world) is seen as itself part of the healing process whereby he Corinthian church is built up in faith, renewed in Christ. And perhaps the most famous passage where this comes to expression, a passage I have increasingly seen as central and climactic for Pauline and indeed New Testament theology as a whole, is Romans 8.18–27.

There, within the context of the hope for the renewal (healing?) of the whole creation, Paul sketches a picture of the church's task. The church is not called to stand on the sidelines, watching the world from a distance as it groans in travail, longing for redemption. The church finds itself caught up in the same groaning, suffering at the heart of a world in pain. But within the church's groaning Paul detects the groaning of the Spirit, the Spirit of Jesus, the Spirit of the living God. God does not stand aloof from the pain of the church and hence from the pain of the world. Rather, God is present in the church, calling forth prayer, even inarticulate prayer, precisely at the place of the world's pain. Thus the church is called to be for the world what Jesus was for Israel: not just a moral lecturer, nor even a moral example, but the people who, in obedience to God's strange vocation, learn to suffer and pray at the place where the world is in pain, *so that the world may be healed.* And this healing takes place both in the future, when God remakes heaven and earth, and here and now, in those strange moments of healing that, though unpredictable and sometimes open to challenge, catch us by surprise as moments of true revelation. Such prayer is thus both worship and mission. Whether the healing that results is physical, mental, emotional, psychological, political, sociological, or whatever, when it happens we are awed and humbled.

Thus the wheel of Christian experience comes full circle. The church's ministry of healing, at this deep level, is carried on in the midst of the suffering that comes from engaging with the powers; it is the very embodiment of characteristic and authentic Christian spirituality; and it is explained by the richest Christian theology—the doctrine of the Trinity, set within an eschatological framework in which the creator God designs to heal and renew the whole creation. Within this broad framework there is, I believe, a lot more room for mainline churches to explore the meaning of healing on a day-to-day basis. Many are already moving in this direction. Healing is far too important and central to the stories about Jesus for those who wish to follow him today to ignore it. And, like the other three aspects of discipleship I have highlighted in this chapter, healing draws together worship and mission. It is as we worship the God revealed in Jesus, in the power of the Spirit, that this power is unleashed, always strange and sovereign, never at our disposal, in the mission of healing to and for the world.

## JESUS AND INTEGRATION

I have not used the word *reconciliation* in this chapter, but it is of course central to all I have been saying—reconciliation between God and the world, between humans, and so on. I have scarcely spoken of forgiveness, but it is one of the best words for what the worshiper of God in Jesus experiences and wishes to communicate in mission to the world— one of the best indexes of true Christian spirituality and theology, politics and healing. I suppose the main thing I have been trying to say, and the main reason why, despite our friendship, I still find it impossible to agree with Marcus in his analysis, has to do with integration.

Integration, first, between the Jesus of history and the Christ of faith—or, in Marcus's language (not that these are exactly the same), between the pre-Easter Jesus and the post-Easter Jesus. Marcus sees some continuity between these two figures; it is still, he claims, the same Jesus, despite being in various ways radically different. There are of course striking differences, strongly evident in the New Testament itself. The pre-Easter Jesus does not appear through locked doors, breathe his spirit on his followers, or ascend to heaven. But from where I sit it always appears, to put it bluntly, that in Marcus's picture there is too much discontinuity and not enough continuity—just as I expect he will find the opposite in my account. A full discussion of the question would require that we pay attention to what we mean by "identity" in the case of persons, which is a hoary old philosophical puzzle in itself. But at stake, ultimately, is the resurrection and what we mean by it (back to chapter 7 once more). I see, as has become clear, far more direct continuity between Jesus before and after Easter than Marcus does.

In particular, I see continuity between the things the church claimed about Jesus after Easter and the aims and beliefs of Jesus before Easter. The obvious retort, that the church invented a Jesus to suit its subsequent beliefs, misses the point, as I argued at length in *Jesus and the Victory of God:* there is precisely continuity, not identity, since the early church did not express its beliefs in, for instance, Jesus' achievement on the cross in the same way as Jesus himself had done. The point, for me, is that I am committed to worshiping Jesus the first-century Palestinian Jew; to saying, indeed, that this Jesus, whom I may discover to have thought thoughts that contemporary westerners, Marcus included, find distasteful or even shocking, is identical with the messiah of Israel, the Lord of the world, the one I worship. Unless I am prepared to do this, how do I know if the Jesus I am worshiping is not simply an idol, made in the image either of myself or of my favored ideologies?

Integration, therefore, second—and more specifically—between Jesus the Jewish messiah and Jesus the Lord acclaimed by Christians. This is of course a minefield into which I cannot stray very far. Yet I persist in believing that it is historically far more useful to use "emic" categories than "etic" ones (that is, the categories the subjects themselves would have recognized rather than the categories we impose upon them). We are much more likely to get into the minds of our subjects that way. And when we do so, the categories that Jesus' own world offered to describe someone doing and saying the sort of things Jesus was doing and saying were: prophet, messiah, martyr. Jesus could and, I have argued, did believe that he, in filling these roles, was doing something for Israel that Israel could not do for itself, something that in its scriptures only its God, YHWH, could and would do. If, as Marcus suggests, these roles make us nervous, with our late-twentieth-century perceptions and prejudices, so be it. *Nervous?* They scare me stiff. Is that not precisely what we should expect if we come face-to-face with ultimate and deeply personal reality—that is, God? Ought we to expect to be able to appraise God coolly, neutrally, rationally? Would God be God if we could?

Integration, third, between the different facets of Christian experience. Many Christians integrate two of the four areas I have outlined; some attempt three; very few draw together all four. I said earlier that many Christians lived their lives on the basis of spirituality and theology, leaving politics and healing out of the question. Some liberation theologians have integrated politics and theology while holding themselves aloof from spirituality and healing. Some charismatic Christians have developed rich spiritualities and healing ministries but sit light to theology and avoid politics like the plague. No doubt there are other combinations and permutations. I suggest that following the Jesus I have described enables us to bring together things that are often separated within the practice of the faith. I regard this as a sign of health.

Integration, fourth, between history and eschatology. One of my biggest problems with Marcus's account of Jesus is this: despite his fine insistence throughout his work on the this-worldly meaning of eschatological or apocalyptic language in the gospels, he has screened out of his account (as far as I can see) the very first-century Jewish belief, characteristically expressed in the language of apocalyptic, that Israel's whole history was reaching its decisive climax. Instead, Marcus seems to me to have embraced a form of (what one might call) Christian Platonism, in which allegory takes the place of eschatology. I propose, rather, that history—the study of Jesus within his actual context—reveals Jesus as having used eschatological language to indicate his belief that Israel's history was indeed reaching its God-ordained climax, even though that climax would not look like his contemporaries thought it would.

Integration, fifth, between history and faith. I return to the point at which I started. Yes, there is, as Marcus notes, a risk in allowing faith any say in the activity of history, but not half so much of a risk as pretending (not that Marcus does) to a neutral and presuppositionless historiography. Both history and faith cry out to be described in wider terms yet: both are mental and emotional activities, which in principle could be practiced by a disembodied spirit (equipped, one assumes, with a disembodied library in which to do research). The historian/believer is not disembodied. He or she lives in the created world, the sacramental world, the human world, the political world, the world of a reality simultaneously mundane and shot through with glory. Once we have widened our horizons to include all this—and if we do not we are again pretending to a disengagement that is out of tune with all our actual experiences—we will find, I believe, that the tension supposed to exist between history and faith is much more oblique, much less of a problem and more of a stimulus, than usually conceived. And once we focus both history and faith on Jesus of Nazareth, discovering him to be as I have tried to describe him, we may perhaps find that creation, sacraments, human life, politics, history, and faith come rushing together in new integrations for which as yet we have no language but worship. That, too, seems to me to possess the ring of truth.

What, after all, is the end of all this endeavor? Is it that we, as historians, theologians, cultural critics, or whatever, should analyze a question to our own satisfaction, provide an answer that neatly ties everything together, and go off shopping or playing golf, secure in a good little job well done? Is not a book about Jesus merely a step toward something far more important? Is not the ultimate aim that we should come face-to-face—and hope and pray to bring others face-to-face—with the one in whose face (wounded yet glorious) we see the face of the creator God, the covenant God, the one who loves us more than we can ever guess? Is it not that we should be transformed by that meeting, that gaze, so that we can share the same love with the world around? Books about Jesus can be an aid toward worship, a guide in mission. But if it really is Jesus we are talking about, worship and mission are more important even than books.

# A VISION OF THE CHRISTIAN LIFE

*Marcus Borg*

---

THUS FAR I HAVE described a vision—a way of seeing—the historical Jesus and post-Easter traditions about him, including the stories of his death, resurrection, and birth, as well as traditions relevant to Christology and the second coming. The question of meaning, though occasionally addressed, has remained mostly implicit. My task in this concluding chapter is to become consistently explicit.[1]

In the first part of the chapter I explore some central differences between my vision and Tom's vision of Jesus. In the second part I describe a vision of the Christian life as I see it, flowing out of how I see Jesus, the gospels, and Scripture as a whole.

What will emerge is a relational understanding of the Christian life. Its central dynamic is not believing, but living within the Christian tradition as a sacrament whose purpose is to mediate the Spirit and transform our lives. Put compactly, I see the Christian life as a relationship to God, mediated by Scripture and tradition, and transforming our sense of ourselves and our relationship to the world of the everyday.

## DIFFERENCES BETWEEN OUR VISIONS OF JESUS

There is much with which I agree in Tom's last chapter. I affirm his vision of the Christian life whole-heartedly: the two poles of Christian existence as worship and mission, and his exposition of what this means under the categories of spirituality, theology, politics, and healing. I admire his vision's elegance and eloquence. Indeed, I think Tom's vision of the Christian life and the one I describe later in this chapter are remarkably similar, despite differences in language and topic headings.

Our essential agreement about the image of the Christian life that emerges out of our study of Jesus and early Christianity is important. We have reached similar conclusions about what it means to take Jesus seriously, even as we have disagreements about historical matters related to Jesus. Our agreement also provides the framework for speaking about our differences.

Some of the differences between Tom and me concern details of relatively minor importance. Others might be more apparent than real and might be reconciled through sustained dialogue. Still others are not merely apparent, but real and major. I will comment, respectfully and affectionately, and (I trust) clearly and fairly, about how I see the major differences. I do not think of these comments as a final opportunity for rebuttal, but rather as a laying out of major choices to be made as we think about how we might envision the historical Jesus.

## *Our Foundational Categories*

The foundational categories with which we develop our sketches of Jesus are quite different. My categories—namely, the five primary strokes of my sketch of Jesus as a Spirit person, healer, wisdom teacher, social prophet, and movement initiator—are drawn from the cross-cultural study of religion. Tom uses categories native to the Jewish tradition: Jesus as messiah and prophet of the kingdom of God, the need for the real return from exile, Israel's vocation to be the light to the nations, and so forth. We both agree that Jesus was a deeply Jewish figure, but we follow different strategies as we seek to describe him; Tom uses emic categories (categories from within the culture), I using etic (categories from outside the culture) categories. And I can translate my etic categories back into Jewish categories, just as Tom presumably could also translate his Jewish categories into more etic language.

I choose a cross-cultural approach in part because my audience over the last twenty-five years has been quite secularized and pluralistic college and university students. In that setting, I have found a comparative religions approach to the study of Jesus and early Christianity to be an effective pedagogical strategy.

But there is also another reason for my use of a cross-cultural approach with its emphasis on religious experience. Namely, my involvement with mainline churches in North America suggests that many people are experiencing a crisis of confidence about the meaning and truthfulness of the Christian tradition. An older understanding of Christianity has ceased to be compelling to millions of people over the last thirty to forty years and is the major cause of the loss of membership in mainline denominations. I have described that older understanding elsewhere with five adjectives: in harder and softer forms, it was literalistic, doctrinal, moralistic, exclusivistic, and afterlife oriented.[2] It has ceased to work for a large number of people. They find that if they must take the Bible literally, they cannot take it at all. Moreover, the notion that Christian doctrines are true, and the teachings of other religions false, sounds increasingly dubious, as does the related notion that only Christians can be "saved." Thus the form of Christianity to which many people have been exposed sounds doubtful at best. As a result, many have left the church, while others remain in the church and struggle to make sense of things.

Two hundred years ago, the German Protestant theologian Friedrich Schleiermacher called this group "the cultured despisers of religion."[3] Though a harsh-sounding phrase, it simply means people whose education into a different worldview had called into question the truth of traditional Christian convictions. In his day, they were a small group of intellectuals who had embraced the new thought of the Enlightenment. In our time, they number in the millions. Yet many of today's cultured despisers of religion are also cultured yearners and seekers. They are looking for a way of being religious that makes persuasive sense without tearing out the heart of the matter.

For these religious seekers, within the church as well as on its margins, an emphasis upon the experience of the sacred across cultures has a credibility that a focus on a single religious tradition does not. A single religious tradition can easily be doubted as merely a human creation and projection, but when one sees that the great religious traditions share much in common, especially at the level of experience and practice, one begins to wonder if there might be something to religion.

That has been my experience, both in my own religious journey, and in my work in mainline denominations. People find that the approach I and many of my colleagues represent provides a way back into the life of the church and, for those who never left, a way of quickening and deepening their life with God.[4]

As already mentioned, Tom's approach uses categories and language drawn mostly from the Jewish and Christian traditions. It accomplishes the same end; his readers consistently report that it leads to a fresh seeing of the tradition and to a deeper immersion in the Christian life.

Both approaches and angles of vision are useful and valid, it seems to me. They need not be seen as requiring an either-or choice but can be combined easily as a both-and. In my study of Jesus, I have sought to do so myself, not only seeing Jesus through cross-cultural lenses, but also seeking consistently to relate what I see to the language and history of ancient Judaism. The two perspectives are complementary and not competitive. Indeed, I can imagine somebody combining not only our angles of vision but even our major conclusions. One might conclude that Jesus was a Jewish Spirit person, healer, wisdom teacher, social prophet and movement initiator, as I do, *and also* that he saw himself as having a messianic awareness and vocation, as Tom does. I do not reach that conclusion myself, but combining what one sees from our two angles of vision is not intrinsically contradictory.

## Epistemology and Faith

By the phrase "epistemology and faith," I mean the role of faith in knowing about Jesus. My comments begin with the opening line of Tom's chapter 2: "We know about Jesus in two ways: history and faith." As I read his section on faith as a way of knowing, I was both impressed and moved by his description of what he knows about Jesus through his own faith relationship with Jesus.

Using my terminology, I would say that the Jesus he knows through faith is the post-Easter Jesus, that is, the living risen Jesus who is a figure of the present. But I remain unclear about the significance of this kind of knowing for making historical judgments about which teachings and events go back to Jesus of Nazareth. Does knowing by faith, for example, help in making a judgment about whether the story of Jesus walking on the water or feeding the multitude with a few loaves and fishes is based on history remembered rather than being a metaphorical narrative? I have heard people do this. Usually they say something like, "I don't care if some scholars say it's a symbolic story; I believe it happened." Here faith (understood as belief) becomes a basis for historical affirmation. I doubt that this is what Tom means. But I'm uncertain about what he does mean, and I get nervous about the way the expression can be understood.

Rather than saying that faith is a way of knowing about the historical Jesus, I prefer to speak of the role of metahistorical factors in the study of Jesus. Metahistorical factors are convictions that go beyond what a historian as historian can affirm. Examples of the metahistorical factors that shape my work include the conviction that God is real and can be experienced, that reality is far more mysterious than our categories can capture, and that the risen living Christ is real and can be known. I think I can make plausibility arguments for all of these, but, like all arguments for the reality of God, they fall short of a proof. My affirmation of all of these is what William James usefully called an "over-belief": a conviction grounded in experience but going beyond experience.[5]

One could reach different conclusions. For example, one could grant that people have experiences of God and the risen Christ but that there are psychological and cultural explanations of such experiences that do not require the affirmation, "The sacred is real." And what a historian thinks about experiences like this will affect his or her historical work. If one thinks that experiences of the sacred do not happen, either because there is no sacred or because the sacred is so transcendent that it cannot be experienced, then one will not make experiences of the sacred central in one's understanding of Jesus and Christian origins. If one thinks that the limits of the possible are defined by the Newtonian worldview, then one will not see stories that violate those limits as historically factual. All of this illustrates what I mean by the role of metahistorical factors in historical work.

If this, or something like this, is what Tom means, then we do not differ at this point. But I remain uneasy about his formulation. Faith as a way of knowing, if it is applied to making judgments about the past, is too easily misunderstood and opens the door to tipping the balance scales in favor of a positive judgment by saying, "I have faith that it happened this way."[6] But whether or not I believe something to have happened has nothing to do with whether it did.

## How Much is Historical?

The remaining differences strike me as real and important. They involve a twofold question combining historical and theological issues. Namely, how much of what the gospels report about Jesus is historical, and how much needs to be historical? The former is a historical judgment; the latter is a theological judgment.

Tom and I agree that the gospels combine historical material with metaphorical significance. Tom powerfully affirms that the gospel narratives resound with rich metaphorical resonances. What we disagree about is how much is history remembered, and whether gospel texts (beyond the parables) can be metaphorically true without also being historically factual.

As I understand Tom's position, he sees the gospel narratives as essentially historical in two senses of the word. First, they report (with perhaps a few exceptions?) events that really happened. Second, their historicity is essential in the sense of needful or necessary; that is, the truth of the Christian gospels depends upon the basic factuality of their reports about Jesus.

On the other hand, I see the gospel traditions about Jesus as falling into three categories: some are simply history remembered, some combine history remembered with history metaphorized, and some are only history metaphorized (that is, the story is not a historically factual report). Examples of material I place in the last category include the birth stories, the multiplication of loaves, walking on water and stilling a storm, the transfiguration story, and sayings reporting that Jesus had a messianic self-awareness and saw his death as having a salvific purpose.

Moreover, I do not think the metaphorical truth of a gospel narrative depends upon it also reporting a specific historical event. We thus disagree not only about how much is historically factual, but about how much needs to be.

The issue is not whether history matters. I think history mattered deeply to Jesus, and to the God of Jesus and Israel. The past of his own people, especially Moses and the prophets, mattered to Jesus. History in the sense of the contemporary life of his society, with its complex web of ideational, religious, moral, social and political systems, mattered to Jesus. For Jesus and Israel, history is the place where the will and passion of God are known. The issue, rather, is whether the truth of a gospel story is dependent upon its being grounded in a particular historical event. Tom says "yes," and I say "no."

I have not thought through what is the bare minimum that must be historical in order for the gospels to be true. I am not sure it would be useful to do so. What I am confident about is that we know enough about the historical Jesus to give substantial content to the claim that in Jesus we see what God is like and what a life full of God is like.

## Sources and Method

The differences already mentioned flow to a large extent out of differences about our sources and our method for using them. About one step of the methodological process, we agree: historical context is utterly crucial. Traditions about Jesus that we think are historical must be set in the total context of the Jewish homeland in the first third of the first century. What they meant is what they would have meant in that context.

But we disagree significantly about the other step of the methodological process, namely, our understanding of the sources of the gospels and how to use them. Radically to crystallize what I said in chapter 1, my method for using the gospels has three stages. First, a decision about sources—about what is earlier and what is later; second, constructing a hypothesis from early layers, using multiple (typically double) independent attestation; third, using single-source material that is congruent with the hypothesis constructed at stage two. Tom essentially bypasses this and uses a one-stage method for using the gospels.

My summary understanding of the sources as described in chapter 1 is, as Tom acknowledges, a fairly standard scholarly understanding. The most important element is the claim that Mark is the earliest of our existing gospels and that Matthew and Luke used Mark. Of next importance (though not as crucial) is the existence of Q, a hypothetical early document consisting mostly of the wisdom teaching of Jesus, also used by Matthew and Luke.

Tom is right that there is not unanimity among scholars about the priority of Mark and the existence of Q. Then he uses this lack of unanimity as a justification for setting aside these widely accepted claims. I don't know if he would make a case for rejecting them, but he does bracket them—he goes about his historical work without a decision about earlier and later sources.

He proposes instead a method based on hypothesis and verification: the most satisfactory hypothesis is the one that enables us to incorporate the greatest amount of data. The effect of this methodological move on his work is important: everything in the synoptic gospels becomes a candidate for inclusion in his reconstruction of Jesus, the criterion being primarily whether it can be accommodated in an overall hypothesis.

In doing so, he in effect sets aside two hundred years of scholarly work on the sources. Of course, Tom is deeply conversant with that scholarship; he has not ignored it. His reasons for not beginning with it are twofold. He is not confident that the most common scholarly understanding of the sources is correct; and he does not think that conclusions about earlier and later sources are the necessary gateway to historical Jesus research.

Of course, the common scholarly understanding of the sources could be mistaken. It is the nature of historical work that we are always involved in probability judgments. Granted, some judgments are so probable as to be certain; for example, Jesus really existed, and he really was crucified, just as Julius Caesar really existed and was assassinated. But many judgments have varying degrees of probability.

We make different probability judgments about the sources. In the case of the priority of Mark, it seems to me that the probability is very high indeed, even though I am aware that highly intelligent scholars (though relatively few) have reached a different conclusion. Slightly less higher in probability is the existence of Q, though still more probable than not, in my judgment.

The consequence for our historical work is considerable. When Mark and Matthew and/or Luke all report the same story or saying, I understand the differences among them to be the product of Matthew and Luke's modification of Mark. They are the product of editorial revision and thus are not candidates for historical data about Jesus. Tom, by setting this view of the sources aside, can sometimes treat differences among Matthew, Mark, and Luke as the product of independent witnesses to the same event or saying.[7] He can also treat material found in only one source as equally eligible for inclusion in an overall reconstruction of Jesus. All of this is included in what I mean when I say that Tom has essentially a one-stage method for using the gospels.[8]

This raises a crucial question: what if Tom's method of hypothesis and verification is seeking to accommodate data that are not data? That is, by bracketing the most common scholarly understanding of the sources, he may very well be treating as evidence for the historical Jesus material that is in fact the voice of the community. Tom is not alone in facing this problem; all of us involved in historical Jesus research are. But because of his decision not to make a decision about earlier and later layers of the tradition, the problem in his case is more acute, it seems to me.

The work of a historian has often been compared to that of a detective: trying to figure out what happened. In detective work, there are three stages, sometimes done by the same person, but often done by separate persons. There is the work of the "street detective"—the gathering of all possible evidence, without a clear notion that all of it actually is evidence. Then there is the work of the "forensic detective"— analyzing the evidence gathered by the street detective. Third, there is the "hunching" stage—suggesting overall scenarios that make cumulative sense of the evidence. At both the forensic and hunching stages, some of the evidence gathered by the street detective may be seen not to be evidence after all. Of course, the stages are not completely independent of one another. A bad hunch may leave too much of the evidence unaccounted for and will need to be corrected by a hunch that makes sense of more of the evidence. But a hunch that is based on everything that the street detective has collected may also be seriously wrong.

The point of the analogy, I suspect, is obvious. By seeking to accommodate as much of the data as possible, Tom may be seeking to accommodate material that in fact is not evidence. And it seems to me that his claim that Jesus saw his own death as central to his messianic vocation may be using data that are likely to be the product of the community after Easter. But, of course, I could be wrong. We are always dealing with probability judgments.

And this leads to my final point. The Christian conviction that Jesus is the messiah cannot, it seems to me, be based on the probability judgment that Jesus thought he was. It is instead a confessional statement: in this person, I see the messiah (and the Son of God, the Wisdom of God, the Word of God, the light of the world, the way made flesh, and so forth). These affirmations need not be understood as facts about Jesus and his own sense of who he was. Rather, they are a commitment to see in the kind of person he was the decisive revelation of God and of what a life full of God is like.

## A VISION OF THE CHRISTIAN LIFE

In the rest of this chapter, I will describe a vision of the Christian life that flows out of my way of looking at Jesus and the gospels. As I do so, I am no longer speaking about differences between Tom and me; I am simply describing what I see as central implications for understanding and living the Christian life today.

### A Relational Understanding

I begin with a story. Each year at Oregon State University, I teach an introductory-level course on the Bible. From teaching the course for almost twenty years, I know that roughly 20 percent of the students will be very conservative in their attitude toward the Bible, either from their upbringing or because they are recent converts to conservative forms of college Christianity.

For the sake of these students, I use the first class period to explain as clearly as I can the vantage point from which the course will be taught: namely, the perspective of the academic discipline of biblical scholarship. I tell them about the history of the discipline since it began a few centuries ago and the way it sees things. I emphasize in particular that it does not see the Bible as divine in origin but as human, namely, as the product of two ancient communities. The Hebrew Bible is the product of ancient Israel, the Christian Testament is the product of the early Christian movement. As such, the Bible tells us not how God sees things, but how those two ancient communities saw things. It tells us about their life with God, as they saw it: about their convictions about God and about their understanding of the kind of life that flowed out of those convictions.

Finally, I tell the class that in order to understand the course and do well in it, they have to be willing to enter into this way of looking at the Bible. I tell them that they don't have to change their beliefs; they simply need to be willing to look at the Bible this way for the sake of the course. But, despite all of my careful explanation, the first two weeks of each term typically involve a fair amount of squabbling between me and the more bold and articulate of the conservative students.

A few years ago, a very bright Muslim engineering student took the course. A senior, he did so because he needed another humanities course for graduation and the course fit his schedule. One day, after witnessing the first few weeks of my interaction with the more conservative students, he said to me, "I think I understand what's going on here. You're saying the Bible is like a lens through which we see God, and they're saying that it's important to believe in the lens." And I said, "Yeah, that's what I'm saying."

Obviously, I very much liked his lens analogy: the Bible is a lens, and as a lens, it is not the object of belief but a means whereby we see. And from his analogy, I wish to draw two points that are central to the rest of this chapter.

The first is a relational understanding of the Christian life. I do not think being a Christian is primarily about believing. It is not about believing in the lens, but about entering a deepening relationship to that which we see through the lens. It is not about believing in the Bible or the gospels or Christian teachings about Jesus, but about a relationship to the One whom we see through the lens of the Christian tradition as a whole.

The notion that the central dynamic of the Christian life is "believing" is widespread in the modern world.

Our common religious questions, asked of one another and in public opinion polls, center on belief. "Do you believe in God?" "Do you believe the Bible is the Word of God?" "Do you believe Jesus is the Son of God?" "Do you believe Jesus was born of a virgin?" "Do you believe he will come again?"

Our preoccupation with believing is because many of the central teachings of Christianity have come into question in the modern world. Thinking of the Christian life as being primarily about believing in God, the Bible, and Jesus is thus a modern mistake, with profound consequences. Beliefs have little ability to change our lives. One can believe all the right things and remain a jerk, or worse. Saints have been heretical, and people with correct beliefs have been cruel oppressors and brutal persecutors. Rather, the Christian life is about a relationship to the God to whom the tradition points. What matters is the relationship, for it can and does and will transform our lives.

The second point I wish to draw from my student's analogy is what it means to see the Bible as a lens.[9] Through the lens of the Bible we see God. And because the Bible is not just about God, but about the divine-human relationship, through that lens we also see our life with God. To expand the metaphor to the Christian tradition as a whole: the Bible, Jesus, and central postbiblical traditions are a lens through which we see God and our relationship with God. What matters is not believing in the lens but seeing through the lens.

Or, to use a hearing metaphor for a moment, what matters is hearing the voice that speaks to us through the tradition, not believing in the tradition. Of course, the Bible contains a plurality of voices: in it, we hear the voices of the communities out of which it came and the voices of the writers who composed it. The voices sometimes conflict with one another, for the Bible is a human product: it contains voices of oppression and protest against oppression, voices of conventional wisdom and subversion of conventional wisdom. But in, with, and under those voices, we are to listen for and respond to the divine voice. What matters, as Buber put it, is that we hear the voice.

## JESUS AS LENS

In all of this, for us as Christians, Jesus is central. I define the Christian life most compactly as a relationship with God as revealed in Jesus Christ. A revelation is a disclosure: something is unveiled. A revelation is an epiphany: something is manifested. Language of revelation connects to seeing: something is revealed, and we behold it.

The core Christian christological affirmation is twofold: Jesus is, for us as Christians, the decisive revelation of what God is like and of what a life full of God is like. Jesus is the revelation, disclosure, and epiphany of both. As both "true God" and "true human," Jesus is a lens through which we see God and what a life full of God is like.

### WHAT GOD IS LIKE

As a lens through which we see God, Jesus enables us to see much. What we see is deeply Jewish. Everything that Jesus discloses about God is found in the Jewish tradition prior to him in the voices of Spirit persons like Moses and the prophets, psalmists, and teachers of a wisdom that challenged convention and tradition. In Jesus, those voices come together with particular power and eloquence. Or, to return to the sight metaphor, Jesus as a lens becomes a magnifying glass of what is most central about God.

1. God is near, at hand, and can be experienced. So Jesus' life as a Jewish mystic suggests. God is not a distant being "out there" but the one in whom we live and move and have our being.[10] God is "Spirit" in the rich biblical sense of the word. In both Hebrew and Greek, the word also means "wind" and "breath." God as Spirit is like the wind that moves around us and the breath that moves within us, both transcendent and immanent.

2. The near God is immediately accessible, apart from convention, tradition, and institution. Jesus' experience as a mystic, his activity as a healer, his wisdom teaching, and his inclusive community all point to this. The opposite is thinking of God as accessible only through the observance of sacred tradition and the mediation of sacred institution. The notion that God is accessible only through such mediation was widespread in Jesus'

day, as it has been also in the history of Christianity. Voices in both Jewish and Christain traditions have often claimed a monopoly on access to God, even as other voices in both traditions have challenged the claim. Jesus did so: he taught and embodied an unmediated relationship to the sacred. God was accessible to those who were "not much" or worse, including the radically marginalized and outcasts.

3. God is compassionate. Jesus embodied the compassion of God and taught that God is compassionate: be compassionate as God is compassionate. Compassion is not simply the will of God, but the very quality of God. God as compassionate is life giving, nourishing, embracing: God feeds the birds, clothes the lilies, makes the sun rise on the just and the unjust, and sends rain on the righteous and wicked. God as compassionate feels for us, for all of us, even the birds and the lilies, as a mother feels for the children of her womb. And like a mother who sees some of her children being victimized by others, God's compassion can become fierce. The compassion of God is commonly and more abstractly spoken of as the love of God. God is love—and it can be a fierce love.

4. God is passionate about justice. God's passion for justice is central to Moses and the prophets, voices of religious social protest against the domination systems of their day. Jesus stood in this stream of the Jewish tradition. God's passion for justice led Jesus to side with the poor and marginalized and to indict the religious and political elites, including Jerusalem and the temple as the center of the native domination system. Indeed, Jesus' passion for justice in the name of God was the cause of his death: he challenged and suffered the wrath of the powers.

### A Life Full of God

Jesus is also the decisive revelation of what a life full of God is like. He is the incarnation of the word and wisdom, the compassion and passion, of God. He is thus a lens through which we see what a life filled with God's Spirit looks like.

An ancient and widespread vision of the Christian life boldly affirms: we are to become like him. Known as the *imitatio Christi*, the imitation of Christ, this vision is central to the New Testament itself. Paul speaks of imitating Christ, and the gospel image of discipleship means "following after Jesus": taking seriously what Jesus took seriously.

What is it about Jesus that we are to imitate? Not everything, of course. To say that we should dress as he did or all become artisans or all become itinerants seems obviously foolish. It also seems obvious that imitating his marital status (assuming he was single) is not central to taking him seriously, even though some may be called to the single life.

Granting that not everything we can glimpse of him is to be imitated, what is to be? The vision of Jesus I have sketched suggests five characteristics as most central: a life centered in the Spirit, lived by an alternative wisdom, marked by compassion, concerned about justice, and lived within the alternative community of Jesus. The five are connected to one another.

A life centered in the Spirit means, of course, a life of relationship to God. To a large degree, the subversive and alternative wisdom of Jesus is an invitation to such a life. His wisdom teaching calls us to a life centered not in religious tradition or institution or convention, but in that which is beyond all of our domestications of reality: the One in whom we live and move and have our being. Life in the Spirit leads beyond convention to the still and wild place where God is known.

Life in the Spirit means that spirituality is one of the major focal points of the Christian life. Spirituality is entering into a *conscious* and *intentional* relationship to God. I emphasize *conscious* because we are already in a relationship with God and have been from our beginning, whether we realize that or not; spirituality is about becoming conscious of that relationship. *Intentional* means seeking to deepen the relationship with God, which happens in a variety of ways. It typically involves regular prayer, whether verbal or nonverbal, and perhaps other traditional spiritual practices. It also happens through worship that manifestly mediates the Spirit, whether the charismatic worship of Pentecostals, the silent gatherings of Quakers, or the sacramental worship of more liturgical traditions. What matters is opening to the Spirit.

A deepening relationship to the Spirit is transforming. It transforms our sense of identity. We are not simply or primarily who our cultural conventions say we are. It can liberate us from the anxieties and preoc-cupations that mark so much of our lives. It is a source of courage as well as endurance. It enables us to face suffering in a new way.

Life in the Spirit transforms our relationship to the world of the everyday. Our sense of moral responsibility—our ethic—is strongly af-fected by how we see. A deepening relationship to the Spirit leads us to see everybody and everything (though not everything that happens) as a manifestation of the Spirit—in more traditional Christian language, as created by God. Seeing all that is as a manifestation of the Spirit does not blot out differences—but we can momentarily see, and can stead-fastly know, "what is" without the valuations imposed by culture.

There is such seeing, and it awakens compassion: we see people and nature itself as creations of God, and we are led to be compassionate as God is compassionate. It is how Jesus saw, and how mystics and saints in all traditions saw: the Buddha, Paul, and St. Francis; in our own cen-tury, Martin Buber, Thomas Merton, and Mother Teresa. The Spirit leads us to see other people not in cultural categories of attractive and unattractive, successful and unsuccessful, interesting and uninterest-ing, deserving and undeserving. It leads us to see that common cate-gories of "good behavior" and "bad behavior," and thus of "good people" and "bad people," are very often simply based on deeply in-grained cultural convention.

Life in the Spirit grounded in the wisdom of Jesus does not mean the complete rejection of convention. We cannot live without conven-tional wisdom; I am grateful that people stop at stop signs and that cannibalism is a taboo so that I don't have to wonder if somebody is looking at me as their potential supper. But the kind of conventional wisdom we affirm matters greatly. Neither can we live without institu-tions, though of course the structures and ends of our institutions mat-ter greatly. Similarly, religious tradition understood as a lens or pointer to the sacred serves the very important function of mediating the sa-cred; it is only when it is mistaken as "the thing itself" that it becomes a snare and even idolatrous.

A vision of the Christian life that takes Jesus seriously awakens not only compassion but also a passion for justice. Like those who stood in the Jewish prophetic tradition before him, Jesus knew that the desperation of peasant life flowed from systemic injustice. Destitution and degradation, in his world and ours, are neither natural nor inevitable but are the product of domination systems created and maintained by the rich and powerful to serve their own interests. Such structures are neither ordained by God nor mandated by scarcity.

Compassion thus includes social justice. Of course, compassion is a virtue for individuals, but compassion that does not see that much of the world's misery flows from systemic injustice is a compassion that is still partially blind. We are called to become politically aware as well as loving. "The dream of God," to use Verna Dozier's wonderful phrase for the sociopolitical vision of the Bible, is the kingdom of God: what life in this world would be like if God were king, and the rulers of the present age were not.[11]

Life in the Spirit is also life in community. The vision of Jesus is not individualistic, even though of course individuals mattered to him. Like the Jewish tradition in which he stood, he saw the covenant with God as not simply about our relationship to God, but also about our relationship with one another. The community that gathered around him, enacted in his open meal practice, was both symbol and reality: it embodied his inclusive social vision, even as it also met genuine human needs for sustenance and belonging. For us today, life in the community of Jesus nourishes life in the Spirit. Our worship together celebrates and mediates the reality of God, our learning together draws us deeper into the way of Jesus, and our acting together seeks to incarnate "the dream of God," namely, compassion and justice in the world of the everyday.

A vision of the Christian life that takes Jesus seriously would not be very much concerned with the afterlife. Jesus' message was not about how to get to heaven. The widespread impression that it was grew, to a large extent, out of a misunderstanding of two phrases in the gospels: the Jesus of Matthew's gospel regularly speaks about "the kingdom of heaven," and the Jesus of John's gospel often speaks of "eternal life." But both phrases meant something different from what they convey in English. Matthew used "kingdom of heaven" for Mark's "kingdom of God" because he shared a common Jewish reverential reluctance to use the word *God*. The phrase thus really means "kingdom of God." In

John, "eternal life" translates a phrase that means "life of the age to come," not "life in heaven." Moreover, John sometimes speaks of "the life of the age to come" as a present reality, not simply as a state we can enter into after death.

My point is not that Jesus didn't believe in an afterlife. He seems to have. But he didn't talk about it very much. On one occasion, he spoke about it because somebody else brought it up. He was asked about the woman who had been married to seven husbands: in the afterlife, whose wife will she be? His response suggested that the afterlife is radically different from what the question presupposed.[12] Jesus did not often bring up the subject himself, and when he did, he typically subverted common understandings of it.[13]

My point is also not to deny an afterlife. But it wasn't central to Jesus' teaching. The vision of the Christian life that flows out of taking him seriously is about a relationship with the Spirit of God that transforms our lives in the present, not about a reward that only comes later. It is the vision of Christian life that Paul wrote about with evocative and extravagant eloquence: "And we all, with unveiled faces, beholding the glory of the Lord, are being transformed into the likeness of Christ, from one degree of glory to another. And this comes from The Lord, who is the Spirit."[14] Beholding the radiant presence of God, we are transformed by the Spirit into the likeness of Christ.

## The Gospels as Lens

In much of this book, I have treated the gospels as sources for constructing a historical understanding of Jesus. That is the nature of the quest for the historical Jesus. I have also affirmed the importance of the gospels as the testimony of the early Christian movement to what Jesus had become in their lives. Now I want to underline their centrality for the Christian life today.

In the history of Jesus scholarship, scholars have sometimes put the historical Jesus and the Jesus of the gospels in opposition to each other. Some have argued that the gospels (and the rest of the New Testament, especially Paul) have fundamentally distorted Jesus of Nazareth and his message. Their message has been, "Choose the historical Jesus, not the

Jesus of the gospels." Critics of the quest have often responded by emphasizing the opposite choice: "Choose the Jesus of the gospels, not the historical Jesus."

Both advocates and critics thus have sometimes seen the issue as a sharp either-or choice. I am not among them. I see it as a both-and affirmation. The historical Jesus and the canonical gospels both matter. Both are normative for the Christian life.

But the gospels have become a problem for many Christians in the modern period. Many things in the gospels stretch our sense of what is possible, often beyond the breaking point. Fundamentalist Christians see the same difficulty and respond by insisting that faith means believing the gospels (and the Bible as a whole) to be literally and factually true. Indeed, one could almost define their understanding of faith as "believing that which doesn't make sense." Most mainline Christians cannot accept this option, but many are unsure what to do with the gospels and the Bible. Believe the parts that do make sense? Rescue a few facts from the fire?

As part of my vision of the Christian life, I suggest a way of hearing the gospels that neither depends on hearing them as literally and factually true nor reduces them to a few facts rescued from the fire. Namely, we need to develop the ability to hear the gospels (and the Bible as a whole) in a state of *postcritical naïveté*. It is a state beyond the childhood stage of *precritical naïveté* and the adolescent and adult stage of *critical thinking*.[15]

These quite technical sounding phrases are greatly illuminating. To illustrate what they mean, think of any biblical story that narrates a spectacular event: the story of Noah and the flood, the Exodus story with its plagues and parting of the sea, the stories of Jesus walking on the water and feeding the multitude, the birth stories. Those of us who grew up in the church first heard these stories as young children in a state of precritical naïveté. In that state, we took it for granted that they really happened the way they were told.

To speak from my own experience, when I heard the Christmas stories as a child, I took it for granted that Jesus really was born of a virgin and that there really were a magic star, wise men, birth in a stable, angels singing to the shepherds, and so forth. It didn't occur to me to wonder, "Now, did these things really happen, or are these stories metaphorical narratives?" Nor did it take faith to believe them; I had no reason to think otherwise. I simply heard them as true stories.

Then we enter the stage of critical thinking, which involves evaluating things we believed and were taught in childhood. The process happens naturally; we do not decide deliberately to do it, and nobody has to tell us to do so. If we grew up with Santa Claus and the tooth fairy, we early on let go of them. If we grew up with the Bible, the process eventually affects our attitude toward it as well. We begin to wonder if the biblical stories really happened the way they're told. It begins to take faith to believe them. We may even become convinced that they didn't happen. But whether that happens or whether we simply have serious doubts, we are no longer able to hear them as true stories.

In our time, this stage is intensified and is often prolonged by the modern identification of truth with factuality. To use language I used in chapter 1, skeptics and biblical literalists alike in the modern world are often "fact fundamentalists": if something didn't happen, it isn't true. Although the progression from precritical naïveté to critical thinking is virtually automatic, moving beyond the skepticism of a critical mode of thinking wedded to the modern worldview is not. Many people get stuck in this stage, sometimes for their whole lives.

Beyond critical thinking is postcritical naïveté. Put simply, postcritical naïveté is the ability to hear the central stories of the Christian tradition once again as true stories. Importantly, postcritical naïveté is not a return to precritical naïveté, for one knows that the stories may not be historically factual. But one also knows that their truth does not depend upon their historical factuality.

It is the ability to affirm, in words I have often quoted from a Native American storyteller, "I don't know if it happened this way or not, but I know this story is true." It is the ability to hear the Christmas stories once again as true stories, as we did when we were children, even as we know that they are almost certainly not historical narratives. As T. S. Eliot wrote:

> And the end of all our exploring
> will be to arrive where we started
> and know the place for the first time.

Hearing the gospels in a state of post-critical naïveté is similar to what is often called "narrative theology." But unlike some advocates of narrative theology who declare the bankruptcy of the historical-critical method, post-critical naïveté as I understand it affirms insights from the historical-critical stage and integrates them into a larger paradigm. We need to be liberated from the tyranny of the historical-critical method, but we deceive ourselves if we think we can simply abandon it. A post-critical reading does not disavow the critical, but brings the critical with it.

Without using the phrase earlier in this book, I have already provided many examples of reading the gospels in a state of post-critical naïveté. Among them are the Christmas stories, just mentioned and treated more fully in chapter 12. Reading the community's interpretations of the death and resurrection of Jesus in the ways that I suggest in chapter 8 provides another example. So also the Emmaus Road story: I hear it as a true story, though I do not think that it reports a particular event on a particular afternoon.

Hearing the gospel of John's language about Jesus as "the bread of life" as true is yet another. As a Christian, I know that Jesus is the bread of life, independently of whether Jesus ever fed a multitude with a few loaves and fishes, and independently of whether he ever said this about himself. We live in a tradition which speaks of abundance and not scarcity, and of meals in the wilderness on our path to liberation. We are fed by spiritual food, even as the gospels' emphasis on material food for embodied people reminds us that the gospel is not simply about spiritual food.

Because I combine historical Jesus research with a metaphorical and narrative reading of the gospels, I can affirm that both the historical Jesus and the canonical Jesus matter. One does not need to choose between the two.

## Living Within the Tradition

Postcritical naïveté provides a way of hearing the gospel stories of Jesus as deeply true. The gospels and the Bible generally are full of stories whose truth is known in Christian experience. We live in a tradition that speaks of the oppressed being set free, exiles coming home, blind people seeing, deaf people hearing, the paralyzed and lame being able to walk again, life coming out of death, light shining in the darkness, a banquet at which the wine never runs out and the best is saved for last. Being a Christian involves living within this tradition and letting it shape our lives. It means letting these stories have their way with us.

The lens metaphor I have been using throughout this chapter needs to be modified slightly but importantly. Ultimately, I think of the Christian tradition not simply as a lens, but as a sacrament. A sacrament is a means of grace, a mediator of the sacred. More than a lens through which we see, the tradition is also a sacrament that mediates to us that which we behold. If we let these stories shape our understanding of reality, life, and ourselves, they begin to mediate the life of which they speak and lead us into that life. Within this framework, being Christian is not about believing, but about a relationship with the God who is sacramentally mediated to us through the Christian tradition in a comprehensive sense of the word: the Bible, the gospels, Jesus himself, and the worship and practices of our life together in Christian community.

Celtic Christianity speaks of "thin places." The metaphor has its home in a vision of reality that affirms that reality has at least two layers or levels or dimensions: the visible world of our ordinary experience, and the sacred, understood not only as the source of everything but also as a presence interpenetrating everything. In "thin places" the boundary between the two levels becomes soft and permeable, the veil becomes diaphanous and sometimes lifts. Jesus was a "thin place," as are the stories and practices of the tradition that remembers and celebrates him. Through these ways and more, the living Christ comes to us and transforms our lives, even today.

# ○ NOTES

---

## CHAPTER 1

1. For a more extended treatment of the subject of this chapter, see chap. 8 of my *Jesus at 2000* (Boulder, CO: Westview, 1997), 121–47.

2. Instead of "history metaphorized," I could say "history interpreted," for the function of metaphor in the gospels is interpretation. But I prefer the former phrase, for the language of interpretation in the gospels is primarily metaphorical and not yet conceptual. With Paul Ricoeur, I see metaphor (or symbol and story) as the first language of religious experience, with conceptualization second.

3. Metaphor simultaneously affirms and negates: x is y, x is not y. To use an obvious example: when I say, "My love is a red, red rose," I am affirming that my love is a rose, even as (of course) my love is not a rose. And though no one thinks the statement means that I am in love with a flower, it can nevertheless be heard as a true statement about my love for my beloved.

4. To illustrate: the central section of Mark's gospel (8.27–10.45) treats the "way" of Jesus and what it means to follow him. Mark frames it with two stories of sight being given to blind people: the blind man of Bethsaida in 8.22–26, and blind Bartimaeus in 10.46–52 (whose passionate petition is, "I want to see again"). This framing suggests that seeing the way of Jesus is like having one's sight restored. The point: Mark's arrangement of the material results in history metaphorized, even though there may be a historical basis to the stories.

5. It is important to realize that Jesus himself used metaphor, and used it often. The presence of metaphor in a saying and story thus does not in itself mean that it does not go back to Jesus.

6. Albert Nolan, *Jesus Before Christianity* (Maryknoll: Orbis Books, 1978), 117.

7. For the fullest development of his interdisciplinary approach, see John Dominic Crossan, *The Historical Jesus: The Life of a Mediterranean Jewish Peasant* (San Francisco: HarperSanFrancisco, 1991).

8. For a fuller treatment of this subject, see my essay "Root Images and the Way We See," in *Jesus in Contemporary Scholarship* (Valley Forge, PA: Trinity Press International, 1994), 127–39.

9. Commonly, individuals will have the worldview of their culture; the process of socialization involves internalizing one's culture's understanding of what is real.

10. See W. T. Stace, *Religion and the Modern Mind* (Philadelphia: Lippincott, 1952), 10: "In the majority of people, it [our worldview] works unseen, a dim background in their minds, unnoticed by themselves because taken for granted."

11. To use Huston Smith's apt phrase, it has turned us into "fact fundamentalists." See his essay in *Jesus at 2000* (Boulder, CO: Westview, 1997), 116–17.

12. For an exceptionally fine treatment of the contrast between the modern worldview and the worldview of virtually every other culture in history, see Huston Smith, *Forgotten Truth* (San Francisco: HarperSanFrancisco, 1976; reprint, 1992).

13. This has already happened in postmodern science. Indeed, one can make a good case that postmodern science and religion not only agree that there is "more than this," but that "the more" is a *stupendous more*. See Smith, *Forgotten Truth,* chapter 5.

14. Though I accept the existence of Q, I am skeptical that we can separate Q into redactional layers (some scholars speak of Q1, Q2, Q3). I am even more skeptical about constructing further hypotheses based upon a layering of Q.

15. For a significant minority point of view that disputes both the priority of Mark and the existence of Q, see W. R. Farmer, *The Gospel of Jesus* (Louisville, KY: Westminster/John Knox 1994). Farmer and his colleagues argue that Matthew is the earliest gospel, that Luke used Matthew, and that Mark used both Matthew and Luke (and is thus the latest of the synoptics, rather than the earliest).

16. I thus do not agree with those who argue for a sharp either-or choice between the two. Some Jesus scholars do this, explicitly or implicitly affirming that *only* the historical Jesus matters. Some critics of Jesus scholarship also do this by affirming the opposite choice: *only* the canonical Jesus matters, not the historical Jesus.

## CHAPTER 2

1. After writing this paragraph I discovered remarkably similar sentiments in Richard A. Horsley, ed., *Paul and Empire: Religion and Power in Roman Imperial Society* (Harrisburg, PA: Trinity Press International, 1997), 2.
2. cf. N. T. Wright, *The New Testament and the People of God*, vol. 1 of *Christian Origins and the Question of God* (Minneapolis: Fortress, 1992), 98–109.
3. N. T. Wright, *Jesus and the Victory of God*, vol. 2 of *Christian Origins and the Question of God* (Minneapolis: Fortress, 1996).
4. George B. Caird, *The Language and Imagery of the Bible*, 2d ed. (Grand Rapids: Eerdmans, 1997), 271.
5. See, for example, N. T. Wright, "Doing Justice to Jesus: A Response to J. D. Crossan, 'What Victory? What God?'" *Scottish Journal of Theology* 50, no. 3 (1997): 359–79.
6. Philippians 3.10.
7. John 10.14.

## CHAPTER 3

1. It is clearly impossible to argue in detail for all the positions I will state in this brief treatment. Full argument and documentation can be found in N. T. Wright, *The New Testament and the People of God*, vol. 1 of *Christian Origins and the Question of God* (Minneapolis: Fortress, 1992), and *Jesus and the Victory of God*, vol. 2 of *Christian Origins and the Question of God* (Minneapolis: Fortress, 1996). On Jesus' own beliefs, see particularly *Jesus and the Victory of God*, 651f.
2. This includes the scrolls, whose writers saw their own little group as the advance guard of the real "return." Thus, precisely because they thought that "return" was already beginning with them, they bore witness to the prevailing belief that it hadn't happened yet. On the whole theme of exile and return in second-temple Judaism, see *The New Testament and the People of God*, 268–70; *Jesus and the Victory of God*, xviif.; and copious references in both places.
3. For Jesus as a prophet, see *Jesus and the Victory of God*, chap. 5.
4. For the details, compare *The New Testament and the People of God*, 302–7, and *Jesus and the Victory of God*, chap. 6, esp. 202–9.
5. *Antiquities* 18.4–10, 23–5; cf. *The New Testament and the People of God*, 173, 302–7.
6. Alluding to the messianic prophecy of Numbers 24.17 (the star that would come forth from Jacob).

7. Mishnah, Aboth 3.5; cf. *NTPG*, 199.

8. This raises the question of Jesus' literacy. In common with the great majority of scholars, I assume that Jesus could and did read the Hebrew scriptures. The Jews' deep attachment to their scriptures make them the exception to the normal expectations about peasant illiteracy—even supposing Jesus really was a peasant.

9. There is no equivalent, in this period, to what happened when Solomon dedicated the temple, when the glory of YHWH filled the house (1 Kings 8.10–11; 2 Chronicles 5.13; 7.2; cf. Isaiah 6.4).

10. On the parables in this light, see *Jesus and the Victory of God*, 174–82; and, for examples, 125–31 (the prodigal son); 230–39 (the sower), etc.

11. For this point, see *Jesus and the Victory of God*, 467–72. The Jewish evidence does not lead me to agree with Marcus that the kingdom of God can be reduced to terms of God's power, presence, or social program.

12. They backdated it to 1792, when the critical liberating events were regarded as having taken place.

13. On this section see the full discussion in *Jesus and the Victory of God*, chap. 7.

14. Compare Josephus, *Life* 110, with the discussion in *Jesus and the Victory of God*, 250f.

15. I have explored this further in my article "Jesus" in *Early Christian Thought in Its Jewish Context*, ed. John Barclay and John Sweet (Cambridge: Cambridge Univ. Press), 43–58, esp. 50–52.

16. Matthew 8.11. For this theme, see *Jesus and the Victory of God*, 308–10, 431.

17. For what follows, see esp. *Jesus and the Victory of God*, chap. 8.

18. See *Jesus and the Victory of God*, 339–67.

19. cf. *The New Testament and the People of God*, 291–97; *Jesus and the Victory of God*, 360–65, 510–19.

20. For example, 1 Kings 18.17; Amos 7.10–13.

21. On the whole topic, see *Jesus and the Victory of God*, chap. 9, where I discuss in detail the possible objections to my view and explain particularly the relationship between Jesus and the Pharisees, for which there is no space here.

22. What about the "den of thieves" (Mark 11.17 and parallels)? Here I gladly acknowledge the illumination of Marcus Borg's *Conflict, Holiness, and Politics in the Teaching of Jesus* (Harrisburg, PA: Trinity Press International, 1998), 181–89. As so often, the context of the relevant Old Testament quotation (in this case Jeremiah 7.3–15) is all-important. Jeremiah was not advocating a reform of the temple; he was predicting its destruction. The Greek word *lestes,* here translated "thieves," is in fact the regular word used by Josephus to denote "brigands" or "rebels." The temple had become the focal point for

the nationalists in their eagerness for revolt against Rome, as well as for the rich and powerful in their oppression of the rest of the nation. How could it then symbolize, as Isaiah had said it should, the desire of Israel's god that it should become the beacon of hope and light for the nations, the city set on a hill that could not be hidden?

23. Matthew 16.14.
24. *Rule of the Congregation* (usually known as 1Qsa) 2.3–11.
25. Healing and restoration are joined together in various biblical passages, for example, Isa. 35.
26. *The New Testament and the People of God,* 234f.
27. Zechariah 8.19.
28. Mark 2.19f.
29. Deducing things from Jesus' central actions is not, then, an inference merely. Again and again, what he did was more important than what he said. As I have argued in *Jesus and the Victory of God,* chap. 11, Jesus' central symbolic actions spoke louder and clearer than words could have done. If we are sitting patiently awaiting a lecturer, and someone comes into the room and begins to lecture, she does not need to begin by saying, "I am the lecturer." The performative claim is all the more powerful for being unspoken. I have argued, further, that Jesus' central messianic acts—his entry into Jerusalem and cleansing of the temple—were surrounded by several "messianic riddles," whose form and content proclaim powerfully that they must be original to Jesus and must bear this significance.
30. *Messiah* is not, of course, a divine predicate, however much later Christian usage has muddied that bit of water.
31. Historians are of course at liberty to employ "etic" approaches, projecting categories from outside the culture onto a culture that did not describe itself in those ways; but these usually need balancing with an "emic" approach, discovering the categories that the culture itself used. When we do this, we come up again and again, when studying Jesus, with the first-century Jewish categories of "prophet" and "messiah."
32. *Life* 110.
33. On the meanings of *eschatology,* see *Jesus and the Victory of God,* 207–9.

CHAPTER 4

1. To avoid a possible misunderstanding: I am not arguing that Jesus *became* messiah, Son of God, and so forth, only after Easter, a position known in the history of theology as "adoptionism." Rather, I am speaking about *when such language was first used* about Jesus. Thus my point here is not ontological but, rather, concerns a chronological sequence in the use of language.

2. Decisive, but not exclusive. That is, I do not think that Jesus is the only or only adequate disclosure of the sacred; I am convinced that the sacred is known in all of the world's major religious traditions. The affirmation that Jesus is the ultimate disclosure of God defines what it means to be Christian, but need not mean that God has not been disclosed elsewhere. For more on this point, see my chapter on Christology.

3. Mark 8.27–30.

4. *Christ* and *messiah* are synonyms. *Messiah* is the English form of Hebrew *mashiah,* and *Christ* is the English form of *christos,* the Greek word used to translate *mashiah.*

5. To guard against a misunderstanding: the subject comes up again in Mark's story of Jesus' trial. Mark 14.62 reports that Jesus apparently responded affirmatively to the high priest's question, "Are you the messiah, the Son of the blessed?" I am skeptical that this text has a historical basis (see my next chapter). But even if one accepted it as historical, it would not affect what is most central to the claim I am making: an explicit messianic claim was not part of Jesus' own teaching in Mark. The subject comes up only at the end of his life, and then not in public.

6. Matthew 16.16–17. The text continues with the designation of Peter as "the rock" upon which Jesus will build his church, and the giving of "the keys of the kingdom of heaven" to Peter. All of this is part of Matthew's addition to Mark.

7. Mark 6.45–52.

8. Matthew 14.32.

9. This is very different from Mark, who never portrays people worshiping Jesus and even reports that Jesus rebuffed the description of him as "good": "Why do you call me good? No one is good but God alone" (Mark 10.17–18). It is interesting to note how Matthew changes this verse as he copies Mark: Matthew has Jesus say, "Why do you ask me about what is good?" (Matthew 19.17).

10. John's gospel contains the great "I am" sayings ("the light of the world," "bread of life," "the way, truth and life," etc.) and statements like "I and the Father are one" and "Whoever has seen me has seen God." Most mainline scholars do not see these self-affirmations as going back to Jesus himself but view them rather as the product of John's community. I note that Tom also does not use Jesus' self-statements in John in his treatment of the historical Jesus.

11. A further reason why messianic self-awareness does not play a role in my sketch of Jesus: even if there were persuasive evidence that Jesus thought of himself as the messiah, it wouldn't tell us much. The word means "anointed

by God" and was associated with the hope for a deliverer; but beyond that, there was no generally accepted notion in first-century Judaism of what the messiah would be like. It is therefore a relatively empty category, which would need to be filled by what we know of Jesus.

12. I am referring to what commonly happens, and not to Tom's position in particular.

13. Mark begins here, as does Q. So do the summaries of early Christian preaching in the book of Acts, as well as the gospel of John.

14. Some argue that the word translated as "carpenter" can mean "stone cutter." In either case, Jesus would have been an artisan. Artisans in that world were not middle-class; rather, they came from families who had lost their land. Thus artisan families were generally more marginalized than peasant families who still owned a piece of land.

15. Sepphoris had also been a center of the Jewish revolts that broke out at the death of Herod the Great in 4 B.C.E. Partially destroyed by the Romans as they put down the rebellion, it was rebuilt by Herod's son Herod Antipas shortly thereafter. Historians have speculated that Joseph and perhaps Jesus may have worked there. Herod Antipas later built the city of Tiberias, beginning in 19 C.E., which then replaced Sepphoris as the capital of Galilee.

16. Especially compared to other religious founders: the public activity of the Buddha, Confucius, and Muhammad lasted decades.

17. When pressed for an even more compact summary, I reduce the five-stroke sketch to three phrases: there was to Jesus the Jew a spirit dimension, a wisdom dimension, and a social-political dimension.

18. William James, *The Varieties of Religious Experience*, first published in 1902 and available in a variety of editions. The distinction between firsthand religious experience and secondhand religious belief is the premise of the book as a whole and is explicitly treated near the end of chap. 1.

19. My statement is not initially ontological but phenomenological: my claim is simply that some people have experiences that seem manifestly to them to be experiences of the sacred. Whether these experiences are to be understood as disclosures of the way things really are—that is, as ontological—is a separate question. My own answer to that question is yes. But a yes answer is not a prerequisite for taking such experiences seriously.

20. How broadly or narrow to define mystical experience is a matter of choice. Some scholars of mysticism define it as one major category of religious experience and distinguish it from personal encounter with the sacred, such as visions and shamanic journeys. Others include visions and shamanic journeys. There is value in both a narrower and broader definition, and I use the term in both senses: inclusively, to include visions and shamanic

journeys, and also more narrowly to refer to experiences marked by a sense of communion or union.

21. The great twentieth-century scholar of religions Mircea Eliade refers to the "other world" of religious experience as "the Golden World." Cited by Robert A. Johnson (with Jerry M. Ruhl) in his newest book, *Balancing Heaven and Earth* (San Francisco: HarperSanFrancisco, 1998), 2; it is the central metaphor of Johnson's opening chapter, in which he describes his own experiences of "the golden world."

22. For a fuller treatment of such experiences, see my *The God We Never Knew* (San Francisco: HarperSanFrancisco, 1997), 39–41.

23. James, *Varieties of Religious Experience,* chap. 16.

24. Though James does not include "transformative" in his four defining characteristics, it is implicit and is treated explicitly in his description of "saintliness" as the mature fruit of religious experience.

25. Panentheism and dialectical theism are alternative terms for a root concept of God that affirms both transcendence and immanence. The Greek roots of *panentheism* point to a way of thinking about this: *pan*(everything) *en*(in) *theos* (God). That is, rather than thinking of God as a being separate from the universe, panentheism affirms that the universe (everything that is) is in God. God is not somewhere else; rather, God is the encompassing Spirit in which everything that is is. Importantly, panentheism is very different from pantheism, which affirms only the immanence of God: God is present in everything, but not more than everything. For these terms and fuller development, see my *The God We Never Knew,* chap. 2.

26. Anglican theologian Kenneth Leech refers to God as a separate supernatural being as "the god of conventional western theism," *Experiencing God: Theology as Spirituality* (San Francisco: Harper and Row, 1985), p.7. I note that supernatural theism exists in both a deist and interventionist form. The former affirms a distant God who in the beginning created a universe separate from God, which now operates in accord with natural laws set up by God. But God has done nothing since. The interventionist form accepts this basic model, and simply adds to it that God does occasionally intervene from "out there," especially in the dramatic events reported in the biblical tradition, and perhaps to this day.

27. Thus dialectical theism or panentheism has a better claim to be orthodox than does supernatural theism.

28. The pattern is also widespread across the developing traditions of early Christianity. Luke very deliberately portrays Jesus as a Spirit person: Jesus' first public words in Luke are, "The Spirit of the Lord is upon me" (Luke 4.18). The gospel of Thomas portrays Jesus as teaching the kind of wisdom

characteristic of one who has had an enlightenment experience. The gospel of John (known from the late second century as "the spiritual gospel") is shaped by a mystical sensitivity.

29. For a compact treatment of the issues raised in this whole section, see my *Jesus: A New Vision* (San Francisco: Harper and Row, 1987), chap. 4, 57–75. For an extended treatment with superb footnotes and bibliography, see John Meier, *A Marginal Jew: Rethinking the Historical Jesus*, vol. 2 (New York: Doubleday, 1994), 507–1038.

30. Josephus, *Jewish Antiquities* 18.3.3 (written around 90 C.E.), provides the earliest non-Christian reference to Jesus and the only one from the first century. His full statement reads: "At this time there appeared Jesus, a wise man. For he was a doer of startling deeds, a teacher of people who receive the truth with pleasure. And he gained a following both among Jews and among many of Greek origin. And when Pilate, because of an accusation made by the leading men among us, condemned him to the cross, those who loved him previously did not cease to do so. And up until this very day the tribe of Christians (named after him) has not died out." For a careful and persuasive case for the authenticity of this text, see John Meier, *A Marginal Jew: Rethinking the Historical Jesus*, vol 1 (New York: Doubleday, 1991), pp. 56-88.

31. Mark 1.32–34, 1.39, 3.10.

32. Because John's gospel is not very much "history remembered," it is not included here. John has no exorcisms, though it does have a few healing stories.

33. Called "leprosy" in the gospels, but not the same as modern leprosy, which we know as "Hansen's disease."

34. About a second category of "mighty deeds," commonly called "nature miracles" (including walking on water, stilling a storm, multiplying loaves and fishes, and changing water into wine), my historical judgment and the judgment of mainline scholars generally is negative. Most see them as symbolic or metaphorical narratives, primarily because the stories manifestly make use of an inherited religious tradition, namely, language and symbols derived from the Hebrew Bible. They are history metaphorized and not history remembered. Thus I do not think these stories happened, but as metaphorical narratives I find them to be powerfully and persuasively true stories. See my *Jesus: A New Vision*, 67–70.

35. Most basically: it presumes that God is "out there" and not normally here, with all the theological and intellectual problems created by that view; and it leaves impossibly unexplained why, if God sometimes intervenes, God does not do so more often. How does one explain the noninterventions? If,

for example, God could have intervened to stop the Holocaust but chose not to do so, what does that imply about God? Is that an acceptable notion of God? The issue is not the reality of God or of God's involvement with the world, but whether it makes sense to think of God with an interventionist model.

36. Matthew 12.28 = Luke 11.20.

37. Matthew 11.4 = Luke 7.22. I am uncertain whether this saying goes back to Jesus. At the very least, however, it indicates how the mighty deeds of Jesus were seen by the time of Q: as signs that the time of deliverance spoken of by Isaiah had arrived.

38. A major theme of Crossan's work. See in particular *The Historical Jesus: The Life of a Mediterranean Jewish Peasant* (San Francisco: HarperSanFrancisco, 1991), esp. pp. 303–353; and *Jesus: A Revolutionary Biography* (San Francisco: HarperSanFrancisco, 1994), pp. 75–101.

39. Though there are important differences between Jesus and the Buddha, I think their understandings of "the way" are very similar. See *Jesus and Buddha: The Parallel Sayings,* ed. Marcus Borg and Ray Riegert (Berkeley: Ulysses Press, 1997), esp. v–xvii.

40. In one sense, culture is tradition, so that they are synonyms. Yet culture can be broader than tradition, for a given culture can contain multiple traditions.

41. A clarification about my use of the word *new* here. I do not mean new in the sense of hitherto unknown within Judaism, for I think this way was known in Judaism prior to the time of Jesus. Rather, I mean new in the life of a person: a transformation from an old way of seeing and being to a new way of seeing and being.

42. Many sayings in Jesus' wisdom teaching express this understanding: treasures on earth versus treasures in heaven; serving God or serving mammon; emptying oneself versus exalting oneself; saving and losing one's life. In the New Testament as a whole, a central metaphor for the process of de-centering and recentering is death and resurrection, taking up one's cross, and being born anew. Whether some of this imagery goes back to Jesus or whether it is all a post-Easter creation, it crystallizes this dimension of his wisdom teaching: his way involved dying to an old life and being born into a new life, brought about through a radical centering in God.

43. Luke 6.36. The language of perfection in the parallel in Matt. 5.48 is probably Matthew's redaction.

44. Amos 1.2, 3.8, 7.15.

45. Walter Wink, *Engaging the Powers* (Minneapolis: Fortress, 1992); and *The Powers That Be* (New York: Doubleday, 1998).

46. Walter Brueggemann, *The Prophetic Imagination* (Philadelphia: Fortress Press, 1978), chap. 1. For my own more extended exposition, see *Meeting Jesus Again,* chap. 3; *Jesus in Contemporary Scholarship* (Valley Forge, PA: Trinity Press International, 1994), chap. 5; and *Conflict, Holiness and Politics in the Teaching of Jesus* (Harrisburg, PA: Trinity Press International, 1998), esp. pp. 10–16.

47. Compare Luke 6.20–26 with Matthew 5.3–6.

48. The application of this message to reasonably well-to-do people in the very different social world of modern society is unclear. See chapter 6 in my *The God We Never Knew.*

49. There is sharp disagreement about this among contemporary Jesus scholars. Ed Sanders and Paula Fredriksen in particular have argued that I have seriously misunderstood Jewish purity laws, and that they were not much of an issue for Jesus. For more about this, see my introduction to the paperback edition of *Conflict, Holiness, and Politics,* pp. 8–10.

50. We differ considerably in what it means to say this.

51. For my reasons, see esp. chapters 3 and 4 of my *Jesus in Contemporary Scholarship.*

52. Luke 17.21, Thomas 113. A similar note is sounded in Thomas 3: "The Kingdom of God is within you, and outside you." Not everybody accepts the Thomas sayings as going back to Jesus, of course. For me, their similarity to Luke 17.21 and their consistency with my understanding of Jesus as a mystic count in their favor.

53. I owe this way of putting it to John Dominic Crossan. It is a frequent theme of his work.

### CHAPTER 5

1. John 3.16, quoted in the non-gender-inclusive language in which most of us first heard it.

2. Mark 8.31. The other two predictions of the passion are in Mark 9.31 and 10.33–34. Matthew and Luke also make these predictions central to their story of Jesus' final journey to Jerusalem.

3. Luke 24.25–27.

4. 1 Corinthians 15.3. This letter was written around 54 C.E. Paul's conversion experience on the Damascus Road probably happened within three years or so of Jesus' death. Thus, if this tradition goes back to what Paul was told soon after his conversion, we are here in touch with very early tradition indeed.

5. Chap. 8.

6. I mention "majority" not to give my own position authority, but simply to let readers know that my position is not idiosyncratic. Of course, majorities

can be wrong, and I have often disagreed with majority opinions myself.

7. In Luke 24.21, after recounting the death of Jesus, the two disciples on the Emmaus Road say, "But we had hoped that he was the one to redeem Israel." So also in Mark: the way Jesus' followers react during Jesus' arrest and execution suggests that the death of Jesus took them by surprise.

8. From Tom's chapter six.

9. Tom thus locates the germ of Christian atonement theology in the intention of Jesus himself. He does not attribute the fully-developed atonement theology of later Christian thought to Jesus, in which Jesus is understood as having made the necessary sacrifice which makes it possible for God to forgive sins. But he is saying that a very Jewish understanding of atonement on behalf of others was present in the mind of Jesus.

10. I can accept that Jesus might have believed some strange things, and that he was wrong about some things; but I have trouble accepting that strange convictions were at the center of his life. The difficulty I have with Tom's understanding is in some ways the same difficulty I have with Ed Sanders' understanding of Jesus as a prophet of temple restoration eschatology: that the central conviction of Jesus' life was that God would build a new temple from which Jesus and his followers would rule over the messianic age. See Sanders, *Jesus and Judaism* (Philadelphia: Fortress, 1985) and *The Historical Figure of Jesus* (London: Penguin, 1993). I have difficulty putting that together with what else I see going on in the Jesus tradition.

11. Matthew and Luke basically follow Mark's account of the final week, with minor additions. John's gospel adds little if anything of historical value.

12. Mark 11.1–10. The colt may have had a symbolic meaning as well. As Matthew copies Mark's story, he connects it to Zechariah 9.9, which speaks of a king of peace riding a colt and banishing the war horse from Jerusalem.

13. The Pharisees were a renewal group committed to the extension of priestly purity laws into everyday life; the Sadducees were a group associated with the priestly aristocracy.

14. These incidents are all found in Mark 11–12.

15. Mark 11.15–17. For my fuller exposition of this incident, see *Jesus in Contemporary Scholarship* (Valley Forge, PA: Trinity Press International, 1994), 112–16. Note that Mark frames this story with the cursing of the fig tree, suggesting that the temple (like the fig tree) was not producing the fruit it was meant to. Like the fig tree, it is cursed.

16. Mark 12–13.

17. Mark 11.18. See also 12.12 for the reaction of the temple authorities to the parable of the wicked tenants.

18. For recent scholarly treatments of the passion stories, see Raymond Brown's massive two-volume study, *The Death of the Messiah* (New York: Doubleday, 1994); John Dominic Crossan, *Who Killed Jesus* (San Francisco: HarperSanFrancisco, 1995); John T. Carroll and Joel B. Green, *The Death of Jesus in Early Christianity* (Peabody, MA: Hendrickson, 1995); and Gerard S. Sloyan, *The Crucifixion of Jesus* (Minneapolis: Fortress, 1995).

19. The Jewish historian Josephus also tells us a bit: "Pilate, because of an accusation made by the leading men among us, condemned Jesus to the cross." A few details can perhaps be teased from Paul. Crossan has argued that the Gospel of Peter contains the earliest passion narrative. About his case, I find myself saying, "It is possible." But I am unpersuaded by this particular part of his scholarly work, and I remain a happy agnostic about the Gospel of Peter.

20. I owe the phrases "history remembered" and "prophecy historicized" to Crossan.

21. To see this for yourself, read any of the passion stories in a Bible that has good footnotes or cross-references to the Hebrew Bible, and keep track of how many references there are.

22. Mark 15.34, quoting Psalm 22.1.

23. Mark 15.29, echoing Psalm 22.7.

24. Mark 15.24, echoing Psalm 22.18

25. Examples could be multiplied. One more: Mark 15.33 reports that darkness covered the land for three hours, from noon until Jesus' death. Are we to think of this as history remembered, or as a detail created in order to call to mind the Hebrew Bible's association of darkness at midday with a day of judgment? The latter seems much more likely.

26. Mark 14.36.

27. There is nothing improbable about Jesus praying shortly before his arrest, and I can imagine that he might have prayed something very much like this; the words are appropriate and in character.

28. Matt. 27.25.

29. 1 Corinthians 15.3.

30. I am open to the possibility that Luke's passion story may preserve some independent tradition. But if so, it would not affect my understanding in any major way.

31. Even though they have double early independent attestation. They are found in very early tradition in 1 Corinthians 11.23–25 and Mark 14.22–24. If I could imagine a plausible meaning for them as words of Jesus, I would be very open to seeing them as history remembered.

32. For two recent and somewhat unconventional views of Judas, see William Klassen, *Judas: Betrayer or Friend of Jesus?* (Minneapolis: Fortress, 1996); and John Spong, *Liberating the Gospels* (San Francisco: HarperSanFrancisco, 1996), 257–76. Spong argues that Judas was a Christian invention.

33. Mark 11.18, followed by Matthew and Luke. Much less plausibly, John 11.45–53 says that the resurrection of Lazarus was the trigger event.

34. Mark 14.50.

35. It is not impossible, of course, that somebody who was there later became a source of information for the early Christian community. But Crossan's terse comment needs to be given weight: those who knew didn't care, and those who cared didn't know. See *Who Killed Jesus?*, p. 219.

36. If you were an ordinary murderer or robber, you were not likely to be crucified. The use of the word *robbers* for those crucified with Jesus is a translation mistake. The Greek word used in Mark is the same word used by Josephus for Jewish resistance fighters; it is a pejorative term, with connotations like the modern *terrorist.*

37. The remains were found in 1968. See John J. Rousseau and Rami Arav, *Jesus and His World* (Minneapolis: Fortress, 1995), 74–78.

38. Matthew 27.24–25. Matthew also adds the story of Pilate's wife's dream in 27.19. There is no reason to think of these scenes as history remembered; they seem clearly to be Matthew's elaboration.

39. Tom interprets this scene quite differently, including the meaning of "Son of Man" in this exchange. He sees it not only as attributable to Jesus, but also as referring to the coming vindication of Jesus and the historical destruction of Jerusalem. But it seems more plausible to me that Mark and his hearers understood "Son of Man" in this text to refer to Jesus and specifically to the return of Jesus as the Son of Man, i.e., to the second coming.

### CHAPTER 6

1. For all this and more, see N. T. Wright, *Jesus and the Victory of God*, vol. 2 of *Christian Origins and the Question of God* (Minneapolis: Fortress, 1996), 576–92, and the numerous texts cited there.

2. I owe this information to Dr. Philip Turner, sometime dean of the Berkeley Divinity School at Yale and a former missionary in Uganda.

3. *Jesus and the Victory of God*, 133–36.

4. This includes the passion narratives in John, which are, despite Marcus's caution, regularly regarded as possessing a strong claim to containing good historical information.

5. The fact that the stories have, in some later circles, been read as supporting various doctrines, on the one hand, and various sociopolitical attitudes, on

the other, has nothing to do with the historical point. Thus I refuse to read back, say, Luther's theology of the cross—and, by the same token, Luther's anti-Judaism—into the gospel narratives. At this point (to use a politically incorrect metaphor) a politically correct hermeneutic of suspicion shoots itself in the foot. After all, several readers of the great masters of suspicion, Freud, Nietzsche, and Marx, have used them to support massively destructive and dehumanizing policies.

6. On all this, see *Jesus and the Victory of God,* chap. 12.
7. For this and subsequent paragraphs, see *Jesus and the Victory of God,* 597–604.
8. Which related to his own fate and that of the nation, not to a "second coming." See chap. 14, below.
9. See my response to Crossan on this point, in "Doing Justice to Jesus: A Response to J. D. Crossan, 'What Victory? What God?'," *Scottish Journal of Theology* 50, no. 3 (1997): 370–73.
10. Compare *Jesus and the Victory of God,* 577–79.
11. See *Jesus and the Victory of God,* 131–33.
12. Mark 14.55–64.
13. 1 Corinthians 15.3.
14. Acts 2.40.
15. Galatians 2.20.
16. 1 John 2.2.
17. Such as Galatians 4.1–11.
18. In several of my nonscholarly writings, I try to answer this at a homiletic, pastoral, and practical level. See, for instance, *The Crown and the Fire,* (Grand Rapids: Eerdmans, 1995); *Bringing the Church to the World,* (Minneapolis: Bethany House, 1992); *Following Jesus,* (Grand Rapids: Eerdmans, 1995), and *For All God's Worth* (Grand Rapids: Eerdmans, 1997).
19. Gustaf Aulén, *Christus Victor* (New York: Macmillan, 1931).
20. Romans 8.18–27.
21. Ephesians 3.10.
22. 1 Corinthians 11.26.
23. Colossians 2.14f.

## CHAPTER 7

1. Much of this chapter presents in abbreviated form arguments that I have spelled out at more length in three articles under the title "The Resurrection of the Messiah" in *Sewanee Theological Review* 41, no. 2 (Easter 1998): 107–56. I hope to expand them further in due course.

2. For this section, compare N. T. Wright, *The New Testament and the People of God,* vol. 1 of *Christian Origins and the Question of God* (Minneapolis: Fortress, 1992), 320–32.

3. Isaiah 26.19; Ezekiel 37.1–14; Daniel 12.2–3.

4. Daniel 11.32–35.

5. Daniel 12.2.

6. Wisdom 3.7–8.

7. *Genesis Rabba* 14.5; *Leviticus Rabba* 14.9. The house of Shammai took the first view, treating Ezekiel as a literal prophecy of the eventual resurrection and envisaging continuity between present and future physicality; the house of Hillel took the second, envisaging an entirely new creation, having no necessary continuity with present physical remains.

8. Mark 6.16.

9. Wisdom 3.1–7.

10. Acts 11.15.

11. In Acts 23.8 Luke explains that the Sadducees do not believe in resurrection, "neither angel nor spirit," but the Pharisees "acknowledge them both." The best way to understand this, not least in view of Luke 24.37–39, where it is explicitly denied that the risen Jesus is "a spirit," is to see "angel" and "spirit" as two ways of describing the intermediate state between death and resurrection. The Sadducees deny the future reembodiedness and also deny the two ways in which the Pharisees express the temporary preresurrection state.

12. Again Acts 23 is relevant. In verse 9 the Pharisees, trying to shield Paul from accusation, ask: "What if an angel or spirit spoke to him?" Resurrection was what happened *after* the invisible, tangible, nonembodied angel or spirit mode of existence.

13. See esp. 1 Corinthians 9.1, with 15.8 (on which, see below).

14. Gerd Lüdemann, *The Resurrection of Jesus: History, Experience, Theology* (London: SCM, 1994).

15. 1 Corinthians 15.8.

16. It is impossible to argue from the word *ophthe,* as some have tried to do, that these were "seeings" of a nonobjective type. In 9.1 Paul uses the regular verb: "Have I not *seen* [*heoraka*] Jesus our Lord?"

17. 1 Corinthians 15.12–28. On the Lordship of Jesus, see further, chap. 10 below.

18. 1 Corinthians 15.28.

19. 1 Corinthians 15.35–41.

20. 1 Corinthians 15.42–49.

21. A question Marcus's reading of 1 Corinthians 15 ought to face is: in what way is his account of Jesus' resurrection a model, as Paul indicates it should be, for that which will happen to all those who are in Christ?

22. 1 Corinthians 15.50.

23. In 1 Corinthians 15.44 and 46.

24. 1 Corinthians 15.29–34, 50–58.

25. John 1.1–18. John 21, though it also fits very well where it is, is an after-thought, a postscript.

26. John 21.12; Matthew 28.17.

27. Tertullian, *On the Flesh of Christ*, 5. The actual quotation is *Certum est quia impossibile est.*

28. Matthew 28.20.

29. See chap. 10.

30. Colossians 3.1–11.

### CHAPTER 8

1. The Easter stories fall into two major categories: tomb stories and appearance stories. The story of the empty tomb (with variations of detail) is found in all four gospels. Appearance stories in which the risen Christ appears to his followers are found in three of the gospels (not Mark) and the book of Acts and are referred to by Paul.

2. Portions of this section are adapted from my contribution to *Will the Real Jesus Please Stand Up?*, ed. by Paul Copan (Grand Rapids, MI: Baker, 1998). The book contains a debate about the resurrection of Jesus between William Lane Craig and John Dominic Crossan, moderated by William Buckley, and chapters commenting on the debate by several scholars.

3. Tom agrees that resuscitation and resurrection are very different, and he agrees that Easter is not about resuscitation. He would not agree with the point that I build upon this, however, since he argues that the resurrection of Jesus involved the transformation of his corpse.

4. Written around the year 54, roughly fifteen years before Mark, our first gospel.

5. 1 Corinthians 15.3–8.

6. And thus our first reference to an empty tomb is in the gospel of Mark, written around 70.

7. The phrase "last of all" in this verse need not mean what Tom suggests: that Paul was claiming that resurrection experiences like his were now over with, and thus qualitatively different from experiences of the risen Christ ever since. The phrase could simply mean that Paul's experience is the last one he's going to mention in his list, or, alternatively, that he was the last of those who could be be called "apostles" to receive such an experience.

8. 1 Corinthians 15.35. The rest of the chapter is his response.

9. Explicitly in 1 Corinthians 15.44 and 46, though the whole context is relevant to the question of their meaning.

10. The disagreement and uncertainty are reflected in the variety of words used to translate the contrast between the two bodies. In the RSV, NRSV, and TEV ("Good News Bible"): "physical body" and "spiritual body." In the NEB: "animal body" and "spiritual body." In the KJV and NIV: "natural body" and "spiritual body." In the Jerusalem Bible, the first kind of body "embodies soul," the second kind "embodies spirit."

11. It is important to note that one can speak of a bodily resurrection without meaning *physical* body. Thus, for example, affirming the line in the creed, "I believe in the resurrection of the body" need not mean physical body.

12. Luke 24.13–35.

13. Crossan, *Jesus: A Revolutionary Biography*, makes this point especially effectively. After a similar analysis of the story, he says: it is "the metaphoric condensation of the first years of early Christian thought and practice into one parabolic afternoon." Then he concludes with two three-word sentences, both of which must be equally emphasized: "Emmaus never happened. Emmaus always happens" (197).

14. There are also theological reasons why I do not like an emphasis upon the historical factuality of the empty tomb. (1) It can have a distorting effect on the meaning of Easter faith: Easter faith easily becomes believing in the factuality of a past event, rather than living within a present relationship, and the truth of Christianity becomes grounded in the "happenedness" of this past event rather than in the continuing experience of the risen Christ. (2) In conservative Christian apologetic, the factuality of the empty tomb is often used to prove the truth of Christianity and even its superiority to all other religious traditions. But I do not believe that the truth of Christianity can be proved in this fashion, and I do not believe that God is known primarily or only in our tradition. The claim conflicts with what I know of other religions, and it is difficult to reconcile with the Christian notion of grace. (3) Finally, this emphasis virtually requires an interventionist notion of God, which I do not accept (see chap. 4). I do not know if Tom would affirm any of these implications, so these points are addressed, not specifically to him, but to a fairly common Christian line of argument.

15. John 20.28.

16. I suspect, though I cannot prove, that both "God raised Jesus from the dead" and "God raised Jesus to God's right hand" are earlier than the story of the empty tomb. I do not mean simply that these two phrases occur in an earlier written source (though they do: Paul uses them, and our earliest written source referring to an empty tomb is Mark), but that the early community spoke of "raised from the dead" and "raised to God's right hand"

before there was a story of an empty tomb. Within this way of looking at it, the story of the empty tomb becomes a parable of the resurrection: Jesus will not be found in the land of the dead, for God has raised him up. My suggestion is that "raised from the dead" and "raised to God's right hand" are alternative ways of saying the same thing; they do not point to two separate moments of being raised from the tomb and then being raised to God's right hand.

17. Acts 2.36. See also 2.23–24, 3.13–15, 4.10–11.

18. For a treatment of this theme in the history of Christian theology, see Gustaf Aulén, *Christus Victor*.

19. The most thorough contemporary study of the powers is by Walter Wink, author of a three-volume treatment. See especially volume three, *Engaging the Powers*, and his one-volume summary, *The Powers That Be*. See also a book on the powers from a generation ago by George B. Caird, mentor to both Tom and me: *Principalities and Powers* (Oxford: Clarendon Press, 1956).

20. Colossians 2.15.

21. Galatians 2.20. See also Romans 6, where Paul uses the language of death and resurrection to speak of the meaning of baptism as a dying and rising.

22. Mark 8.34. Following Jesus as he journeys from Galilee to Jerusalem, the place of death and resurrection, is a major theme of the great central sections of each of the synoptic gospels. It is also a major theme of the season of Lent: Lent invites us to participate in the journey of death and resurrection.

23. Isaiah 43.4.

24. Technically, of course, he was executed just outside the walls of Jerusalem.

25. Hebrews 7.27; 9.12, 26; 10.10, 12.

26. Romans 10.4.

## CHAPTER 9

1. I have treated this topic in a number of places. See especially chap. 5 of *Meeting Jesus Again for the First Time*, chap. 4 of *The God We Never Knew*, and chap. 2 of *Jesus at 2000*. Because I have written about this several times, there will inevitably be some repetition in this chapter.

2. John Knox, *The Death of Christ* (New York: Abingdon, 1958).

3. The phrase comes from Luke 4.18 and cites Isaiah 61.1. Because it is Jesus' "inaugural address" in Luke, it is probably Luke's creation. But I see such language as reflecting an experience that I think Jesus had. Different phrases can be used to name it, such as being filled with the Spirit or experiencing the Spirit coming upon one.

4. See chap. 4, pp. 61–62.

5. I want to emphasize that I am describing a popular-level way of imagining this, not the way the church's theological voices through the centuries have thought about it. I also am not attributing this view to Tom.

6. I am sometimes asked, "Doesn't this mean that anybody could be like Jesus?" My response is, "Yes—in the same sense that anybody could be a Mozart." That is, the recognition that being a Mozart (or Jesus) is a human possibility does not mean that any of us could become one by really working at it. People like Jesus and Mozart don't come along very often.

7. John 6.35, 53. John 6 as a whole treats this theme.

8. Exodus 4.22 and Hos. 11.1.

9. 2 Samuel 7.14.

10. Psalm 2.7. This psalm also speaks of the king as God's anointed, that is, as *mashiah* (messiah).

11. Job 1.6.

12. See Geza Vermes, *Jesus the Jew* (New York: Macmillan, 1973), 210–13.

13. For further development, see *Meeting Jesus Again,* chap. 5.

14. In Proverbs: wisdom and creation, 8.22–31; as prophet: 1.20–33; and banquet, 9.1–6. See also Sirach 24 and Wisdom of Solomon, esp. 7.22–8.1 and chap. 10.

15. It may have been the movement's earliest Christology, though this is very difficult to discern. See, for example, James D. G. Dunn, *The Partings of the Ways* (Philadelphia: Trinity Press International, 1991), 195–201; Elisabeth Schüssler Fiorenza, *In Memory of Her* (New York: Crossroad, 1985), 130–40, 188–92; Elizabeth Johnson, *She Who Is* (New York: Crossroad, 1992), 94–100, 156–67.

16. John 14.6 and Acts 4.12. Many scholars think that John's gospel was written in a time when some Christians were tempted to leave the community and return to their ancestral religious tradition. In this setting, John 14.6 does not have all of the world's religions in mind but says, in effect: *Jesus* is the way—don't return to the old way that you left.

17. The quoted phrases are from John Hick. Author of many books, especially about Christianity in the context of the world's religions, Hick is a contemporary theologian and philosopher whose writing is marked by exceptional clarity. I recall reading these words several years ago, but I have not been able to find the reference.

18. Colossians 1.15.

## CHAPTER 10

1. I have written about contemporary divinities in *Bringing the Church to the World* (Minneapolis: Bethany House, 1992).

2. For full discussion, see N. T. Wright, *The New Testament and the People of God*, vol. 1 of *Christian Origins and the Question of God* (Minneapolis: Fortress, 1992), chap. 9.

3. Pliny the Younger, *Letters*, 10.96.9f.

4. Deuteronomy 6.4, the opening words of the prayer known as the *Shema*. There are various other possible ways of translating the underlying Hebrew, for example, "YHWH our God is one YHWH," or "YHWH is our God, YHWH alone."

5. Psalm 147.9.

6. See above, chap. 3.

7. All five, in Hebrew, are represented by feminine nouns.

8. John 1.1–18.

9. John 1.14; compare Sirach 24. On the comparison, see *The New Testament and the People of God*, 413–16.

10. For which, see the detailed studies in my books *The Climax of the Covenant* (Minneapolis: Fortress, 1992), chaps. 4, 5, and 6; and *What St. Paul Really Said* (Grand Rapids: Eerdmans, 1997), chap. 4.

11. Often regarded as pre-Pauline, though Paul intends every word to bear weight within the wider letter.

12. Galatians 4.8–11.

13. Galatians 4.4 and 4.6.

14. For instance, the remarkable Romans 8.3–4.

15. For example, Exodus 4.22.

16. Such as 2 Samuel 7.14, Psalm 2.7, and Psalm 89.27.

17. In 4Q174. The meaning of the same phrase in 4Q246 is disputed.

18. See, too, Romans 1.3–4, where, though "son of God" means more than "messiah," it does not mean less.

19. In *Jesus and the Victory of God*, vol. 2 of *Christian Origins and the Question of God* (Minneapolis: Fortress, 1996), chap. 13.

20. On throne imagery, and the idea of sharing God's throne, see *Jesus and the Victory of God*, 624–29.

21. For this, and what follows, see the close listing of material, and the argument, of *Jesus and the Victory of God*, 645–51.

22. *Jesus and the Victory of God*, 648–50.

23. *Jesus and the Victory of God*, 653.

24. See Mark 3.21. I believe I owe this point to Bishop Rowan Williams.

## CHAPTER 11

1. Paul speaks of Jesus as descended from David in Romans 1.3. In Galatians 4.4 he describes Jesus as "born of a woman." Commentators have not been able to agree why he says this here.

2. Since I believe that the beginning of Mark is lost—see N. T. Wright, *The New Testament and the People of God,* vol. 1 of *Christian Origins and the Question of God* (Minneapolis: Fortress, 1992), 390, n. 67—I cannot say whether or not the book originally contained a birth narrative.
3. Compare, for example, Matthew 11.2–19, much of which is cryptic anti-Herod material.
4. Isaiah 7.14, quoted in Matthew 1.23.
5. Matthew 2.5, fulfilling Micah 5.1–3.
6. Matthew 1.21.
7. It is beside the point to question whether *'almah,* the Hebrew original behind the LXX *parthenos,* "virgin," really meant what that word means today. For the record, the only texts where it is possible to tell whether the Hebrew term refers to a virgin or not are Genesis 24.43, Exodus 2.8, and Song 6.8, and there the women in question are certainly unmarried.
8. Acts 5.37. This may perhaps reinforce the possibility that the right way to read Luke 2.2 is "this census took place *before the time when* Quirinius was Governor of Syria." Why would Luke call it the "first" one?
9. The careful study of R. E. Brown, *The Birth of the Messiah: A Commentary on the Infancy Narratives in Matthew and Luke* (Garden City, NY: Doubleday, 1977), appendix IV (517–33), remains among the most thorough introductions to the question. See, too, C. E. B. Cranfield, "Some Reflections on the Subject of the Virgin Birth," *Scottish Journal of Theology* 41, no. 2 (1988): 177–89.
10. Or those of Alexander the Great or Romulus, or the Buddha.

CHAPTER 12

1. For the birth of Jesus in recent scholarship, see above all Raymond Brown, *The Birth of the Messiah* (1977; New York: Doubleday, 1993). See also John P. Meier, *A Marginal Jew: Rethinking the Historical Jesus,* 1: 205–52; John Dominic Crossan, *Jesus: A Revolutionary Biography,* 1–28; Crossan's essay in Hershel Shanks, ed., *The Search for Jesus* (Washington, DC: Biblical Archaeology Society, 1994), 59–82; Richard Horsley, *The Liberation of Christmas* (New York: Crossroad, 1989); Jane Schaberg, *The Illegitimacy of Jesus* (San Francisco: Harper & Row, 1987). For a Jungian approach informed by biblical scholarship, see Eugen Drewermann, *Discovering the God Child Within,* trans. Peter Heinegg (New York: Crossroad, 1994).
2. It is also absent from Q, which may not be significant, given that Q has little narrative material.
3. If a virgin birth is historical, one might think that the genealogy of Joseph is irrelevant, since he was not the genetic father. However, in Jesus' world, the

legal father (whether biological or not) was thought of as the "real" father. Yet it is also plausible to argue, as some scholars have, that the genealogies date from a time when it was thought that Joseph was the biological father.

4. Matthew 1.23, citing Isaiah 7.14; 2.6, citing Micah 5.2; 2.15, citing Hosea 11.1; 2.18, citing Jeremiah 31.15; 2.23, citing an unknown passage. It is instructive to look these up in the Hebrew Bible and to see to what extent they seem like predictions of events surrounding the birth of Jesus.

5. These magnificent hymns are virtually a recitation of images of deliverance from the Hebrew Bible. Some scholars see them as Luke's creation; others see them as early Christian hymns that Luke has adapted for his birth stories. The latter suggestion is intriguing; if correct, it means that we are hearing the early Christian community at worship in these hymns.

6. 4 B.C.E. is the most commonly accepted date for Herod's death, though this is being reevaluated in scholarly circles.

7. The argument has been made that a man other than Joseph was the father, either because Mary was the victim of rape or had been sexually indiscreet. See Schaberg, *Illegitimacy of Jesus,* and John Spong, *Born of a Woman: A Bishop Rethinks the Birth of Jesus* (San Francisco: HarperSanFrancisco, 1992). I think it more probable that Joseph was the father.

8. Psalm 119.105.

9. Isaiah 9.2.

10. Isaiah 60.1–3. Imagery from this chapter of Isaiah may have supplied ingredients for Matthew's story of the wise men: nations (Gentiles) coming to the light (verse 3), bringing gifts of gold and frankincense (verse 6).

11. John 1.9. See also 1.5.

12. John 8.12, 9.5.

13. Luke 2.10–11, 14.

14. I owe the central insight in this section to Crossan's analysis in the two works cited in note 1 of this chapter.

15. John 1.13. John, of course, does not have a story of Jesus' birth. Interestingly, these words refer not to Jesus but to those who become children of God through Jesus. The point: language like this need not point to a literal (biological) conception by the Spirit.

16. Mark 9.7.

CHAPTER 13

1. From the Nicene Creed (fourth century). The Apostles' Creed uses almost the same language at this point.

2. Because of the ambiguous range of meanings of this word among scholars, I do not often use it. See *Jesus in Contemporary Scholarship* (Valley Forge,

PA: Trinity Press International, 1994), 70–74. I do not object to other scholars using it, so long as they specify what they mean.

3. Often used by scholars as shorthand for the second coming of Jesus, *parousia* is a Greek word meaning "presence."

4. A survey from *U.S. News and World Report,* cited by Reginald Stackhouse, *The End of the World? A New Look at an Old Belief* (New York: Paulist, 1997), 2. This very readable book is an excellent survey of Christian beliefs about the second coming and the end of the world, treating both the variety and history of such beliefs.

5. 1 Thessalonians 4.14–17.

6. Passages like this raise an interesting question: how literally did the New Testament authors understand their own language? In this instance, Paul's purpose is clearly pastoral; he is seeking to reassure people about members of the community who have died (see 4.13 and 18). Is the passage to be understood primarily as words of pastoral assurance and not as a carefully described eschatological scenario that he thought literally would come to pass? That is, if one were able to ask Paul, "What do you really mean? Can you say it another way?," would he put his statement quite differently? Or would he say, "No, this is exactly what I mean"? Obviously, no answer to this speculation is possible, but it does lead to reflection about how literally we are to read passages like this. Perhaps there were literalists and nonliteralists then, even as there are now.

7. This passage is one of the foundations for the notion of "the rapture" in some Christian circles: when the end is near, those who are "true believers" will be taken up from the earth and spared the final tribulation (a period of great suffering, spoken of in the visions of the book of Revelation), which those left on earth will have to endure. "The rapture" is a relatively recent notion, and I know of no New Testament scholar who takes it seriously. Note that "the rapture" reading of this passage understands "we who are alive" to refer not to Paul's contemporaries, but to those alive at the time of the end, whenever it occurs.

8. Other passages also suggest that Paul expected this soon. See, for example, 1 Corinthians 15.51–52. Later in his life, he envisioned the possibility of dying before the second coming; see, for example, Philippians 1.21–24.

9. Mark 13.24–27. Tom understands this text quite differently, arguing that the coming of "the Son of Man" does refer not to the second coming of Jesus but to Jesus' vindication and the coming destruction of Jerusalem (which happened in the year 70). But I am persuaded that Mark thought "the Son of Man" in this passage referred to Jesus and that Mark therefore thought of this text as a second-coming-of-Jesus text.

10. Mark 13.30.

11. Matthew not only includes the little apocalypse of Mark 13 but supplements it with parables that he sets in this context: the wise and foolish virgins, money in trust, and the sheep and goats, all in Matthew 25. See also Matthew 10.23, which speaks of the coming of the Son of Man before the followers of Jesus will have managed to reach all the towns of Israel. Though the gospel of John has what scholars often call a "realized" or "present" eschatology, it also contains traces of apocalyptic eschatology. See, for example, John 5.25–29 and 21.21–23, both of which imply that some had expected the imminent return of Jesus.

12. The author identifies "the beast from the sea" in chap. 13 and "the great whore" of chap. 17 with the Roman empire of his time.

13. Revelation 1.1, 3 and 22.12, 20. See also 22.10.

14. Most scholars see 2 Peter as written in Peter's name but not by Peter himself, and as dating from somewhere between the end of the first century and the middle of the second.

15. 2 Peter 3.4, 8.

16. This view dates back to the work of Johannes Weiss and Albert Schweitzer near the beginning of this century. It became the dominant position in much of German and North American scholarship. British scholars were less persuaded.

17. Mark 9.1. See also Mark 1.15, which speaks of the nearness of the kingdom.

18. Matthew 10.23. Another example is Mark 13.24–27, already quoted in this chapter.

19. This is one of the hot issues in contemporary New Testament studies, and scholars are quite divided. Among those affirming the older majority position are E. P. Sanders, John Meier, and others. Among those denying it are John Dominic Crossan, Robert Funk, the Jesus Seminar generally, Burton Mack, myself, and Tom. I note that Tom thinks Jesus did use apocalyptic language, but sees it as a way of investing events in the space-time world with their ultimate meaning. Thus Tom and I agree that Jesus did not have an apocalyptic eschatology, as the phrase is commonly understood, even though he "saves" apocalyptic language by giving it a different meaning.

20. For further development, see esp. chaps. 3 and 4 of my *Jesus in Contemporary Scholarship*.

21. I note that the gospel of Mark was written near the time of Jerusalem's destruction. I am inclined to see the apocalyptic elements in Mark (including the imminent expectation of the kingdom, as in Mark 9.1, and the "little apocalypse" of Mark 13) as reflecting heightened eschatological expectation due to the events of 70.

22. Most of us have heard jokes about whether Jesus will return to Rome or to Salt Lake City or to some other place. The serious point of the jokes: if we think of Jesus coming back, we have to think of him coming back *somewhere*. To make the point another way, several years ago a student showed me a fund-raising letter from a televangelist. Its purpose was to raise money to make sure that airborne television crews would be able to cover the second coming. The notion that the second coming could be televised is, of course, ludicrous. But it also makes us wonder whether we can imagine the second coming as an event within the space-time world.

23. Matthew 25.31–46.

## CHAPTER 14

1. John 3.1–12.

2. Luke 23.43: "Today you will be with me in paradise."

3. Wisdom 3.1–8; N. T. Wright, *The New Testament and the People of God*, vol. 1 of *Christian Origins and the Question of God* (Minneapolis: Fortress, 1992), 329f. (See also p. 113 above.)

4. This is the meaning, then, of passages like 1 Peter 1.4. Salvation "kept in heaven for you" does not mean that you need to go to "heaven" to get it; it is waiting, as we say, in the wings, ready to be brought onstage when the time is right. When Paul says "our citizenship is in heaven" (Philippians 3.20), he goes on at once to say that Jesus the Lord will come *from* heaven to transform earthly existence.

5. Compare Psalm 115.16.

6. 2 Kings 6.15–19.

7. Revelation 4–5.

8. *The New Testament and the People of God*, 459–64.

9. 1 Corinthians 15:50–58.

10. Verses 52–5; compare 2 Corinthians 5:1–10.

11. Verses 54, 57.

12. 1 Corinthians 15.25.

13. In Luke's writings the fresh truth is revealed to the apostles at the ascension: Acts 1.11.

14. 1 Thessalonians 4.16; cf. 1 Corinthians 15.51–2, Philippians 3.20f.

15. And also the theme of biblical prophets being seized by the Spirit and transported elsewhere: cf. Ezekiel 3.12; 8.3; 11.1, 24; 37.1; 43.5; 1 Kings 18.12; 2 Kings 2.16. The word used in the LXX of these passages is different; but Paul uses the term again in 2 Corinthians 12.2, 4 to denote the mystical experience of being "caught up to heaven."

16. See, again, Philippians 3.20f.

17. On this question cf. *The New Testament and the People of God,* 462–4.
18. Compare *Jesus and the Victory of God,* vol. 2 of *Christian Origins and the Question of God* (Minneapolis: Fortress), 1996), chaps. 8, 11.
19. Read 2 Corinthians 5.1–10 in the light of 1.8–11.
20. The same indeterminacy is visible in, for instance, John 21.20–23.

CHAPTER 15

1. See, for instance, my various collections of sermons and addresses: *The Crown and the Fire* (Grand Rapids: Eerdmans, 1995); *Following Jesus* (Grand Rapids: Eerdmans, 1994); *The Lord and His Prayer* (Grand Rapids: Eerdmans, 1996); *For All God's Worth* (Grand Rapids: Eerdmans, 1997).
2. 1 Samuel 4–5.
3. Colossians 2.9.
4. Mark 12.30 and parallels; Romans 12.1–2.
5. Galatians 2.5, 14; cf. 4.16, 5.7.
6. For all this, see N. T. Wright, *The New Testament and the People of God,* vol. 1 of *Christian Origins and the Question of God* (Minneapolis: Fortress, 1992), chap. 14.
7. Acts 17.7.
8. On all this, see the very interesting collection of essays edited by Richard A. Horsley, *Paul and Empire: Religion and Power in Roman Imperial Society* (Harrisburg, PA: Trinity Press International, 1997).
9. Two books that I have found enormously stimulating on these topics, in very different ways: Oliver O'Donovan, *The Desire of the Nations: Rediscovering the Roots of Political Theology* (Cambridge: Cambridge Univ. Press, 1996); Miroslav Volf, *Exclusion and Embrace: A Theological Exploration of Identity, Otherness, and Reconciliation* (Nashville: Abingdon, 1996).
10. See the carefully researched and documented account by Paul Marshall, *Their Blood Cries Out* (Dallas: Word Publishing, 1997).
11. See also the concluding section of chap. 6 above.

CHAPTER 16

1. That I have "the last word" in this book is an accident of design: Tom and I agreed to alternate the sequence in which we treat each topic. If the book had had one more topic, he would have had the final word. I seek not to abuse the privilege.
2. I describe this more fully in the introduction to my *The God We Never Knew* (San Francisco: HarperSanFrancisco, 1997). I do not see Tom as holding this understanding of Christianity. Rather, I am describing a widespread understanding in our culture.

3. Friedrich Schleiermacher, *On Religion: Speeches to Its Cultured Despisers*, ed. Richard Crouter (Cambridge: Cambridge Univ. Press, 1988).

4. The remarkable level of public interest in recent Jesus scholarship in North America is evidence of the appetite. Five Jesus books by scholars have been on *Publishers' Weekly* ten-best-selling books in religion in the last six years. Most of the people buying and reading them are connected to a religious community and are looking for ways of making sense of things, not reasons to disbelieve.

5. See the concluding chapter of his *Varieties of Religious Experience* (first published in 1902). In my judgment, it is one of the most illuminating chapters in the history of academic religious publishing.

6. On the issue of the role of faith in making historical judgments, see especially Van A. Harvey, *The Historian and the Believer* (New York: Macmillan, 1966).

7. He does this explicitly in his treatment of the stories of the empty tomb, suggesting that the differences among the synoptic accounts look like the kind of testimony that different eyewitnesses to the same event report. On Tom's view, the synoptic gospels thus contain three independent traditions about the empty tomb. On my view, they contain one (Mark's), and Matthew and Luke revise that one account.

8. I am also skeptical that memory works the way that Tom suggests: namely, that in oral cultures, a story once told retains essentially its form and content. It is difficult for me to imagine the passion story in its present form in Mark emerging within a few days or weeks of the death of Jesus and then being told essentially the same way until it was written down some forty years later. For a suggestive analysis of how memory works, see part 2 of John Dominic Crossan's new book, *The Birth of Christianity* (San Francisco: HarperSanFrancisco, 1998), 49–93.

9. Ultimately, I don't think "lens" is a completely adequate metaphor, and later in this chapter I will speak of the tradition not simply as "lens," but as "sacrament." That is, I think the tradition is not only a lens for seeing, but also a mediator (sacrament) of that which is seen. But for now I will use the lens metaphor.

10. I am aware that I am here echoing words attributed to Paul in Acts 17.28, not a saying of Jesus. But my claim is that the experience of a mystic like Jesus points to seeing God in this way.

11. Verna Dozier, *The Dream of God: A Call to Return* (Boston: Cowley, 1991). See also chap. 6 of my *The God We Never Knew*.

12. Mark 12.18–27.

13. Examples: In Luke 11.31–32 = Matthew 12.41–42, Gentiles (the people of Nineveh and the Queen of the South) will fare better in the judgment than those of "this generation" who failed to heed Jesus' message, reversing the notion that of course Jews would do better than Gentiles. A similar subversion occurs in the famous parable of the sheep and goats in Matthew 25.31–46: there will be one standard of judgment for Jews and Gentiles alike, namely deeds of compassion done for "the least of these." The point of these sayings is not to teach that there will be a judgment and an afterlife; rather, these sayings accept the common belief that there will be and then subvert commonly accepted beliefs about it.

14. 2 Corinthians 3.18.

15. I owe this way of thinking about the gospels to Paul Ricoeur, who spoke of the movement from "first naïveté" to "second naïveté." I believe the intellectual lineage of the notion goes back at least to William Blake, who spoke of "first innocence" and "second innocence."

# INDEX